Summary

The Congressional Research Service (CRS) developed the *Congressional Oversight Manual* over 30 years ago, following a three-day December 1978 Workshop on Congressional Oversight and Investigations. The workshop was organized by a group of House and Senate committee aides from both parties and CRS at the request of the bipartisan House leadership. The *Manual* was produced by CRS with the assistance of a number of House committee staffers. In subsequent years, CRS has sponsored and conducted various oversight seminars for House and Senate staff and updated the *Manual* as circumstances warranted. Worth noting is the bipartisan recommendation of the House members of the 1993 Joint Committee on the Organization of Congress (Rept. No. 103-413, Vol. I):

> [A]s a way to further enhance the oversight work of Congress, the Joint Committee would encourage the Congressional Research Service to conduct on a regular basis, as it has done in the past, oversight seminars for Members and congressional staff and to update on a regular basis its *Congressional Oversight Manual*.

Over the years, CRS has assisted many Members, committees, party leaders, and staff aides in the performance of the oversight function: the review, monitoring, and supervision of the implementation of public policy. Understandably, given the size, reach, cost, and continuing growth of the modern executive establishment, Congress's oversight role is even more significant—and more demanding—than when Woodrow Wilson wrote in his classic *Congressional Government* (1885): "Quite as important as lawmaking is vigilant oversight of administration." Today's lawmakers and congressional aides, as well as commentators and scholars, recognize that Congress's work, ideally, should not end when it passes legislation. Oversight is an integral way to make sure that the laws work and are being administered in an effective, efficient, and economical manner. In light of this destination, oversight can be viewed as one of Congress's principal responsibilities as it grapples with the complexities of the 21st century.

Contents

Tables

Appendixes

Contacts

Purposes, Authority, and Participants

Throughout its history, Congress has engaged in oversight—broadly defined as the review, monitoring, and supervision of the implementation of public policy—of the executive branch. The first several Congresses inaugurated such important oversight techniques as special investigations, reporting requirements, resolutions of inquiry, and use of the appropriations process to review executive activity. Contemporary developments, have only increased Congress's capacity and capabilities *to check on and check the Executive.* Public laws and congressional rules have measurably enhanced Congress's implied power under the Constitution to conduct oversight.

Despite its lengthy heritage, oversight was not given explicit recognition in public law until enactment of the Legislative Reorganization Act of 1946.[1] That act required House and Senate standing committees to exercise *"continuous watchfulness"* over programs and agencies within their jurisdiction.

Since the late 1960s, according to such scholars as political scientist Joel Aberbach, Congress has shown increasing interest in oversight for several major reasons. These reasons include the expansion in number and complexity of federal programs and agencies; increases in expenditures and personnel, including contract employees; the rise of the budget deficit; and the frequency of divided government, with Congress and the White House controlled by different parties. Major partisan disagreements over priorities and processes also heighten conflict between the legislature and the executive branches.

Oversight occurs in virtually any congressional activity and through a wide variety of channels, organizations, and structures. These range from formal committee hearings to informal Member contacts with executive officials, from staff studies to support agency reviews, and from casework conducted by Member offices to studies prepared by non-congressional entities, such as statutory commissions and offices of inspector general.

Purposes

Congressional oversight of the executive is designed to fulfill a number of purposes:

Ensure Executive Compliance with Legislative Intent

Congress, of necessity, must delegate discretionary authority to federal administrators. To make certain that these officers faithfully execute laws according to the intent of Congress, committees and Members can review the actions taken and regulations formulated by departments and agencies.

Improve the Efficiency, Effectiveness, and Economy of Governmental Operations

A large federal bureaucracy makes it imperative for Congress to encourage and secure efficient and effective program management, and to make every dollar count toward the achievement of

---

[1] P.L. 79-601, 60 Stat. 812 (1946).

program goals. A basic objective is strengthening federal programs through better managerial operations and service delivery. Such steps can improve the accountability of agency managers to Congress and enhance program performance.

Evaluate Program Performance

Systematic program performance evaluation remains a relatively new and still-evolving technique in oversight. Modern program evaluation uses social science and management methodologies, such as surveys, cost-benefit analyses, and efficiency studies, to assess the effectiveness of ongoing programs.

Prevent Executive Encroachment on Legislative Prerogatives and Powers

Beginning in the late 1960s, many commentators, public policy analysts, and legislators argued that Presidents and executive officials overstepped their authority in various areas such as impoundment of funds, executive privilege, war powers, and the dismantling of federal programs without congressional consent. Increased oversight—as part of the checks and balances system— was called for to redress what many in the public and Congress saw to be an executive arrogation of legislative prerogatives.

Investigate Alleged Instances of Poor Administration, Arbitrary and Capricious Behavior, Abuse, Waste, Dishonesty, and Fraud

Instances of fraud and other forms of corruption, the breakdown of federal programs, incompetent management, and the subversion of governmental processes arouse legislative and public interest in oversight.

Assess Agency or Officials' Ability to Manage and Carry Out Program Objectives

Congress's ability to evaluate the capacity of agencies and managers to carry out program objectives can be accomplished in various ways. For example, numerous laws require agencies to submit reports to Congress; some of these are regular, occurring annually or semi-annually, for instance, while others are activated by a specific event, development, or set of conditions. Reporting requirement may promote self-evaluation by the agency. Organizations outside of Congress, such as offices of inspector general and study commissions, also advise Members and committees on how well federal agencies are working.

Review and Determine Federal Financial Priorities

Congress exercises some of its most effective oversight through the appropriations process, which provides the opportunity to review recent expenditures in detail. In addition, most federal agencies and programs are under regular and frequent reauthorizations—on an annual, two-year, four-year, or other basis—giving the authorizing committees the same opportunity. As a consequence of these oversight efforts, Congress can abolish or curtail obsolete or ineffective programs by cutting off or reducing funds or it may enhance effective programs by increasing funds.

Ensure That Executive Policies Reflect the Public Interest

Congressional oversight can appraise whether the needs and interests of the public are adequately served by federal programs, and thus lead to corrective action, either through legislation or administrative changes.

Protect Individual Rights and Liberties

Congressional oversight can help to safeguard the rights and liberties of citizens and others. By revealing abuses of authority, for instance, oversight hearings and other efforts can halt executive misconduct and help to prevent its recurrence, either directly through new legislation or indirectly by putting pressure on the offending agency.

Other Specific Purposes

The general purposes of oversight—and what constitutes this function—can be stated in more specific terms. Like the general purposes, these unavoidably overlap because of the numerous and multifaceted dimensions of oversight. A brief list includes:

- review the agency rulemaking process;
- monitor the use of contractors and consultants for government services;
- encourage and promote mutual cooperation between the branches;
- examine agency personnel procedures;
- acquire information useful in future policymaking;
- investigate constituent complaints and media critiques;
- assess whether program design and execution maximize the delivery of services to beneficiaries;
- compare the effectiveness of one program with another;
- protect agencies and programs against unjustified criticisms; and
- study federal evaluation activities.

Thoughts on Oversight and its Rationales from...

James Wilson (The Works of James Wilson, 1896, vol. II, p. 29), an architect of the Constitution and Associate Justice on the first Supreme Court:

> The House of Representatives ... form the grand inquest of the state. They will diligently inquire into grievances, arising both from men and things.

Woodrow Wilson (Congressional Government, 1885, p. 297), perhaps the first scholar to use the term "oversight" to refer to the review and investigation of the executive branch:

> Quite as important as legislation is vigilant oversight of administration.

> It is the proper duty of a representative body to look diligently into every affair of government and to talk much about what it sees. It is meant to be the eyes and the voice, and to embody the wisdom and will of its constituents.

> The informing function of Congress should be preferred even to its legislative function.

John Stuart Mill (Considerations on Representative Government, 1861, p. 104), British utilitarian philosopher:

> ... the proper office of a representative assembly is to watch and control the government; to throw the light of publicity on its acts; to compel a full exposition and justification of all of them which any one considers questionable....

Authority to Conduct Oversight

United States Constitution

The Constitution grants Congress extensive authority to oversee and investigate executive branch activities. The constitutional authority for Congress to conduct oversight stems from such explicit and implicit provisions as:

- *The power of the purse.* The Constitution provides that "No Money shall be drawn from the Treasury, but in Consequence of Appropriations made by Law."[2] Each year the Committees on Appropriations of the House and Senate review the financial practices and needs of federal agencies. The appropriations process allows Congress to exercise extensive control over the activities of executive agencies. Congress can define the precise purposes for which money may be spent, adjust funding levels, and prohibit expenditures for certain purposes.

- *The power to organize the executive branch.* Congress has the authority to create, abolish, reorganize, and fund federal departments and agencies. It has the authority to assign or reassign functions to departments and agencies, and grant new forms of authority and staff to administrators. Congress, in short, exercises ultimate authority over executive branch organization and generally over policy.[3]

- *The power to make all laws for "carrying into Execution" Congress's own enumerated powers as well as those of the executive.* Article I grants Congress a wide range of powers, such as the power to tax and coin money; regulate foreign and interstate commerce; declare war; provide for the creation and maintenance

---

[2] U.S. CONST. art. I, § 9, cl. 7.

[3] U.S. CONST. art. I, § 9; *see also* U.S. CONST. art. II, § 2, cl. 2.

of armed forces; and establish post offices.[4] Augmenting these specific powers is the Necessary and Proper Clause, also known as the "Elastic Clause," which gives Congress the authority "To make all Laws which shall be necessary and proper for carrying into Execution the foregoing Powers, and all other Powers vested by this Constitution in the Government of the United States, or in any Department or Officer thereof."[5] Clearly, these provisions grant broad authority to regulate and oversee departmental activities established by law.

- *The power to confirm officers of the United States.* The confirmation process not only involves the determination of a nominee's suitability for an executive (or judicial) position, but also provides an opportunity to examine the current policies and programs of an agency along with those policies and programs that the nominee intends to pursue.[6]

- *The power of investigation and inquiry.* A traditional method of exercising the oversight function, an implied power,[7] is through investigations and inquiries into executive branch operations. Legislators often seek to know how effectively and efficiently programs are working, how well agency officials are responding to legislative directives, and how the public perceives the programs. The investigatory method helps to ensure a more responsible bureaucracy, while supplying Congress with information needed to formulate new legislation.

- *Impeachment and removal.* Impeachment provides Congress with a powerful, ultimate oversight tool to investigate alleged executive and judicial misbehavior, and to eliminate such misbehavior through the convictions and removal from office of the offending individuals.[8]

The Supreme Court on Congress's Power to Oversee and Investigate

McGrain v. *Daugherty*, 273 U.S. 135, 177, 181-182 (1927):

Congress, investigating the administration of the Department of Justice during the Teapot Dome scandal, was considering a subject "on which legislation could be had or would be materially aided by the information which the investigation was calculated to elicit." The "potential" for legislation was sufficient. The majority added, "We are of [the] opinion that the power of inquiry—with process to enforce it—is an essential and appropriate auxiliary to the legislative function."

Eastland v. *United States Servicemen's Fund*, 421 U.S. 491, 509 (1975):

Expanding on its holding in *McGrain*, the Court declared, "To be a valid legislative inquiry there need be no predictable end result."

---

[4] U.S. CONST. art. I, § 8.

[5] U.S. CONST. art. I, § 8, cl. 18.

[6] *See* U.S. CONST. art. II, § 2, cl. 2.

[7] For a more detailed discussion of constitutional authority to investigate, *see* *"Constitutional Authority to Perform Oversight and Investigative Inquiries."*

[8] *See* U.S. CONST. art. II, § 4.

Principal Statutory Authority

Direct Expansions of Congress's Oversight Power

A number of laws directly augment Congress's authority, mandate, and resources to conduct oversight, including assigning specific duties to committees. Among the most important, listed chronologically, are:

1. *1912 Anti-Gag Legislation and Whistleblower Protection Laws for Federal Employees.*

   a. The 1912 act countered executive orders, issued by Presidents Theodore Roosevelt and William Howard Taft, which prohibited civil service employees from communicating directly with Congress.

   b. It also guaranteed that "the right of any persons employed in the civil service ... to petition Congress, or any Member thereof, or to furnish information to either House of Congress, or to any committee or member thereof, shall not be denied or interfered with." 37 Stat. 555 (1912), codified at 5 U.S.C. §7211 (2006).

   c. The Whistleblowers Protection Act of 1978, as amended, makes it a prohibited personnel practice for an agency employee to take (or not take) any action against an employee that is in retaliation for disclosure of information that the employee believes relates to violation of law, rule or regulation or which evidences gross mismanagement, waste, fraud or abuse of authority (5 U.S.C. § 2302 (b)(8)). The prohibition is explicitly intended to protect disclosures to Congress: "This subsection shall not be construed to authorize the withholding of information from the Congress or the taking of any personnel action against an employee who disclosures information to the Congress."

   d. Intelligence Community Whistleblower Protection Act (P.L. 105-272) establishes special procedures for personnel in the Intelligence Community, to transmit urgent concerns involving classified information to inspectors general and the House and Senate Select Committees on Intelligence.

   e. Section 714 of the Consolidated Appropriations Act, 2010, P.L. 111-117, 123 Stat. 3034 (2010), prohibits the payment of the salary of any officer or employee of the Federal Government who prohibits or prevents or attempts or threatens to prohibit or prevent, any other Federal officer or employee from having direct oral or written communication or contact with any Member, committee or subcommittee. This prohibition applies irrespective of whether such communication was initiated by such officer or employee or in response to the request or inquiry of such Member, committee or subcommittee. Further, any punishment or threat of punishment because of any contact or communication by an officer or employee with a Member, committee, or subcommittee is prohibited under the provisions of this act.

   f. Section 716 of the Consolidated Appropriations Act, 2010, P.L. 111-117, 123 Stat. 3034 (2010), prohibits the expenditure of any appropriated funds for use in implementing or enforcing agreement in Standard Forms 312 and 4414 of the Government or any other non-disclosure policy, form, or agreement if such policy, form, or agreement does not contain a provision that states that the restrictions are consistent with and do not supersede, conflict with, or otherwise alter the employee obligation, rights and liabilities created by E.O. 12958; 5 U.S.C. § 7211 (Lloyd-LaFollette Act); 10 U.S.C. §1034 (Military Whistleblower Act); 5 U.S.C. § 2303 (b)(8) (Whistleblower Protection Act); 50 U.S.C. § 421 et seq. (Intelligence Identities Protection Act); and 18 U.S.C. §§ 641, 793, 794, 798, and 952 and 50 U.S.C. § (783)(b).

2. *1921 Budget and Accounting Act Establishing the General Accounting Office (GAO)*, renamed the Government Accountability Office in 2004.

   a. Insisted that GAO "*shall be independent of the executive* departments and under the control and direction of the Comptroller General of the United States." 42 Stat. 23 (1921) (emphasis added); and

   b. Granted authority to the Comptroller General to "*investigate, at the seat of government or elsewhere*, all matters relating to the receipt, disbursement, and application of public funds." 42 Stat. 26 (1921) (emphasis added).

3. *1946 Legislative Reorganization Act*

   a. Mandated House and Senate committees to exercise "*continuous watchfulness*" of the administration of laws and programs under their jurisdiction. 60 Stat. 832 (1946) (emphasis added);

   b. Authorized for the first time in history, *permanent professional and clerical staff* for committees. 60 Stat. 832 (1946) (emphasis added);

   c. Authorized and directed the *Comptroller General* to make administrative management analyses of each executive branch agency. 60 Stat. 837 (1946) (emphasis added); and

   d. Established the Legislative Reference Service, renamed the Congressional Research Service by the 1970 Legislative Reorganization Act (see below), as a separate department in the Library of Congress and called upon the Service "to advise and assist any committee of either House or joint committee in the analysis, appraisal, and evaluation of any legislative proposal ... and *otherwise to assist in furnishing a basis for the proper determination of measures* before the committee." 60 Stat. 836 (1946) (emphasis added).

4. *1968 Intergovernmental Cooperation Act*

   a. Required that House and Senate committees having jurisdiction over *grants-in-aid* conduct studies of the programs under which grants-in-aid are made. 82 Stat. 1098 (1968); and

   b. Provided that studies of these programs are to determine whether: (1) their purposes have been met, (2) their objectives could be carried on without further assistance, (3) they are adequate to meet needs, and (4) any changes in programs or procedures should be made. 82 Stat. 1098 (1968).

5. *1970 Legislative Reorganization Act*

    a. Revised and rephrased in more explicit language the oversight function of House and Senate standing committees: "... each standing committee shall *review and study, on a continuing basis, the application, administration, and execution* of those laws or parts of laws, the subject matter of which is within the jurisdiction of that committee." 84 Stat. 1156 (1970) (emphasis added);

    b. Required most House and Senate committees to issue *biennial* oversight reports. 84 Stat. 1156 (1970) (emphasis added);

    c. Strengthened the *program evaluation* responsibilities and other authorities and duties of the GAO. 84 Stat. 1168-1171 (1970) (emphasis added);

    d. Redesignated the Legislative Reference Service as the *Congressional Research Service*, strengthening its *policy analysis* role and expanding its other responsibilities to Congress. 84 Stat. 1181-1185 (1970) (emphasis added);

    e. Recommended that House and Senate committees ascertain whether *programs* within their jurisdiction could be *appropriated for annually*. 84 Stat. 1174-1175 (1970) (emphasis added);

    f. Required most House and Senate committees to include in their committee reports on legislation *five-year cost estimates* for carrying out the proposed program. 84 Stat. 1173-1174 (1970) (emphasis added); and

    g. *Increased by two the number of permanent staff for each standing committee, including provision for minority party hirings*, and provided for hiring of *consultants* by standing committees. 84 Stat. 1175-1179 (1970) (emphasis added).

6. *1972 Federal Advisory Committee Act*

    a. Directed House and Senate committees to make a *continuing review* of the activities of each advisory committee under its jurisdiction. 86 Stat. 771 (1972) (emphasis added); and

    b. The studies are to determine whether: (1) such committee should be abolished or merged with any other advisory committee, (2) its responsibility should be revised, and (3) it performs a necessary function not already being performed. 86 Stat. 771 (1972).[9]

7. *1974 Congressional Budget Act, as amended*

    a. *Expanded* House and Senate committee *authority for oversight*. Permitted committees to appraise and evaluate programs themselves "or by contract, or (to) require a Government agency to do so and furnish a report thereon to the Congress." 88 Stat. 325 (1974);

---

[9] Advisory committee charters and reports can generally be obtained from the agency or government organization being advised.

b. Directed the Comptroller General to *"review and evaluate the results of Government programs and activities,"* on his own initiative, or at the request of either House or any standing or joint committee and to assist committees in analyzing and assessing program reviews or evaluation studies. Authorized GAO to establish an Office of Program Review and Evaluation to carry out these responsibilities. 88 Stat. 326 (1974) (emphasis added);

c. Strengthened GAO's role in *acquiring fiscal, budgetary, and program-related information.* 88 Stat. 327-329 (1974) (emphasis added);

d. Established House and Senate Budget Committees and the Congressional Budget Office (CBO). The CBO director is authorized to *"secure information, data, estimates, and statistics directly* from the various departments, agencies, and establishments" of the government. 88 Stat. 302 (1974) (emphasis added).

e. Required any House or Senate legislative committee report on a public bill or resolution to include an *analysis* (prepared by CBO) providing an *estimate and comparison of costs* which would be incurred in carrying out the bill during the next and following four fiscal years in which it would be effective. 88 Stat. 320 (1974) (emphasis added); and

Indirect Expansions of Congress's Oversight Power

Separate from expanding its own authority and resources directly, Congress has strengthened its oversight capabilities *indirectly*, by, for instance, establishing study commissions to review and evaluate programs, policies, and operations of the government. In addition, Congress has created various *mechanisms, structures, and procedures within the executive branch* that improve the executive's ability to monitor and control its own operations and, at the same time, provide additional information and oversight-related analyses to Congress. These statutory provisions include:

1. *Inspector General Act of 1978*, as amended, 5 U.S.C. Appendix 3: Establishing offices of inspector general in all cabinet departments and larger agencies and numerous boards, commissions, and government corporations;

2. *Chief Financial Officers Act of 1990*, 107 Stat. 2838 (1990): Establishing chief financial officers in all cabinet departments and larger agencies;

3. *Financial Integrity Act of 1982*, 96 Stat. 814-815 (1982): Improving the government's ability to manage its programs;

4. *Cash Management Improvement Act of 1990*, 104 Stat. 1058 (1990): Improving the efficiency, effectiveness, and equity in the exchange of funds between the federal government and state governments;

5. *Government Performance and Results Act of 1993*, 107 Stat. 285-296 (1993), as amended by the *GPRA Modernization Act of 2010* (P.L. 111-352; 124 Stat. 3866-3884): Increasing efficiency, effectiveness, and accountability within the government;

6. *Government Management and Reform Act of 1994*, 108 Stat. 3410 (1994): Improving the executive's stewardship of federal resources and accountability;

7. *Paperwork Reduction Act of 1995*, 109 Stat. 163 (1995): Controlling federal paperwork requirements;

8. *Information Technology Improvement Act*, 110 Stat. 679 (1996): Establishing the position of chief information officer in federal agencies to provide relevant advice for purchasing the best and most cost-effective information technology available;

9. *Single Audit Act of 1984*, as amended, 98 Stat. 2327 (1984) and 110 Stat. 679 (1996): Establishing uniform audit requirements for state and local governments and nonprofit organizations receiving federal financial assistance;

10. *Small Business Regulatory Enforcement Fairness Act of 1996*, 110 Stat. 857-874 (1996), codified at 5 U.S.C. §§801-808 (2006): Creating a mechanism, the Congressional Review Act (CRA), by which Congress can review and disapprove virtually any federal rule or regulation; and

11. Enacting other laws to assist the House and Senate in their reviews of various programs. For example, *the Economic Stabilization Act of 2008* (P.L. 110-343):

    a. The act permits the Secretary of the Treasury to purchase and insure "troubled assets" to help promote the strength of the economy and financial system. The act established two organizations to provide broad oversight of the program—a Financial Stability Oversight Board and a Congressional Oversight Panel.

    b. The act also placed audit responsibilities for the program with two individuals—a new Special Inspector General for the Troubled Asset Relief Program and the Comptroller General of the United States, who heads the GAO. And in 2010, Congress called on GAO to report annually, identifying "areas of potential duplication, overlap, and fragmentation, which, if effectively addressed, could provide financial and other benefits" (P.L. 111-139; 124 Stat. 29).

Responsibilities in House and Senate Rules

House Rules

1. House rules grant the *Committee on Oversight and Government Reform* a comprehensive role in the conduct of oversight (Rule X, clause 4). For example, pertinent review findings and recommendations of this committee are to be considered by the authorizing committees, if presented to them in a timely fashion. In addition, the authorizing committees are to indicate on the cover of their reports on public measures that they contain a summary of such findings when that is the case (Rule XIII, clause 3).

2. The Committee on Oversight and Government Reform has *additional* oversight duties to:

    a. review and study on a continuing basis, the operation of government activities at all levels to determine their economy and efficiency (Rule X, clause 3);

    b.   receive and examine reports of the Comptroller General and submit recommendations thereon to the House (Rule X, clause 4);

    c.   evaluate the effects of laws enacted to reorganize the legislative and executive branches of the government (Rule X, clause 4);

    d.   study intergovernmental relationships between the United States and states, municipalities, and international organizations of which the United States is a member (Rule X, clause 4); and

    e.   *report an oversight agenda*, not later than March 31 of the first session of a Congress, based upon oversight plans submitted by each standing committee and after consultation with the Speaker of the House, the majority leader, and the minority leader. The oversight agenda is to include the oversight plans of each standing committee together with any recommendations that it or the House leadership group may make to ensure the most effective coordination of such plans (Rule X, clause 2).

3.   House rules mandate or provide authority for other oversight efforts by *standing committees*:

    a.   Each standing committee (except Appropriations and Budget) shall review and study on a *continuing basis* the application, administration, and execution of all laws within its legislative jurisdiction (Rule X, clause 2). The investigatory authority of committees is outlined Under House Rule XI, clause 1.

    b.   Committees have the authority to *review the impact of tax policies* on matters that fall within their jurisdiction (Rule X, clause 2).

    c.   Each committee (except Appropriations and Budget) has a responsibility for futures research and forecasting (Rule X, clause 2).

    d.   Specified committees have *special oversight authority* (i.e., the right to conduct comprehensive reviews of specific subject areas that are within the legislative jurisdiction of other committees). Special oversight is akin to the broad oversight authority granted the Committee on Government Reform, by the 1946 Legislature Reorganization Act, except that special oversight is generally limited to named subjects (Rule X, clause 3).

    e.   Each standing committee having more than 20 members shall establish an oversight subcommittee, or require its subcommittees, if any, *to conduct oversight* in their jurisdictional areas; a committee that establishes such a subcommittee may add it as a sixth subcommittee, beyond the usual limit of five (Rule X, clauses 2 and 5).

    f.   Committee reports on measures are to include *oversight findings* separately set out and clearly identified (Rule XIII, clause 3). They are also to include a statement of general performance goals and objectives, including outcome-related goals and objectives, for which the measure authorizes funding.

    g.   Costs of stenographic services and transcripts for *oversight hearings* are to be paid "from the applicable accounts of the House" (Rule XI, clause 1).

    h.   *Each standing committee is to submit its oversight plans* for the duration of a Congress by February 15 of the first session to the Committee on Oversight and Government Reform and the Committee on House Administration. Not later than March 31, the Committee on Oversight and Government Reform must report an oversight agenda (discussed above). In developing such plans, each standing committee must, to the extent feasible (Rule X, clause 2):

    i. consult with other committees of the House that have jurisdiction over the same or related laws, programs, or agencies within its jurisdiction, with the objective of ensuring that such laws, programs, or agencies are reviewed in the same Congress and that there is a maximum of coordination between such committees in the conduct of such reviews; and such plans shall include an explanation of what steps have been and will be taken to ensure such coordination cooperation;

    ii. review specific problems with Federal rules, regulations, statutes, and court decisions that are ambiguous, arbitrary, or nonsensical, or that impose severe financial burdens on individuals;

    iii. give priority consideration to including in its plans the review of those laws, programs, or agencies operating under permanent budget authority or permanent statutory authority;

    iv. have a view toward ensuring that all significant laws, programs, or agencies within its jurisdiction are subject to review at least once every 10 years;

    v. have a view toward insuring against duplication of Federal programs; and

    vi. include proposals to cut or eliminate mandatory and discretionary programs that are inefficient, duplicative, outdated, or more appropriately administered by state or local government.

i. *Each committee* must submit to the House not later than June 30 and December 1 a semi-annual activities report (Rule XI, clause 1).

    i. Such report must include *separate sections summarizing the legislative and oversight activities* of that committee during the applicable period;

    ii. in the case of the first such report, a summary of the oversight plans submitted by the committee under clause 2(d) of Rule X;

    iii. a summary of the actions taken and recommendations made with respect to the oversight plans; and

    iv. a summary of any additional oversight activities undertaken by that committee and any recommendations made or actions taken thereon.

j. House Rule XI, clause 2, requires each standing committee to hold at least one hearing during each 120-day period on waste, fraud, abuse, and mismanagement in the government programs that the committee may authorize. Committees are to focus on egregious instances of waste and mismanagement as documented by reports of inspectors general and the Comptroller General. House committees are also obligated to hold a hearing if an agency's financial statements are not in order and if a program under a committee's jurisdiction is deemed by GAO to be at high risk for waste, fraud, and abuse.

4. *The Speaker*, with the approval of the House, is given additional authority to "appoint *special ad hoc oversight committees* for the purpose of reviewing specific matters within the jurisdiction of two or more standing committees." (Rule X, clause 2) (emphasis added).

Senate Rules

1. Each standing committee (except for Appropriations and Budget) must review and study on a continuing basis, the application, administration, and execution of all laws within its legislative jurisdiction (Rule XXVI, clause 8).

2. "Comprehensive policy oversight" responsibilities are granted to specified standing committees. This duty is similar to special oversight in the House. The Committee on Agriculture, Nutrition, and Forestry, for example, is authorized to "study and review, on a comprehensive basis, matters relating to food, nutrition, and hunger, both in the United States and in foreign countries, and rural affairs, and report thereon from time to time." (Rule XXV, clause 1(a)).

3. All standing committees, except Appropriations, are required to prepare regulatory impact evaluations in their committee reports accompanying each public bill or joint resolution (Rule XXVI, clause 11). The evaluations are to include:

    a. an estimate of the numbers of individuals and businesses to be affected;

    b. a determination of the measure's economic impact and effect on personal privacy; and

    c. a determination of the amount of additional paperwork that will result.

4. The Committee on Homeland Security and Governmental Affairs has the following *additional oversight duties* (Rule XXV, clause 1(k)):

    a. review and study on a continuing basis the operation of government activities at all levels to determine their economy and efficiency;

    b. receive and examine reports of the Comptroller General and submit recommendations thereon to the Senate;

    c. evaluate the effects of laws enacted to reorganize the legislative and executive branches of the government; and

    d. study intergovernmental relationships between the United States and states, municipalities, and international organizations of which the United States is a member.

    e. On March 1, 1948 (during the 80th Congress), the Senate adopted S. Res. 189, which established the Permanent Subcommittee on Investigations of the Committee on Homeland Security and Governmental Affairs (then titled the Committee on Government Operations). The Subcommittee was an outgrowth of the famous 1941 Truman Committee (after Senator Harry Truman), which investigated fraud and mismanagement of the nation's war program. The Truman Committee ended in 1948, but the chairman of the Government Operations Committee made the functions of the Truman panel one of his subcommittees: the Permanent Subcommittee on Investigations.

Since then this Subcommittee has investigated scores of issues, such as government waste, fraud, and inefficiency.

Congressional Participants in Oversight

Members

Oversight is generally considered a committee activity.[10] However, both casework and other project work conducted in a Member's personal office can result in findings about bureaucratic behavior and policy implementation; these, in turn, can lead to the adjustment of agency policies and procedures and to changes in public law.

1. *Casework*—responding to constituent requests for assistance on projects or complaints or grievances about program implementation provides an opportunity to examine bureaucratic activity and operations, if only in a selective way.

2. Sometimes *individual Members* will conduct their own investigations or ad hoc hearings, or direct their staffs to conduct oversight studies. Individual Members have no authority to issue compulsory process or conduct official hearings. GAO or some other legislative branch agency, a specially created task force, or private research group might be requested to conduct an investigation of a matter for a Senator or Representative.

Committees

The most common and effective method of conducting oversight is through the committee structure. Throughout their histories, the House and Senate have used their standing committees as well as select or special committees to investigate federal activities and agencies along with other matters.

1. The House Committee on *Government Reform* and the Senate Committee on *Homeland Security and Governmental Affairs*, which have oversight jurisdiction over virtually the entire federal government, have been vested with broad investigatory powers over government-wide activities.

2. The House and Senate Committees on *Appropriations* have similar responsibilities when reviewing fiscal activities.

3. Each *standing* committee of Congress has oversight responsibilities to review government activities within their jurisdiction. These panels also have authority on their own to establish oversight and investigative *subcommittees*. The establishment of such subcommittees does *not preclude* the *legislative* subcommittees from conducting oversight.

4. Certain House and Senate committees have "*special oversight*" or "*comprehensive policy oversight*" of designated subject areas as explained in the previous subsection.

---

[10] For more information on the legal authority of individual Members, *see "Individual Member and Minority Party Authority to Conduct Oversight and Investigations."*

Personal Staff

Constituent letters, complaints, and requests for projects and assistance frequently bring problems and deficiencies in federal programs and administration to the attention of Members and their personal office staffs. The casework performed by a Member's staff for constituents can be an effective oversight tool.

1. Casework can be an important vehicle for pursuing both the oversight and legislative interests of the Member. The Senator or Representative and the staff may be attuned to the *relationship* between *casework* and the *oversight* function. This is facilitated by a regular exchange of ideas among the Member, legislative aides, and caseworkers on problems brought to the office's attention by constituents, and of possible legislative initiatives to resolve those problems.

2. If casework is to be useful as an oversight technique, *effective staffing and coordination are needed*. Casework and legislative staffs maximize service to their Member's constituents when they establish a relationship with the staff of the subcommittees and committees that handle the areas of concern to the Member's constituents. Through this interaction, the panel's staff can be made aware of the problems with the agency or program in question, assess how widespread and significant they are, determine their causes, and recommend corrective action.

3. *Office procedures* enable staff in some offices to identify cases that represent a situation in which *formal* changes in agency procedure could be an appropriate remedy. Prompt congressional inquiry and follow up enhance this type of oversight. Telephone inquiries reinforced with written requests tend to ensure agency attention.

Committee Staff

As issues become more complex and Members' staffs more overworked, professional staffs of committees can provide the expert help required to conduct oversight and investigations. Committee staff typically have the experience and expertise to conduct effective oversight for the committees and subcommittees they serve. Committees may also call upon *legislative support agencies* for assistance, hire *consultants*, or "*borrow*" *staff* from federal departments.

Committee staff, in summary, occupy a central position in the conduct of oversight. The informal contacts with executive officials at all levels constitute one of Congress's most effective devices for performing its "continuous watchfulness" function.

Congressional Support Agencies and Offices

Of the agencies in the legislative branch, three directly assist Congress in support of its oversight function:

- Congressional Budget Office (CBO);

- Congressional Research Service (CRS) of the Library of Congress; and

- Government Accountability Office (GAO).

For further detail on these offices, see "Oversight Information Sources and Consultant Services".

Additional offices that can assist in oversight are the House General Counsel's Office; House Parliamentarian's Office; House Clerk's Office; Senate Legal Counsel's Office; and Senate Historian's Office and Senate Library.

Oversight Coordination and Processes

A persistent problem for Congress in conducting oversight is coordination among committees, both within each chamber as well as between the two houses. As the final report of the House Select Committee on Committees of the 93rd Congress noted, "Review findings and recommendations developed by one committee are seldom shared on a timely basis with another committee, and, if they are made available, then often the findings are transmitted in a form that is difficult for Members to use."[11] Despite the passage of time, this statement remains relevant today. Oversight coordination between House and Senate committees is also uncommon; and it occurs primarily in the aftermath of perceived major policy failures or prominent inter-branch conflicts, as with the Iran-contra affair and the 9/11 terrorist attacks.

Intercommittee cooperation on oversight can prove beneficial for a variety of reasons. It should, for example, minimize unnecessary duplication and conflict and inhibit agencies from playing one committee against another. There are formal and informal ways to achieve oversight coordination among committees.

Oversight Coordination

General Techniques of Ensuring Oversight Coordination Include

1. The House and Senate can establish select or special committees to probe issues and agencies, to promote public understanding of national concerns, and to coordinate oversight of issues that overlap the jurisdiction of several standing committees.

2. House rules require the findings and recommendations of the Committee on Oversight and Government Reform to be considered by the authorizing committees if presented to them in a timely fashion. Such findings and recommendations are to be published in the authorizing committees' reports on legislation. House rules also require the oversight plans of committees to include ways to maximize coordination between and among committees that share jurisdiction over related laws, programs, or agencies.

Specific Means of Ensuring Oversight Coordination Include

1. Joint oversight hearings on programs or agencies.

---

[11] H.Rept. 93-916, at 68 (1974).

2. Informal agreement among committees to oversee certain agencies and not others. For example, the House and Senate Committees on Commerce agreed to hold oversight hearings on certain regulatory agencies in alternate years.

3. Consultation between the authorizing and appropriating committees. The two Committees on Commerce have worked closely and successfully with their corresponding appropriations subcommittees to alert those panels to the authorizing committees' intent with respect to regulatory ratemaking by such agencies as the Federal Communications Commission.

Oversight through Legislative and Investigative Processes

The Budget Process

1. The Congressional Budget and Impoundment Control Act of 1974,[12] as amended, enhanced the legislative branch's capacity to shape the federal budget. The act has major institutional and procedural effects on Congress:

   a. *Institutionally*, Congress created three new entities: the Senate Committee on the Budget; the House Committee on the Budget; and the Congressional Budget Office. CBO

   b. *Procedurally*, the act established methods that permit Congress to: determine budget policy as a whole; relate revenue and spending decisions; determine priorities among competing national programs; and ensure that revenue, spending, and debt legislation are consistent with the overall budget policy.

2. The new budget process coexists with the established authorization and appropriation procedures and significantly affects each.

   a. On the *authorization side*, the Budget Act requires committees to submit their budgetary "views and estimates" for matters under their jurisdiction to their Committee on the Budget within six weeks after the President submits a budget.

   b. On the *appropriations side*, new contract and borrowing authority must go through the appropriations process. Subcommittees of the Appropriations Committees are assigned a financial allocation that determines how much may be included in the measures they report, although less than one-third of federal spending is subject to the annual appropriations process. (The tax and appropriations panels of each house also submit budgetary views and estimates to their respective Committee on the Budget.)

   c. In deciding spending, revenue, credit, and debt issues, Congress is sensitive to trends in the overall composition of the annual federal budget (expenditures for defense, entitlements, interest on the debt, and domestic discretionary programs).

3. In short, these Budget Act reforms have the potential to strengthen oversight by enabling Congress better to relate program priorities to financial claims on the

---

[12] P.L. 93-344, 88 Stat. 297, *codified at* 2 U.S.C. §§ 607-688.

national budget. Each committee, knowing that it will receive a fixed amount of the total to be included in a budget resolution, has an incentive to scrutinize existing programs to make room for new programs or expanded funding of ongoing projects or to assess whether programs have outlived their usefulness.

The Authorization Process

1. Through its authorization power, Congress exercises significant control over any government agency. The entire authorization process may involve a host of oversight tools—hearings, studies, and reports—but the key to the process is the *authorization statute*.

    a. An authorization statute creates and shapes government programs and agencies and it contains the statement of legislative policy for the agency.

    b. Authorization is the *first* lever in congressional exercise of the power of the purse; it usually allows an agency to be funded, but it does *not* guarantee financing of agencies and programs. Frequently, authorizations establish dollar ceilings on the amounts that can be appropriated.

2. The authorization-reauthorization process is an important oversight tool.

    a. Through this process, Members are educated about the work of an agency and given an opportunity to direct the agency's effort in light of experience.

    b. Expiration of an agency's program provides an excellent chance for in-depth oversight:

        i. In recent decades, there has been a mix of permanent and periodic (annual or multi-year) authorizations, although reformers at time press for *biennial budgeting* (acting on a two-year cycle for authorizations, appropriations, and budget resolutions).

        ii. Periodic authorizations improve the likelihood that an agency will be scrutinized systematically.

3. In addition to formal amendment of the agency's authorizing statute, the authorization process gives committees an opportunity to exercise informal, nonstatutory controls over the agency.

    a. Knowledge by an agency that it must come to the legislative committee for renewed authority increases the influence of the committee. This condition helps to account for the appeal of short-term authorizations.

    b. *Non-statutory controls* used by committees to exercise direction over the administration of laws include statements made in:

        i. committee hearings;

        ii. committee reports accompanying legislation;

        iii. floor debates; and

        iv. committee contacts and correspondence with the agency.

4. If agencies fail to comply with these informal directives, the authorization committees can apply sanctions or move to convert the informal directive to a statutory command.

The Appropriations Process

1. The appropriations process is one of Congress's most important forms of oversight.

   a. Its strategic position stems from the constitutional requirement that "no Money shall be drawn from the Treasury, but in Consequence of Appropriations made by Law."[13]

   b. Congress's power of the purse allows the House and Senate Committees on Appropriations to play a prominent role in oversight.

2. The oversight function of the Committees on Appropriations derives from their responsibility to examine and pass on the budget requests of the agencies as contained in the President's Budget.

   a. The decisions of the committees are conditioned on their assessment of the agencies' need for their budget request as indicated by past performance. In practice, the entire record of an agency is fair game for the required assessment.

   b. This comprehensive overview and the "carrot and stick" of the appropriations recommendations make the committees significant focal points of congressional oversight and is a key source of their power in Congress and in the federal government generally.

3. Enacted appropriations legislation frequently contains at least five types of *statutory controls* on agencies:

   a. Such legislation specifies the *purpose* for which funds may be used.

   b. It defines the specified *funding level* for the agency as a whole as well as for programs and divisions within the agency.

   c. It sets *time limits* on the availability of funds for obligation.

   d. Appropriations legislation may contain *limitation* provisions. For example, in appropriating $350 million to the Environmental Protection Agency for research and development, Congress added this condition: "Provided, That not more than $55,000,000 of these funds shall be available for procurement of laboratory equipment, supplies, and other operating expenses in support of research and development." 108 Stat. 2319 (1994).

   e. Appropriations measures may stipulate how an agency's budget can be *reprogrammed* (shifting funds within an appropriations account).

4. *Nonstatutory controls* are a major form of oversight. Legislative language in committee reports and in hearings, letters to agency heads, and other communications give detailed instructions to agencies regarding committee expectations and desires. Agencies are not legally obligated to abide by non-statutory recommendations, but failure to do so may result in a loss of funds and flexibility the following year. Agencies ignore nonstatutory controls at their peril.

---

[13] U.S. CONST. art. I, § 9, cl. 17.

An Example of Nonstatutory Control of Agency Appropriations

The conference report for the Omnibus Consolidated and Emergency Supplemental Appropriations for FY1999 provides guidelines for the reprogramming and transfer of funds for the Treasury and General Government Appropriations Act, 1999. Each request from an agency to the review committee "shall include a declaration that, as of the date of the request, none of the funds included in the request have been obligated, and none will be obligated, until the Committees on Appropriations have approved the request." H.Rept. 105-825, p. 1472 (1998).

The Investigatory Process

Congress's power of investigation is *implied* in the Constitution. Numerous Supreme Court decisions have upheld the legislative branch's right of inquiry, provided it stays within its legitimate legislative sphere. The roots of Congress's authority to conduct investigations extend back to the British Parliament and colonial assemblies. In addition, the Framers clearly perceived the House of Representatives to function as a "grand inquest." Since the Framers expected lawmakers to employ the investigatory function, based upon parliamentary precedents, it was unnecessary to invest Congress with an explicit investigatory power.

1. Investigations and related activities may be conducted by:

   a. individual Members;

   b. committees and subcommittees;

   c. staff or outside organizations and personnel under contract; or

   d. congressional support agencies.

2. Investigations serve several purposes:

   a. they help to ensure honesty and efficiency in the administration of laws;

   b. they secure information that assists Congress in making informed policy judgments; and

   c. they may aid in informing the public about the administration of laws.

See "Investigative Oversight" for greater detail and analysis.

The Confirmation Process

By establishing a public record of the policy views of nominees, congressional hearings allow lawmakers to call appointed officials to account at a later time. Since at least the Ethics in Government Act of 1978,[14] which encouraged greater scrutiny of nominations, Senate committees are setting aside more time to probe the qualifications, independence, and policy predilections of presidential nominees, seeking information on everything from physical health to financial assets. Confirmation can assist in oversight in several ways.

1. The Constitution provides that the President "shall nominate, and by and with the *Advice and Consent of the Senate*, shall appoint Ambassadors, other public Ministers and Consuls, Judges of the supreme Court, and all other Officers of the

President appoints judges etc.

---

[14] P.L. 95-521, 92 Stat. 1824, *codified at* 5 U.S.C. App. §§ 101, *et. seq.*

United States, whose Appointments are not herein otherwise provided for, and which shall be established by Law."[15]

    a. The consideration of appointments to executive branch leadership positions is a major responsibility of the Senate and especially of Senate committees, which review and hold hearings regarding the qualifications of nominees.

2. The confirmation hearing serves as an opportunity for senatorial oversight and influence, providing a forum for the discussion of the policies and programs the nominee intends to pursue. The confirmation process as an oversight tool can be used to:

    i. provide policy direction to nominees;

    ii. inform nominees of congressional interests; and

    iii. extract future commitments.

3. Once a nominee has been confirmed by the Senate, oversight includes following up to ensure that the nominee fulfills any commitments made during confirmation hearings. Subsequent hearings and committee investigations can explore whether such commitments have been kept.

The President has alternative authority to make appointments that do not require the Advice and Consent of the Senate, including recess appointments[16] and designations under the Vacancies Act.[17]

The Impeachment Process

1. The impeachment power of Congress is a unique oversight tool, reserved for unusual circumstances and as a technique of last resort when conventional forms of oversight fail. Impeachment applies to the President, Vice President, and other federal civil officers in the executive and judicial branches.[18] Impeachment offers Congress:

    a. a constitutionally mandated method for obtaining information that might otherwise not be made available; and

    b. an implied threat of punishment for an official whose conduct exceeds acceptable boundaries.

2. Impeachment procedures differ from those of conventional congressional oversight. The most significant procedural differences center on the *roles* played by each house of Congress.

    a. The House of Representatives has the sole power to impeach. A majority is required to impeach.

---

[15] U.S. CONST. art. II, § 2, cl. 2.

[16] U.S. CONST. art. II, § 2, cl. 3. For more information on recess appointments, *see* CRS Report RL33009, *Recess Appointments: A Legal Overview*, by Vivian S. Chu.

[17] 5 U.S.C. §§ 3345, *et. seq.* For more information on the Vacancies Act, *see* CRS Report RS21412, *Temporarily Filling Presidentially Appointed, Senate-Confirmed Positions*, by Henry B. Hogue.

[18] U.S. CONST. art. II, § 4.

b. If the House votes to impeach, the person is tried by the Senate, which has the sole power to try an impeachment. A two-thirds majority is required to convict and remove the individual. Should the Senate deem it appropriate in a given case, it may, by majority vote, impose an additional judgment of disqualification from further federal offices of honor, trust, or profit.

c. In *Nixon v. United States*, 506 U.S. 226 (1993), the Supreme Court held nonjusticiable a constitutional challenge to the use by the Senate in an impeachment proceeding of a 12-member committee appointed to take testimony and gather evidence. Such a committee makes no recommendations as to the ultimate question before the Senate. Nor does the committee rule on questions of relevancy, materiality, and competency. Rather, it reports a certified copy of the transcript of the proceedings before the committee and any evidence received by the committee to the full Senate for its consideration. The full Senate may take further testimony or evidence, or it may hold the entire trial in open Senate. In either event, the full Senate determines whether to convict on one or more of the articles of impeachment involved and, upon conviction, decides the appropriate judgment to be imposed.

3. The impeachment process is cumbersome and infrequently used. The House has voted to impeach in 19 cases. The Senate has voted to convict in eight cases, all pertaining to federal judges. The most recent executive impeachment trial was that of President Clinton in 1998-99; the most recent judicial impeachment trial was that of U.S. District Court Judge G. Thomas Porteous, Jr. in 2010. A number of constitutional and procedural issues were addressed in the Clinton impeachment trial and other past impeachment proceedings, although the answers to some of these questions remain somewhat ambiguous. For example:

   a. An impeachment may be continued from one Congress to the next, although the procedural steps vary depending upon the stage in the process.

   b. The Constitution defines the grounds for impeachment as "Treason, Bribery, or other high Crimes and Misdemeanors."[19] However, the meaning and scope of "high Crimes and Misdemeanors" remains in dispute and depends on the interpretation of individual legislators.

   c. The Constitution provides for impeachment of the "President, Vice President, and all civil Officers of the United States."[20] While the outer limits of the "civil Officers" language are not altogether clear, past precedents suggest that it covers at least federal judges and executive officers subject to the Appointments Clause.

   d. Members of the House and Senate are not subject to impeachment because they are not "civil officers." William Blount, a U.S. Senator from Tennessee, was impeached by the House in 1797, but the Senate chose to *expel* him instead of conducting an impeachment trial.

[handwritten: Can impeach other federal civil officers]

---

[19] U.S. CONST. art. II, § 4.

[20] *Id.*

Investigative Oversight

Congressional oversight and investigations, which are often adversarial and confrontational, can serve to sustain and vindicate Congress's role in the United States' constitutional scheme of separated powers. The rich history of congressional investigations, from the failed St. Clair expedition in 1792 and including Teapot Dome, Watergate, Iran-Contra, and Whitewater, have established, both legally and as a matter of practice, the nature and contours of congressional prerogatives necessary to maintain the integrity of the legislative role.

This section provides an overview of some of the more common legal, procedural, and practical issues that committees may face in the course of conducting oversight and/or congressional investigations. It begins with a general summary of Congress's constitutional authority to perform oversight and investigations. It then turns to a discussion of the legal tools commonly used by congressional committees in conducting oversight and investigations, including the legal basis for subpoenas, staff depositions, and committee hearings, as well as a discussion of the various forms of contempt of Congress, the primary enforcement mechanism available. The section will then discuss limitations on congressional authority to conduct successful oversight and investigations, including constitutional privileges, such as executive privilege. Finally, the section will address a series of frequently encountered legal issues, such as the applicability of the Privacy Act and the Freedom of Information Act, access to grand jury materials and pending litigation files, and access to classified and confidential information.

Constitutional Authority to Perform Oversight and Investigative Inquiries

Generally, Congress's authority and power to obtain information, including classified and/or confidential information, is extremely broad. While there is no express provision of the Constitution or specific statute authorizing the conduct of congressional oversight or investigations, the Supreme Court has firmly established that such power is essential to the legislative function as to be implied from the general vesting of legislative powers in Congress.[21] In *Eastland v. United States Servicemen's Fund*, for instance, the Court stated that the "scope of its power of inquiry ... is as penetrating and far-reaching as the potential power to enact and appropriate under the Constitution."[22] In *Watkins v. United States,* the Court emphasized that the "power of the Congress to conduct investigations is inherent in the legislative process. That power is broad. It encompasses inquiries concerning the administration of existing laws as well as proposed or possibly needed statutes."[23] The Court further stressed that Congress's power to investigate is at its peak when focusing on alleged waste, fraud, abuse, or maladministration within a government department. Specifically, the Court explained that the investigative power "comprehends probes into departments of the federal government to expose corruption, inefficiency, or waste."[24] It also noted that the first Congresses held "inquiries dealing with

---

[21] *See, e.g.*, Nixon v. Administrator of General Services, 433 U.S. 435 (1977); Eastland v. United States Servicemen's Fund, 421 U.S. 491 (1975); Barenblatt v. United States, 360 U.S. 109 (1959); Watkins v. United States, 354 U.S. 178 (1957); McGrain v. Daugherty, 273 U.S. 135 (1927).

[22] *Eastland*, 421 U.S. at 504, n. 15 (quoting *Barenblatt*, 360 U.S. at 111).

[23] *Watkins*, 354 U.S. at 187.

[24] *Id.*

suspected corruption or mismanagement of government officials."[25] Given these factors, the Court recognized "the power of the Congress to inquire into and publicize corruption, maladministration, or inefficiencies in the agencies of Government."[26]

Authority of Congressional Committees

Oversight and investigative authority is implied from Article I of the Constitution and rests with the House of Representatives and Senate. The House and Senate have delegated this authority to various entities, the most relevant of which are the standing committees of each chamber. Committees of Congress only have the power to inquire into matters within the scope of the authority delegated to them by their parent body. However, a committee's investigative purview is substantial and wide-ranging if it satisfies this jurisdictional requirement and has a legislative purpose for conducting the inquiry.

Committee Jurisdiction

Establishing committee jurisdiction is the foundation for any attempt to obtain information and documents from the executive branch or a private entity or person. A claim of lawful jurisdiction, however, does not automatically entitle the committee to access whatever documents and information it may seek. Rather, an appropriate claim of jurisdiction authorizes the committee to inquire and request information. The specifics of such access may still be subject to prudential, political, and constitutionally-based privileges asserted by the targets of the inquiry.

As previously stated, a congressional committee is a creation of its parent house and, therefore, can only inquire into matters within the scope of the authority that has been delegated to it by that body.[27] Thus, the enabling chamber rule or resolution that gives the committee life is also the charter that defines the grant and limitations of the committee's power. In construing the scope of a committee's authorizing charter, courts will look to the words of the rule or resolution itself, and then, if necessary, to the usual sources of legislative history such as floor debate, legislative reports, and prior committee practice and interpretation.

House Rule X and Senate Rule XXV deal with the organization of each chamber's standing committees and establish their jurisdiction.[28] Jurisdictional authority for "special" investigations may be given to a standing committee, a joint committee of both houses, or a special subcommittee of a standing committee, among other vehicles. Given the specificity with which the House and Senate rules now confer jurisdiction on their standing committees, as well as the care with which most authorizing resolutions for special and/or select committees have been drafted in recent years, sufficient models exist to avoid a successful judicial challenge by a witness that his noncompliance was justified by a committee's overstepping its delegated scope of authority.

---

[25] *Id.* at 182.

[26] *Id.* at 200, n.33.

[27] United States v. Rumely, 345 U.S. 41, 42, 44 (1953); *see also Watkins*, 354 U.S. at 198.

[28] *See* House Rule X, 113th Cong. (2013); Senate Rule XXV, 114th Cong. (2013).

Legislative Purpose

While the congressional power of inquiry is broad, it is not unlimited. The Supreme Court has cautioned that the power to investigate may be exercised only "in aid of the legislative function"[29] and cannot be used to expose for the sake of exposure alone. The *Watkins* Court underlined these limitations, stating that:

> There is no general authority to expose the private affairs of individuals without justification in terms of the functions of the Congress ... nor is the Congress a law enforcement or trial agency. These are functions of the executive and judicial departments of government. No inquiry is an end in itself; it must be related to, and in furtherance of, a legitimate task of the Congress.[30]

A committee's inquiry must have a legislative purpose or be conducted pursuant to some other constitutional power of Congress, such as the authority of each House to discipline its own members, judge the returns of their elections, and conduct impeachment proceedings.[31] While the 1881 Supreme Court decision in *Kilbourn v. Thompson*[32] held that the challenged investigation was an improper probe into the private affairs of individuals, courts today generally presume there is a legislative purpose for an investigation.[33] The House or Senate rule or resolution authorizing the investigation does not have to specifically state the committee's legislative purpose.[34] In *In re Chapman*,[35] the Court upheld the validity of a resolution authorizing an inquiry into charges of corruption against certain Senators despite the fact that it was silent as to what might be done when the investigation was completed. The Court stated:

> The questions were undoubtedly pertinent to the subject matter of the inquiry. The resolutions directed the committee to inquire "whether any Senator has been, or is, speculating in what are known as sugar stocks during the consideration of the tariff bill now before the Senate." What the Senate might or might not do upon the facts when ascertained, we cannot say nor are we called upon to inquire whether such ventures might be defensible, as contended in argument, but it is plain that negative answers would have cleared that body of what the Senate regarded as offensive imputations, while affirmative answers might have led to further action on the part of the Senate within its constitutional powers.
>
> Nor will it do to hold that the Senate had no jurisdiction to pursue the particular inquiry because the preamble and resolutions did not specify that the proceedings were taken for the purpose of censure or expulsion, if certain facts were disclosed by the investigation. The matter was within the range of the constitutional powers of the Senate. The resolutions adequately indicated that the transactions referred to were deemed by the Senate reprehensible and deserving of condemnation and punishment. The right to expel extends to

---

[29] Kilbourn v. Thompson, 103 U.S. 168, 204 (1880).

[30] *Watkins*, 354 U.S. at 187.

[31] *See, e.g.*, McGrain v. Daugherty, 273 U.S. 135; In Re Chapman, 166 U.S. 661 (1897).

[32] 103 U.S. 168 (1881).

[33] *McGrain*, 273 U.S. 135.

[34] *Id.*; *see also* Townsend v. United States, 95 F.2d 352 (D.C. Cir. 1938); LEADING CASES ON CONGRESSIONAL INVESTIGATORY POWER, 7 (Comm. Print 1976) [hereinafter LEADING CASES]. For a different assessment of case law concerning the requirement of a legislative purpose, *see* Allen B. Moreland, *Congressional Investigations and Private Persons*, 40 SO. CAL. L. REV. 189, 232 (1967) [hereinafter Moreland].

[35] 166 U.S. 661, 669 (1897).

all cases where the offense is such as in the judgment of the Senate is inconsistent with the trust and duty of a Member.

We cannot assume on this record that the action of the Senate was without a legitimate object, and so encroach upon the province of that body. Indeed, we think it affirmatively appears that the Senate was acting within its right, and it was certainly not necessary that the resolutions should declare in advance what the Senate meditated doing when the investigation was concluded.[36]

In *McGrain v. Daugherty*,[37] the original resolution that authorized the Senate investigation into the Teapot Dome Affair made no mention of a legislative purpose. A subsequent resolution for the attachment of a contumacious witness declared that his testimony was sought for the purpose of obtaining "information necessary as a basis for such legislative and other action as the Senate may deem necessary and proper."[38] The Court found that the investigation was ordered for a legitimate object. It wrote:

The only legitimate object the Senate could have in ordering the investigation was to aid it in legislating, and we think the subject matter was such that the presumption should be indulged that this was the real object. An express avowal of the object would have been better; but in view of the particular subject-matter was not indispensable...

The second resolution–the one directing the witness be attached–declares that this testimony is sought with the purpose of obtaining "information necessary as a basis for such legislative and other action as the Senate may deem necessary and proper." This avowal of contemplated legislation is in accord with what we think is the right interpretation of the earlier resolution directing the investigation. The suggested possibility of "other action" if deemed "necessary or proper" is of course open to criticism in that there is no other action in the matter which would be within the power of the Senate. But we do not assent to the view that this indefinite and untenable suggestion invalidates the entire proceeding. The right view in our opinion is that it takes nothing from the lawful object avowed in the same resolution and is rightly inferable from the earlier one. It is not as if an inadmissible or unlawful object were affirmatively and definitely avowed.[39]

Moreover, it has been held that a court cannot say that a committee of Congress exceeds its power when the purpose of its investigation is supported by reference to specific problems which in the past have been, or in the future may be, the subject of appropriate legislation.[40] In the past, the types of legislative activity which have justified the exercise of investigative power have included the primary functions of legislating and appropriating;[41] the function of deciding whether or not legislation is appropriate;[42] oversight of the administration of the laws by the executive branch;[43] and the essential congressional function of informing itself in matters of national concern.[44] In addition, Congress's power to investigate such diverse matters as foreign and domestic subversive

---

[36] *In re Chapman*, 166 U.S. at 699.

[37] 273 U.S. 135 (1927).

[38] *See id.* at 153.

[39] *Id.* at 179-80.

[40] Shelton v. United States, 404 F.2d 1292, 1297 (D.C. Cir. 1968), *cert denied*, 393 U.S. 1024 (1969).

[41] *Barenblatt*, 360 U.S. 109.

[42] Quinn v. United States, 349 U.S. 155, 161 (1955).

[43] *McGrain*, 273 U.S. at 295.

[44] *Rumely*, 345 U.S. at 43-45; *see also Watkins*, 354 U.S. at 200 n. 3.

activities,[45] labor union corruption,[46] and organizations that violate the civil rights of others[47]—have all been upheld by the Supreme Court.

Despite the Court's broad interpretation of legislative purpose, its scope is not without limits. Courts have held that a committee lacks legislative purpose if it appears to be conducting a legislative trial rather than an investigation to assist in performing its legislative function.[48] However, although "there is no congressional power to expose for the sake of exposure,"[49] "so long as Congress acts in pursuance of its constitutional power, the Judiciary lacks authority to intervene on the basis of the motives which spurred the exercise of that power."[50]

Legal Tools Available for Oversight and Investigations

A review of congressional precedents indicates that there is no single method or set of procedures for engaging in oversight or conducting an investigation.[51] Historically, congressional committees appeared to rely a great deal on public hearings and subpoenaed witnesses to garner information and accomplish their investigative goals. In more recent years, congressional committees have seemingly relied more heavily on staff level communication and contacts as well as other "informal" attempts at gathering information – document requests, informal briefings, etc. – before initiating the necessary formalistic procedures such as issuing committee subpoenas, holding on-the-record depositions, and/or engaging the subjects of inquiries in open, public hearings. This section reviews the legal basis for the formal process of issuing subpoenas, depositions, and holding committee hearings. This section also reviews Congress's authority to grant witnesses limited immunity for the purpose of obtaining information and testimony that may be protected by the Fifth Amendment's right against self-incrimination.

Subpoena Power *- is a writ issued by gov't agency, court, to compel testimony by a witness or production of evidence under a penalty for failure* *witness summons*

As a corollary to Congress's accepted oversight and investigative authority, the Supreme Court has determined that the "[i]ssuance of subpoenas ... has long been held to be a legitimate use by Congress of its power to investigate."[52] In particular, the Court has repeatedly cited the principle that:

> A legislative body cannot legislate wisely or effectively in the absence of information respecting the conditions which the legislation is intended to affect or change; and where the legislative body does not itself possess the requisite information – which not infrequently is true – recourse must be had to others who do possess it. Experience has taught that mere

---

[45] *See, e.g., Barenblatt*, 360 U.S. 109; *Watkins*, 354 U.S. 178; McPhaul v. United States, 364 U.S. 372 (1960).

[46] Hutcheson v. United States, 369 U.S. 599 (1962).

[47] *Shelton*, 404 F.2d 1292.

[48] *See* United States v. Icardi, 140 F. Supp. 383 (D.D.C. 1956); United States v. Cross, 170 F. Supp. 303 (D.D.C. 1959).

[49] *Watkins*, 354 U.S. at 200. However, Chief Justice Warren, writing for the majority, made it clear that he was not referring to the "power of the Congress to inquire into and publicize corruption, mal-administration or inefficiency in agencies of the Government." *Id.*

[50] *Barenblatt*, 360 U.S. at 132.

[51] *See, e.g.,* CONGRESS INVESTIGATES: A CRITICAL AND DOCUMENTARY HISTORY (Roger A. Bruns, David L. Hostetter & Raymond W. Smock eds., 2011).

[52] *Eastland*, 421 U.S. at 504.

requests for such information often are unavailing, and also that information which is volunteered is not always accurate or complete; so some means of compulsion are essential to obtain what is needed. All this was true before and when the Constitution was framed and adopted. In that period the power of inquiry – with enforcing process – was regarded and employed as a necessary and appropriate attribute of the power to legislate—indeed, was treated as inhering in it.[53]

The power of inquiry, with the accompanying process to enforce it, has been deemed "an essential and appropriate auxiliary to the legislative function."[54] A properly authorized subpoena issued by a committee or subcommittee has the same force and effect as a subpoena issued by the parent house itself. Individual committees and subcommittees must be delegated the authority to issue subpoenas. Senate Rule XXVI(1) and House Rule XI(2)(m)(1) presently empower all standing committees and subcommittees to issue subpoenas requiring the attendance and testimony of witnesses and the production of documents. Special or select committees must be specifically delegated that authority by Senate or House resolution. The rules governing issuance of committee subpoenas vary by committee. Some committees require a full committee vote to issue a subpoena while others empower the chairman to issue them unilaterally, or with the concurrence of the ranking minority member.[55]

Congressional subpoenas are served by the U.S. Marshal's office, committee staff, or the Senate or House Sergeants-At-Arms. Service may be effected anywhere in the United States. The subpoena power has been held to extend to aliens physically present in the United States. As will be discussed below, however, securing compliance of United States nationals and aliens living in foreign countries presents more complex problems.[56]

A witness seeking to challenge the legal sufficiency of a subpoena has limited remedies to defeat the subpoena even if it is found to be legally deficient. First, challenges to the legal sufficiency of subpoenas must overcome formidable judicial obstacles. The applicable standard was articulated in *Wilkinson v. United States*:

- the committee's investigation of the broad subject matter area must be authorized by Congress;

- the investigation must be pursuant to "a valid legislative purpose";[57] and

- the specific inquiries must be pertinent to the broad subject matter areas that have been authorized by Congress.[58]

Second, the Supreme Court has ruled that courts may not enjoin the issuance of a congressional subpoena, holding that the Speech or Debate Clause of the Constitution[59] provides "an absolute

---

[53] *McGrain*, 273 U.S. at 175; *see also* Buckley v. Valeo, 424 U.S. 1, 138 (1976); *Eastland*, 421 U.S. at 504-505.

[54] *McGrain*, 273 U.S. at 174-75.

[55] *See, e.g.*, House Committee on Oversight and Government Reform, Rule 12(d); Senate Committee on Homeland Security and Governmental Affairs, Rule 5(c).

[56] *See* "Common Law Privileges".

[57] As to the requirement of "valid legislative purpose," the Supreme Court has made it clear that Congress does not have to state explicitly what it intends to do as a result of an investigation. *In re Chapman*, 166 U.S. 661, 669 (1897).

[58] Wilkinson v. United States, 365 U.S. 399, 408-09 (1961).

[59] U.S. CONST. art. I, §6, cl. 1. *See also* CRS Report R42648, *The Speech or Debate Clause: Constitutional Background and Recent Developments*, by Alissa M. Dolan and Todd Garvey.

bar to judicial interference" with such compulsory process.[60] As a consequence, a witness's sole remedy generally is to refuse to comply, risk being cited for contempt, and then raise the objections as a defense in a contempt prosecution.

Staff Deposition Authority

Committees often rely on informal staff interviews to gather information to prepare for investigative hearings. However, in recent years, when specially authorized, congressional committees have utilized staff-conducted depositions as a tool in exercising their investigatory power. At present, there are only a few standing committees that the House and Senate have expressly authorized to conduct staff depositions.[61] On a number of occasions such specific authority has been granted pursuant to Senate and House resolutions.[62] When granted, a committee will normally adopt procedures for taking depositions, including provisions for notice (with or without a subpoena), transcription of the deposition, the right to be accompanied by counsel, and the manner in which objections to questions are to be resolved.[63]

Staff depositions afford a number of significant advantages for committees engaged in complex investigations, including the ability to:

- obtain sworn testimony quickly and confidentially without the necessity of Members devoting time to lengthy hearings that may be unproductive because witnesses do not have the facts needed by the committee or refuse to cooperate;

- obtain testimony in private, which may be more conducive to candid responses as compared with public hearings;

- verify witness statements that might defame or tend to incriminate third parties before they are repeated publically;

- prepare for hearings by screening witness testimony in advance, which may obviate the need to call other witnesses;

- question witnesses outside of Washington, D.C. without the inconvenience of conducting field hearings with Members present.

Moreover, Congress has enhanced the efficacy of the staff deposition process by re-establishing the applicability of criminal prohibition against false statements to statements made during congressional proceedings, including the taking of depositions.[64]

---

[60] *Eastland,* 421 U.S. at 503-07.

[61] In the House, the only standing committee authorized to take depositions is the Committee on Oversight and Government Reform. *See* House Rules, Rule X(4)(c)(3)(A). In the Senate, the Committees on Agriculture, Nutrition, and Forestry; Ethics; Homeland Security and Governmental Affairs and its the Permanent Subcommittee on Investigations; Indian Affairs; Foreign Relations; Commerce, Science, and Technology;; and the Special Committee on Aging all have deposition authority. *See* S. Doc. 113-20, AUTHORITY AND RULES OF SENATE COMMITTEES 2013-2014, 113th Cong. (2013).

[62] *See* CRS Report 95-949, *Staff Depositions in Congressional Investigations*, by Jay R. Shampansky, at notes 16 and 18.

[63] *See, e.g.*, Rules of the Senate Special Committee on Aging, Rule VII, available at http://www.aging.senate.gov/about/rules.cfm.

[64] 18 U.S.C. § 1001; False Statements Accountability Act of 1996, P.L. 104-292. Congress acted in response to the Supreme Court's decision in *Hubbard v. United States*, 514 U.S. 695 (1995), holding that 18 U.S.C. §1001 applied only (continued...)

Certain disadvantages may also inhere. Unrestrained staff may be tempted to engage in tangential inquiries. Also, depositions present a "cold record" of a witness's testimony and may not be as useful for Members as in-person presentations.

Hearings

House Rule XI(2) and Senate Rule XXVI(2) require that committees adopt written rules of procedure and publish them in the *Congressional Record*. The failure to publish such rules has resulted in the invalidation of a perjury prosecution.[65] Once properly promulgated, such rules are judicially cognizable and must be strictly observed. The House and many individual Senate committees require that all witnesses be given a copy of a committee's rules.

Both the House and the Senate have adopted rules permitting a reduced quorum for taking testimony and receiving evidence. House committees are required to have at least two Members present to take testimony.[66] Senate rules allow the taking of testimony with only one Member in attendance.[67] Most committees have adopted the minimum quorum requirement and some require a higher quorum for sworn rather than unsworn testimony.[68] For perjury purposes, the quorum requirement must be met at the time the allegedly perjured testimony is given, not at the beginning of the session.[69] Reduced quorum requirement rules do not apply to authorizations for the issuance of subpoenas. Senate rules require a one-third quorum of a committee or subcommittee while the House requires a quorum of a majority of the members, unless a committee delegates authority for issuance to its chairman.[70]

Senate and House rules limit the authority of their committees to meet in closed session. For example, the House requires testimony to be held in closed session if a majority of a committee or subcommittee determines it "may tend to defame, degrade, or incriminate any person."[71] Such testimony taken in closed session is normally releasable only by a majority vote of the committee. Similarly, confidential material received in a closed session requires a majority vote for release.

In most oversight and investigative hearings the chair usually makes an opening statement. In the case of an investigative hearing, the opening statement is an important means of defining the subject matter of the hearing and thereby establishing the pertinence of questions asked the witnesses. Not all committees swear in their witnesses; a few committees require that all witnesses be sworn.[72] Most committees leave the swearing of witnesses to the discretion of the chair. If a committee wishes the potential sanction of perjury to apply, it should, in accordance

---

(...continued)

to false statements made in executive branch department and agency proceedings.

[65] United States v. Reinecke, 524 F.2d 435 (D.C. Cir. 1975) (holding that failure to publish committee rule setting one Senator as a quorum for taking hearing testimony was a sufficient ground to reverse a perjury conviction).

[66] House Rule XI(2)(h)(2), 113th Cong. (2013).

[67] Senate Rule XXVI(7)(a)(2), 113th Cong. (2013). *See, e.g.*, S. Doc. 113-20, AUTHORITY AND RULES OF SENATE COMMITTEES 2013-2014, 113th Cong. (2013), Special Comm. on Aging Rule 5.1 at 14.

[68] *See, e.g.*, S. Doc. 113-20, AUTHORITY AND RULES OF SENATE COMMITTEES 2013-2014, 113th Cong. (2013), Comm. on Appropriations Rule II(3) at 19.

[69] Christoffel v. United States, 338 U.S. 84, 90 (1949).

[70] Senate Rule XXVI(7)(a)(1); House Rule XI(2)(m)(3).

[71] House Rule XI(2)(k)(5).

[72] *See, e.g.*, Senate Special Committee on Aging, Rule II(4).

with the statute, administer an oath and swear in its witnesses.[73]However, it should be noted that false statements not under oath are also subject to criminal sanctions.[74]

A witness does not have the right to make a statement before being questioned, however, the opportunity is usually accorded. Committee rules may prescribe the length of such statements and also require written statements be submitted in advance of the hearing. Questioning of witnesses may be structured so that members alternate for specified lengths of time. Questioning may also be conducted by staff at the committee's discretion. Witnesses may be allowed to review a transcript of their testimony and make non-substantive corrections.

The right of a witness to be accompanied by counsel is recognized by House rule and the rules of Senate committees. The House rule limits the role of counsel, who are to serve solely "for the purpose of advising [witnesses] concerning their constitutional rights."[75] Some committees have adopted rules specifically prohibiting counsel from "coaching" witnesses during their testimony.[76]

A committee has complete authority to control the conduct of counsel. Indeed, the House Rules provide that "[t]he chair may punish breaches of order and decorum, and of professional ethics on the part of counsel, by censure and exclusion from the hearings; and the committee may cite the offender to the House for contempt."[77] Some Senate committees have adopted similar rules.[78] There is no right of cross-examination of adverse witnesses during an investigative hearing. However, witnesses are entitled to a range of other constitutional protections, such as the Fifth Amendment right to avoid making self-incriminating statements, that are discussed in more detail below.[79]

Congressional Immunity

The Fifth Amendment to the Constitution provides in part that "no person ... shall be compelled in any criminal case to be a witness against himself...."[80] The privilege against self-incrimination is available to a witness in a congressional investigation.[81] When a witness before a committee asserts this testimonial constitutional privilege, the committee may obtain a court order granting the witness immunity if two-thirds of the full committee votes for the order.[82] Such an order compels the witness to testify and grants him immunity against the *use* of that testimony, and

---

[73] 18 U.S.C. §1621.

[74] 18 U.S.C. §1001.

[75] House Rule XI(2)(k)(3).

[76] *See, e.g.*, S. Prt. 113-20, RULES OF PROCEDURE: SENATE PERMANENT SUBCOMMITTEE ON INVESTIGATIONS OF THE COMMITTEE ON HOMELAND SECURITY AND GOVERNMENT AFFAIRS at 13 (2013) [hereinafter Senate Permanent Subcommittee on Investigations Rules].

[77] House Rule XI(2)(k)(4).

[78] *See, e.g.*, Senate Special Committee on Aging, Rule II(10); Senate Permanent Subcommittee on Investigations Rules, Rule 7.

[79] *See* "Constitutional Limitations."

[80] U.S. CONST. amend. V.

[81] Watkins v. United States, 354 U.S. 178 (1957); Quinn v. United States, 349 U.S. 155 (1955).

[82] *See* 18 U.S.C. §6005.

other information derived therefrom, in a subsequent criminal prosecution.[83]The witness may still be prosecuted on the basis of other evidence.

Grants of immunity have figured prominently in a number of major congressional investigations, including Watergate (John Dean and Jeb Magruder) and Iran-Contra (Oliver North and John Poindexter). The decision to grant immunity involves a number of complex issues, but is ultimately a political decision that Congress makes. As observed by Iran-Contra Independent Counsel Lawrence E. Walsh, "[t]he legislative branch has the power to decide whether it is more important perhaps even to destroy a prosecution than to hold back testimony they need. They make that decision. It is not a judicial decision or a legal decision but a political decision of the highest importance."[84]

In determining whether to grant immunity to a witness, a committee might wish to consider, on the one hand, its need for the witness's testimony to perform its legislative, oversight, and informing functions, and on the other, the possibility that the witness's immunized congressional testimony could jeopardize a successful criminal prosecution. If a witness is prosecuted after giving immunized testimony, the burden is on the prosecutor to establish that the case was not based on the witness's previous testimony or evidence derived therefrom.[85]

Appellate court decisions reversing the convictions of key Iran-Contra figures Lt. Colonel Oliver North and Rear Admiral John Poindexter, who were granted use immunity for their congressional testimony, appear to have made the prosecutorial burden substantially more difficult in high-profile cases. Despite extraordinary efforts by the independent counsel and his staff to avoid being exposed to any of North or Poindexter's immunized testimony, and the submission of sealed packets of evidence to the district court to show that the material was obtained independently of any immunized testimony to Congress, the appeals court in both cases remanded the cases for a further determination on whether the prosecution had directly or indirectly used immunized testimony. Upon remand in both cases, the independent counsel moved to dismiss the prosecutions upon his determination that he could not meet the strict standards set by the appeals court in its decisions.[86] It is unclear whether these rulings created a reluctance on the part of committees to issue immunity grants. Since the enactment of the immunity statute in 1970, congressional committees have obtained more than 300 immunity orders.[87] Of these, almost half were obtained in connection with the 1978 investigation into the assassinations of President John F. Kennedy and Martin Luther King, Jr.[88]

---

[83] *Id.* This type of immunity is known as "use immunity."

[84] Lawrence E. Walsh, *The Independent Counsel and the Separation of Powers*, 25 Hous. L. Rev. 1, 9 (1988).

[85] *See* Kastigar v. United States, 406 U.S. 441, 460 (1972).

[86] *See* United States v. North, 910 F. 2d 843 (D.C. Cir. 1990), *modified*, 920 F. 2d 940 (D.C. Cir. 1990), *cert denied*, 500 U.S. 941 (1991); *see also* United States v. Poindexter, 951 F. 2d 369 (D.C. Cir. 1991).

[87] The most recent immunity order appears to have been granted to Monica Goodling in context of the House Judiciary Committee's investigation of the dismissal of U.S. Attorneys in 2007. Order Immunizing the Testimony of, and Other Information Provided by, Monica Goodling, May 11, 2007, Misc. No. 07-198 (D.D.C. 2007) (on petition of the House Judiciary Committee). *See also* Dan Eggen, Goodling Granted Immunity in Attorney Firings Probe, Wash. Post, May 11, 2007, *available at* http://www.washingtonpost.com/wp-dyn/content/article/2007/05/11/AR2007051100779.html.

[88] *See* H.Rept. 95-1828, *Final Report of the Select Committee on Assassinations*, U.S. House of Representatives (1978).

Enforcement of Congressional Authority

Contempt of Congress

While the threat or actual issuance of a subpoena normally provides sufficient leverage to ensure compliance with a congressional demand for information, the contempt power is Congress's most forceful tool to punish the contemnor and/or to remove the obstruction to compliance. The Supreme Court has recognized the contempt power as an inherent attribute of Congress's legislative authority, reasoning that if it did not possess this power, it "would be exposed to every indignity and interruption that rudeness, caprice or even conspiracy may mediate against it."[89]

There are two different types of contempt proceedings. Both the House and Senate may cite a witness for contempt under their inherent contempt power or under the criminal contempt procedure established by statute.[90]

Inherent Contempt

Under the inherent contempt power, the individual is brought before the House or Senate by the Sergeant-at-Arms, tried at the bar of the body, and, if found in contempt, may be imprisoned. The purpose of the imprisonment or other sanction may be either punitive[91] or coercive.[92] Thus, the witness can be imprisoned for a specified period of time as punishment, or for an indefinite period (but not, at least in the case of the House, beyond the adjournment of a session of Congress) until he agrees to comply. The inherent contempt power has been recognized by the Supreme Court as inextricably related to Congress's constitutionally-based power to investigate.[93] Between 1795 and 1934 the House and Senate utilized the inherent contempt power over 85 times, in most instances to obtain (successfully) testimony and/or production of documents. The inherent contempt power has not been exercised by either house in over 75 years. This procedure appears to be disfavored now because it has been considered too cumbersome and time-consuming to hold contempt trials at the bar of the offended chamber. Moreover, some have argued that the procedure is ineffective because punishment cannot extend beyond Congress's adjournment date.[94]

Statutory Criminal Contempt

Recognizing the practical limitations of the inherent contempt process, in 1857 Congress enacted a statutory criminal contempt procedure as an alternative. The statute, with minor amendments, is now codified at 2 U.S.C. §§ 192 and 194. A person who has been subpoenaed to testify or produce documents before the House or Senate or a committee and who fails to do so, or who

---

[89] Anderson v. Dunn, 19 U.S. (6 Wheat.) 204 (1821).

[90] *See* 2 U.S.C. §§192, 194. For a comprehensive treatment of the history and legal development of the congressional contempt power, *see* CRS Report RL34097, *Congress's Contempt Power and the Enforcement of Congressional Subpoenas: Law, History, Practice, and Procedure*, by Todd Garvey and Alissa M. Dolan.

[91] Jurney v. MacCracken, 294 U.S. 125, 147 (1935).

[92] McGrain v. Daugherty, 273 U.S. 135, 161 (1927).

[93] *See Anderson*, 19 U.S. (6 Wheat.) 204; *see also McGrain*, 273 U.S. 135.

[94] *See* Ernest J. Eberling, CONGRESSIONAL INVESTIGATIONS 289, 302-16 (1928).

appears but refuses to respond to questions, is guilty of a misdemeanor, punishable by a fine of up to $100,000 and imprisonment for up to one year.[95] A contempt citation must be approved by the subcommittee (if applicable), the full committee, and the full House or Senate.[96] After a contempt has been certified by the President of the Senate or the Speaker of the House, it is the "duty" of the U.S. Attorney "to bring the matter before the grand jury for its action."[97]

The criminal contempt procedure was rarely used until the twentieth century, but since 1935 it has been essentially the exclusive vehicle for punishment of contemptuous conduct. Prior to Watergate, no executive branch official had ever been the target of a criminal contempt proceeding. Since 1975, however, 13 cabinet-level or senior executive officials have been cited for contempt for failure to testify or produce subpoenaed documents by either a subcommittee, a full committee, or by a house.[98] Nonetheless, the effectiveness of the criminal contempt process against executive branch officials remains uncertain. For example, following a vote to hold EPA Administrator Anne Gorsuch Burford in contempt in 1982, the Department of Justice questioned whether Congress could compel the U.S. Attorney to submit the citation to a grand jury.[99] In that case, the documents in question were turned over to Congress before the issue was litigated, leaving the question unanswered. A similar issue arose during the contempt proceedings against Attorney General Eric Holder in 2012. Following a successful vote on a criminal contempt citation in the House, the U.S. Attorney refused to forward the contempt citation to a grand jury, effectively ending the criminal contempt process.[100] The question of the U.S. Attorney's "duty" under § 192 to enforce contempt citations remains unresolved.

Statutory Civil Enforcement of Subpoenas in the Senate

As an alternative to both the inherent contempt power and criminal contempt, in 1978 Congress enacted a civil enforcement procedure that is applicable only to the Senate.[101] First, the statute gives the U.S. District Court for the District of Columbia jurisdiction over a civil action to enforce, secure a declaratory judgment concerning the validity of, or prevent a threatened failure or refusal to comply with, any subpoena or order issued by the Senate or a Senate committee or subcommittee.[102] Upon approval of a Senate Resolution, the Senate Office of Legal Counsel is

---

[95] 2 U.S.C. §192.

[96] If the House or Senate is out of session, the contempt citation is filed with the Speaker of the House or the President of the Senate, respectively. *See* 2 U.S.C. §194.

[97] *Id.*

[98] The 13 officials are as follows: Secretary of State Henry Kissinger (1975); Secretary of Commerce Rogers C. B. Morton (1975); Secretary of Health, Education, and Welfare Joseph A Califano, Jr. (1978); Secretary of Energy Charles Duncan (1980); Secretary of Energy James B. Edwards (1981); Secretary of the Interior James Watt (1982); EPA Administrator Anne Gorsuch Burford (1983); Attorney General William French Smith (1983); White House Counsel John M. Quinn (1996); Attorney General Janet Reno (1998); White House Counsel Harriet Miers (2008); White House Chief of Staff Joshua Bolton (2008); and Attorney General Eric Holder (2012). Additionally, Lois Lerner, former director of the Exempt Organizations unit in the Internal Revenue Service (IRS), was held in contempt in 2014.

[99] See *Prosecution for the Contempt of Congress of an Executive Branch Official Who Has Asserted a Claim of Executive Privilege*, 8 Op. Off. Legal Counsel 101 (1984).

[100] Letter from James M. Cole, Deputy Attorney General, to John Boehner, Speaker of the House, June 28, 2012 *available at* http://oversight.house.gov/wp-content/uploads/2012/08/June-28-2012-Cole-to-Boehner.pdf.

[101] Ethics in Government Act of 1978, P.L. 95-521, §§703, 705, 92 Stat. 1877-80 (1978) (codified as amended at 2 U.S.C. §§288b(b) 288d, and 28 U.S.C. §1365 (2012)).

[102] 28 U.S.C. §1365.

---

approved to bring suit seeking one of these remedies. However, this statutory civil enforcement procedure does not apply to subpoenas issued to officers or employees of the executive branch.[103]

Regardless of whether the Senate seeks the enforcement of, or a declaratory judgment concerning a subpoena, the court will first review the subpoena's validity.[104] Even if the court finds that the subpoena is legally deficient, it does not have jurisdiction to enjoin the congressional proceeding. Because of the limited scope of the jurisdictional statute and Speech or Debate Clause immunity for congressional investigations,[105] "when the court is petitioned solely to enforce a congressional subpoena, the court's jurisdiction is limited to the matter Congress brings before it, that is whether or not to aid Congress in enforcing the subpoena."[106]

If the court orders enforcement of the subpoena and the individual still refuses to comply, he may be tried by the court in summary proceedings for contempt of court, with sanctions being imposed to coerce compliance.[107] This civil enforcement procedure provides an element of flexibility, allowing the subpoenaed party to raise possible constitutional and other defenses to the subpoena without risking a criminal prosecution. Since the statute's enactment in 1979, the Senate has authorized the Office of Senate Legal Counsel to seek civil enforcement of a subpoena for documents or testimony at least 6 times, the last in 1995.[108] None of these actions were brought against executive branch officials.

Civil Enforcement of Subpoenas in the House

While the House cannot pursue actions under the Senate's civil enforcement statute discussed above, it can pursue civil enforcement under certain circumstances. The full House must adopt a resolution finding the person in contempt and authorizing the committee and/or the House General Counsel to pursue a civil action in federal district court against the contumacious witness. The committee or the House General Counsel then files suit in the appropriate federal district court, requesting declaratory and/or injunctive relief to enforce the subpoena. This civil enforcement procedure has been employed twice, first in 2008 against Harriet Miers and Joshua Bolten, high ranking officials in the George W. Bush Administration, and most recently in 2012 against Attorney General Eric Holder.[109]

---

[103] *Id.*

[104] *Id.* at 4.

[105] For more information on the Speech or Debate Clause, *see* CRS Report R42648, *The Speech or Debate Clause: Constitutional Background and Recent Developments*, by Alissa M. Dolan and Todd Garvey.

[106] S.Rept. 95-170, 95th Cong., 1st Sess., 94 (1977).

[107] The act specifies that "an action, contempt proceeding, or sanction .... shall not abate upon adjournment sine die by the Senate at the end of a Congress if the Senate or the committee or subcommittee ... certifies to the court that it maintains its interest in securing the documents, answers, or testimony during such adjournment." 28 U.S.C. §1365(b) (2012). In the first case brought under the new procedure, the witness unsuccessfully argued that the possibility of "indefinite incarceration" violated the due process and equal protection provisions of the Constitution, and allowed for cruel and unusual punishment. *Application of the U.S. Senate Permanent Subcommittee on Investigations*, 655 F.2d 1232 (D.C. Cir.), *cert. denied*, 454 U.S. 1084 (1981).

[108] *See* CRS Report RL34097, *Congress's Contempt Power and the Enforcement of Congressional Subpoenas: Law, History, Practice, and Procedure*, by Todd Garvey and Alissa M. Dolan, Table A-3 (Floor Votes on Civil Enforcement Resolutions in the Senate, 1980-Present).

[109] *See generally* Committee on Judiciary, U.S. House of Representatives v. Miers, 558 F. Supp. 2d 53 (D.D.C. 2008); Committee on Oversight and Government Reform, U.S. House of Representatives v. Holder, 973 F. Supp. 2d 1 (D.D.C. 2013).

Perjury and False Statement Prosecutions

Testimony Under Oath

A witness under oath before a congressional committee who willfully gives false testimony is subject to prosecution for perjury pursuant to 18 U.S.C. § 1621. The false statement must be "willfully" made before a "competent tribunal" and involve a "material matter."[110] For a legislative committee to be competent for perjury purposes a quorum must be present.[111] Both houses have adopted rules establishing less than a majority of members as a quorum for taking testimony, normally two members for House committees[112] and one member for Senate committees.[113] The requisite quorum must be present at the time the alleged perjurious statement is made, not merely at the time the session convenes.[114] No prosecution for perjury will lie for statements made only in the presence of committee staff unless the committee has deposition authority and has taken formal action to allow it.[115]

Unsworn Statements

Most statements made before Congress, at both the investigatory and hearing phases of oversight, are unsworn. The practice of swearing in all witnesses at hearings is infrequent. Prosecutions may be brought to punish congressional witnesses for giving willfully false testimony not under oath. Under 18 U.S.C. § 1001, false statements by a person in "any investigation or review, conducted pursuant to the authority of any committee, subcommittee, commission or office of the Congress, consistent with applicable rules of the House and Senate" are punishable by a fine of up to $250,000 or imprisonment for not more than five years, or both.[116]

Limitations on Congressional Authority

Constitutional Limitations

There are constitutional limits not only on Congress's legislative powers, but also on its oversight and investigative powers. The Supreme Court has observed that "Congress, in common with all branches of the Government, must exercise its powers subject to the limitations placed by the Constitution on governmental action, more particularly in the context of this case, the relevant limitations of the Bill of Rights."[117] While not all provisions of the Bill of Rights are applicable to

---

[110] 18 U.S.C. §1621(a).

[111] Christoffel v. United States, 338 U.S. 84, 90 (1949).

[112] House Rule XI(2)(h)(2).

[113] Senate Rule XXVI(7)(a)(2) allows its committees to set a quorum requirement at less than the normal one-third for taking sworn testimony. Almost all Senate committees have set the quorum requirement at one member.

[114] *Christoffel*, 338 U.S. at 90.

[115] Perjury requires that the false statement be made under "an oath authorized by law" and before a "competent tribunal." Unless expressly authorized to take a deposition under oath, conversations with committee staff generally do not fall within the scope of the perjury statute. *See, e.g.*, United States v. Weissman, 1996 U.S. Dist. LEXIS 19125 (S.D.N.Y. 1996).

[116] 18 U.S.C §1001 (2006).

[117] Barenblatt v. United States, 360 U.S. 109, 112 (1959).

---

congressional hearings,[118] this section discusses provisions that may limit Congress's oversight authority.

First Amendment

Although the First Amendment, by its terms, is expressly applicable only to legislation that abridges freedom of speech, press, religion (establishment or free exercise), or assembly, the Court has held that the amendment also restricts Congress in conducting oversight and/or investigations.[119] In the leading case involving the application of First Amendment rights in a congressional investigation, *Barenblatt v. United States*, the Court held that "where First Amendment rights are asserted to bar government interrogation resolution of the issue always involves a balancing by the courts of the competing private and public interests at stake in the particular circumstances shown."[120] Thus, unlike the Fifth Amendment privilege against self-incrimination (discussed below), the First Amendment does not give a witness an absolute right to refuse to respond to congressional demands for information.[121]

The Court has held that in balancing the personal interest in privacy against the congressional need for information, "the critical element is the existence of, and the weight to be ascribed to, the interest of the Congress in demanding disclosure from an unwilling witness."[122] To protect the rights of witnesses, in cases involving the First Amendment, the courts have emphasized the requirements discussed above concerning authorization for the investigation, delegation of power to investigate to the committee involved, and the existence of a legislative purpose.[123]

While the Court has recognized the application of the First Amendment to congressional investigations, and although the amendment has frequently been asserted by witnesses as grounds for not complying with congressional demands for information, the Court has never relied on the First Amendment as grounds for reversing a criminal contempt of Congress conviction.[124]

---

[118] For example, the Sixth amendment right of a criminal defendant to cross-examine witnesses and to call witnesses in his behalf has been held not applicable to a congressional hearing. United States v. Fort, 443 F.2d 670 (D.C. Cir. 1970), *cert. denied*, 403 U.S. 932 (1971).

[119] Watkins v. United States, 354 U.S. 178, 197 (1957).

[120] 360 U.S. 109, 126 (1959).

[121] *Id.*

[122] *Watkins*, 354 U.S. at 198. A balancing test was also used in *Branzburg v. Hayes*, which involved the issue of the claimed privilege of newsmen not to respond to demands of a grand jury for information. *See* Branzburg v. Hayes, 408 U.S. 665 (1972). In its 5-4 decision, the Court concluded that the grand jury's need for the information outweighed First Amendment considerations, but the opinion indicates that "the infringement of protected First Amendment rights must be no broader than necessary to achieve a permissible governmental purpose," and that "a State's interest must be 'compelling' or 'paramount' to justify even an indirect burden on First Amendment rights." *Id.* at 699-700; *see also* Gibson v. Florida Legislative Investigation Committee, 372 U.S. 539 (1963) (applying the compelling interest test in a legislative investigation).

[123] *See, e.g., Barenblatt*, 360 U.S. 109; *Watkins*, 354 U.S. 178; United States v. Rumely, 345 U.S. 41 (1953); *see also* 4 Deschler's Precedents of the U.S. House of Representatives, ch. 15, §10, n. 15 and accompanying text (1994).

[124] LEADING CASES, *supra* note 34, at 42; JAMES HAMILTON, THE POWER TO PROBE: A STUDY OF CONGRESSIONAL INVESTIGATIONS, 234 (1977) [hereinafter Hamilton]. Although it was not in the criminal contempt context, one court of appeals has upheld a witness's First Amendment claim. In *Stamler v. Willis*, the Seventh Circuit Court of Appeals ordered to trial a witness's suit for declaratory relief against the House Un-American Activities Committee in which it was alleged that the committee's authorizing resolution had a "chilling effect" on plaintiff's First Amendment rights. *See* 415 F.2d 1365 (7th Cir. 1969), *cert. denied*, 399 U.S. 929 (1970). Relief has been denied in other cases for declaratory and injunctive relief brought against committees on First Amendment grounds, although courts have (continued...)

However, the Court has narrowly construed the scope of a committee's authority so as to avoid reaching a First Amendment issue.[125] In addition, the Court has ruled in favor of a witness who invoked his First Amendment rights in response to questioning by a state legislative committee.[126]

Potential concerns regarding a witness's First Amendment right may impact a committee's decision on how to proceed in an investigation. In a 1976 investigation of the unauthorized publication in the press of the report of the House Select Committee on Intelligence, the Committee on Standards of Official Conduct subpoenaed four news media representatives, including Daniel Schorr.[127] The Standards of Official Conduct Committee concluded that Mr. Schorr had obtained a copy of the Select Committee's report and had made it available for publication. Although the ethics committee found that "Mr. Schorr's role in publishing the report was a defiant act in disregard of the expressed will of the House of Representatives to preclude publication of highly classified national security information," it declined to cite him for contempt for his refusal to disclose his source.[128] The desire to avoid a clash over First Amendment rights apparently was a major factor in the committee's decision on the contempt matter.[129]

In another First Amendment dispute, the Special Subcommittee on Investigations of the House Committee on Interstate and Foreign Commerce, in the course of its probe of allegations that deceptive editing practices were employed in producing the television news documentary program *The Selling of the Pentagon*, subpoenaed Frank Stanton, the president of CBS. He was directed to deliver to the Subcommittee the "outtakes" of the program.[130] When, on First Amendment grounds, Stanton declined to provide the subpoenaed materials, the Subcommittee unanimously voted a contempt citation; the full Committee voted 25-13 to report the contempt citation to the full House.[131] After extensive debate, the House failed to adopt the committee report, voting instead to recommit the matter to the Committee.[132] During the debate, several Members expressed concern that approval of the contempt citation would have a "chilling effect"

(...continued)

indicated that relief could be granted if the circumstances were more compelling. *See, e.g.*, Sanders v. McClellan, 463 F.2d 894 (D.C. Cir. 1972); Davis v. Chord, 442 F. 2d 1207 (D.C. Cir. 1970); Ansara v. Eastland, 442 F.2d 751 (D.C. Cir. 1971). However, in *Eastland v. United States Servicemen's Fund*, the Supreme Court held that the Constitution's Speech or Debate Clause (Art. I, §6, cl. 1) generally bars suits challenging the validity of congressional subpoenas on First Amendment or other grounds. Thus, a witness generally cannot raise his constitutional defenses until a subsequent criminal prosecution for contempt unless, in the case of a Senate committee, the statutory civil contempt procedure is employed. 421 U.S. 491 (1975); *see also* United States v. House of Representatives, 556 F. Supp. 150 (D.D.C. 1983).

[125] *Rumely*, 345 U.S. 41.

[126] *Gibson*, 372 U.S. 539. In the majority opinion, Justice Goldberg observed that "an essential prerequisite to the validity of an investigation which intrudes into the area of constitutionally protected rights of speech, press, association and petition [is] that the State convincingly show a substantial relation [or nexus] between the information sought and a subject of overriding and compelling state interest. *Id.* at 546.

[127] H. Rept. 94-1754, 94th Cong., 6 (1976).

[128] *Id.* at 42-43.

[129] *Id.* at 47-48 (additional views of Representatives Spence, Teague, Hutchinson, and Flynt).

[130] The outtakes were portions of the CBS film clips that were not actually broadcast. The Subcommittee wanted to compare the outtakes with the tape of the broadcast to determine if improper editing techniques had been used.

[131] H. Rept. 92-349, 92d Cong. (1971). CBS's legal argument was based in part on the claim that Congress could not constitutionally legislate on the subject of editing techniques and, therefore, the subcommittee lacked a valid legislative purpose for the investigation. *Id.* at 9.

[132] *See* 117 CONG. REC. 23922-26, 24603-59, 24720-53 (1971).

on the press and would unconstitutionally involve the government in the regulation of the press.[133]

Fourth Amendment

Several Supreme Court opinions suggest that the Fourth Amendment's prohibition against unreasonable searches and seizures is applicable to congressional committees; however, there has not been an opinion directly addressing the issue.[134] It appears that there must be a legitimate legislative or oversight-related basis for the issuance of a congressional subpoena.[135] The Fourth Amendment protects a congressional witness against a subpoena that is unreasonably broad or burdensome.[136] The Court has outlined the standard to be used in judging the reasonableness of a congressional subpoena:

> Petitioner contends that the subpoena was so broad as to constitute an unreasonable search and seizure in violation of the Fourth Amendment.... 'Adequacy or excess in the breath of the subpoena are matters variable in relation to the nature, purposes, and scope of the inquiry....' The subcommittee's inquiry here was a relatively broad one ... and the permissible scope of materials that could reasonably be sought was necessarily equally broad. It was not reasonable to suppose that the subcommittee knew precisely what books and records were kept by the Civil Rights Congress, and therefore the subpoena could only ' specify ... with reasonable particularity, the subjects to which the documents ... relate.... 'The call of the subpoena for 'all records, correspondence and memoranda' of the Civil Rights Congress relating to the specified subject describes them 'with all of the particularity the nature of the inquiry and the [subcommittee's] situation would permit.... 'The description contained in the subpoena was sufficient to enable [petitioner] to know what particular documents were required and to select them adequately.[137]

If a witness has a legal objection to a subpoena *duces tecum* or is for some reason unable to comply with a demand for documents, he must give the grounds for his noncompliance upon the return of the subpoena. As the D.C. Circuit stated:

> If [the witness] felt he could refuse compliance because he considered the subpoena so broad as to constitute an unreasonable search and seizure within the prohibition of the fourth amendment, then to avoid contempt for complete noncompliance he was under [an] obligation to inform the subcommittee of his position. The subcommittee would then have had the choice of adhering to the subpoena as formulated or of meeting the objection in light of any pertinent representations made by [the witness].[138]

---

[133] *Id.* at 24731-32.

[134] Watkins v. United States, 354 U.S. 178, 188 (1957); *see also* McPhaul v. United States, 364 U.S. 372 (1960).

[135] A congressional subpoena may not be used in a mere "fishing expedition." *See* Hearst v. Black, 87 F.2d 68, 71 (D.C. Cir. 1936) (quoting Federal Trade Commission v. American Tobacco Co., 264 U.S. 298, 306 (1924) (stating that "[i]t is contrary to the first principles of justice to allow a search through all the records, relevant or irrelevant, in the hope that something will turn up.")); *see also* United States v. Groves, 188 F. Supp. 314 (W.D. Pa. 1937) (*dicta*); *But see* Eastland v. United States Servicemen's Fund, 421 U.S. 491, 509 (1975), (recognizing that an investigation may lead "up some 'blind alleys' and into nonproductive enterprises. To be a valid legislative inquiry there need be no predictable end result.").

[136] McPhaul v. United States, 364 U.S. 372 (1960); *see also* Shelton v. United States, 404 F.2d 1292 (D.C. Cir. 1968), *cert. denied*, 393 U.S. 1024 (1969).

[137] *McPhaul*, 364 U.S. at 832 (internal citations omitted).

[138] *Shelton*, 404 F.2d at 1299-1300; *see also* LEADING CASES, *supra* note 34, at 49.

Similarly, if a subpoenaed party is in doubt as to what records are required by a subpoena or believes that a subpoena calls for documents not related to the investigation, he must inform the committee. Where a witness is unable to produce documents he will not be held in contempt "unless he is responsible for their unavailability ... or is impeding justice by not explaining what happened to them."[139]

The application of the exclusionary rule to congressional committee investigation is in some doubt and appears to depend on the precise facts of the situation. It appears that documents that were unlawfully seized at the direction of a congressional investigating committee may not be admitted into evidence in a subsequent unrelated criminal prosecution because of the command of the exclusionary rule.[140] In the absence of a Supreme Court ruling, it remains unclear whether the exclusionary rule bars the admission into evidence in a criminal contempt prosecution arising from a congressional subpoena issued on the basis of documents obtained by a committee following their unlawful seizure by another investigating body (such as a state prosecutor).[141]

Fifth Amendment Privilege Against Self-Incrimination

The Supreme Court has indicated that the privilege against self-incrimination afforded by the Fifth Amendment is available to a witness in a congressional investigation.[142] The privilege is personal in nature,[143] and may not be invoked on behalf of a corporation,[144] small partnership,[145] labor union,[146] or other "artificial" organizations.[147] The privilege protects a witness from being

---

[139] *McPhaul*, 364 U.S. at 382.

[140] Nelson v. United States, 208 F.2d 505 (D.C. Cir. 1953), *cert. denied*, 346 U.S. 827 (1953).

[141] In *United States v. McSurely*, a court of appeals reversed contempt convictions where the subcommittee subpoenas were based on information "derived by the subcommittee through a previous unconstitutional search and seizure by [state] officials and the subcommittee's own investigator." United States v. McSurely, 473 F.2d 1178, 1194 (D.C. Cir. 1972). This decision was rendered in December, 1972. In a civil case brought by the criminal defendants, Alan and Margaret McSurely, against Senator McClellan and the subcommittee staff for alleged violations of their constitutional rights by the transportation and use of the seized documents, a federal district court in June, 1973, denied the defendants' motion for summary judgment. While the appeal from the district court decision in the civil case was pending before the court of appeals, the Supreme Court held, in *Calandra v. United States*, 414 U.S. 338 (1974), that a grand jury is not precluded by the Fourth Amendment's exclusionary rule from questioning a witness on the basis of evidence that had been illegally seized. A divided court of appeals subsequently held in the civil case, that under *Calandra* "a congressional committee has the right in its investigatory capacity to use the product of a past unlawful search and seizure." McSurely v. McClellan, 521 F.2d 1024, 1047 (D.C. Cir. 1975).

The decision of the three-judge panel in the civil case was vacated and on rehearing by the full District of Columbia Circuit, five judges determined that *Calandra* was applicable to the legislative sphere. Another five judges found it unnecessary to decide whether *Calandra* applies to committees, indicating that even if it does not apply to the legislative branch, the exclusionary rule may restrict a committee's use of unlawfully seized documents if it does not make mere "derivative use" of them but commits an independent Fourth Amendment violation in obtaining them. McSurely v. McClellan, 553 F.2d 1277, 1293-94, 1317-25 (D.C. Cir. 1976) (en banc). The Supreme Court granted certiorari in the case, 434 U.S. 888 (1977), but subsequently dismissed certiorari as improvidently granted, with no explanation for this disposition of the case. *See* McAdams v. McSurely, 438 U.S. 189 (1978). Jury verdicts were eventually returned against the Senate defendants, but were reversed in part on appeal. *See* McSurely v. McClellan, 753 F.2d 88 (D.C. Cir. 1985), *cert. denied*, 474 U.S. 1005 (1985).

[142] Watkins v. United States, 354 U.S. 178 (1957); Quinn v. United States, 349 U.S. 155 (1955).

[143] *See McPhaul*, 364 U.S. 372; *see also* McCormick, EVIDENCE §120 (Cleary ed. 1984) [hereinafter McCormick].

[144] Hale v. Henkel, 201 U.S. 43 (1906).

[145] Bellis v. United States, 417 U.S. 85 (1974).

[146] *See* United States v. White, 322 U.S. 694 (1944).

[147] *Bellis*, 417 U.S. at 90; *see also* Rogers v. United States, 340 U.S. 367 (1951).

compelled to testify but generally not against a subpoena for existing documentary evidence.[148] However, where compliance with a subpoena *duces tecum* would constitute implicit testimonial authentication of the documents produced, the privilege may apply.[149]

The basis for asserting the privilege was elaborated upon in a lower court decision:

> The privilege may only be asserted when there is reasonable apprehension on the part of the witness that his answer would furnish some evidence upon which he could be convicted of a criminal offense ... or which would reveal sources from which evidence could be obtained that would lead to such conviction or to prosecution therefore....Once it has become apparent that the answers to a question would expose a witness to the danger of conviction or prosecution, wider latitude is permitted the witness in refusing to answer other questions.[150]

There is no required verbal formula for invoking the privilege, nor does there appear to be a necessary warning by the committee.[151] A committee should recognize any reasonable indication, such as "the Fifth Amendment," that the witness is asserting his privilege.[152] Where a committee is uncertain whether the witness is in fact invoking the privilege against self-incrimination or is claiming some other basis for declining to answer, the committee should direct the witness to specify his privilege or objection.[153]

The committee can review the assertion of the privilege by a witness to determine its validity, but the witness is not required to articulate the precise hazard that he fears. In regard to the assertion of the privilege in judicial proceedings, the Supreme Court has advised:

> To sustain the privilege, it need only be evident, from the implications of the question, in the setting in which it is asked, that a responsive answer to the question or an explanation of why it cannot be answered might be dangerous because injurious disclosure could result.... To reject a claim, it should be 'perfectly clear, from a careful consideration of all the circumstances of the case, that the witness is mistaken, and that the answers cannot possibly have a tendency' to incriminate.[154]

The privilege against self-incrimination may generally only be waived "intelligently and unequivocally."[155] A court will not construe an ambiguous statement of a witness before a

---

[148] Fisher v. United States, 425 U.S. 391, 409 (1976); Andresen v. Maryland, 427 U.S. 463 (1976). These cases concerned business records; there may be some protection available in the case of a subpoena for personal papers. *See* McCormick, *supra* note 143, at §§126, 127.

[149] United States v. Coe, 465 U.S. 605 (1984); *Fisher,* 425 U.S. 391; *see also* Curcio v. United States, 354 U.S. 118 (1957); McCormick, *supra* note 143, at §126.

[150] United States v. Jaffee, 98 F. Supp. 191, 193-94 (D.D.C. 1951); *see also* Simpson v. United States, 241 F.2d 222 (9th Cir. 1957) (privilege inapplicable to questions seeking basic identifying information, such as the witness's name and address).

[151] Although there is no case law on point, it seems unlikely that *Miranda* warnings are required. That requirement flows from judicial concern as to the validity of confessions evoked in an environment of a police station, isolated from public scrutiny, with the possible threat of physical and prosecutorial jeopardy; an environment clearly distinguishable from a congressional context. *See* Miranda v. Arizona, 384 U.S. 436 (1966).

[152] Quinn v. United States, 349 U.S. 155 (1955).

[153] Emspak v. United States, 349 U.S. 190 (1955); *see also* LEADING CASES, *supra* note 34, at 63.

[154] Hoffman v. United States, 341 U.S. 479, 486-87 (1951).

[155] *Emspak,* 349 U.S. at 195.

committee as a waiver.[156] Although routinely hesitant to find an implied waiver of the Fifth Amendment privilege, the Court has held that when a witness voluntarily provides testimony during a criminal proceeding, the witness may waive his right to invoke the Fifth Amendment in response to subsequent questions relating to the details of that disclosure.[157] This "testimonial subject matter" waiver is not an absolute waiver of Fifth Amendment protections, but rather acts as a limited waiver covering only the details of the subject matter disclosed. The application of this doctrine in the congressional context has yet to be clearly established by the Supreme Court.[158]

Under federal statute, when a witness asserts the privilege, the full house or the committee conducting the investigation may seek a court order which (a) directs the witness to testify and (b) grants him immunity against the use of his testimony, or other evidence derived from his testimony, in a subsequent criminal prosecution.[159] As previously discussed, the immunity that is granted is "use" immunity, not "transactional" immunity.[160] Neither the immunized testimony that the witness gives, nor evidence derived therefrom, may be used against him in a subsequent criminal prosecution, except one for perjury or contempt relating to his testimony. However, he may be convicted of the crime (the "transaction") on the basis of other evidence.[161]

An application for a judicial immunity order must be approved by a majority of the House or Senate or by a two-thirds vote of the full committee seeking the order.[162] The Attorney General must be notified at least ten days prior to the request for the order, and he can request a delay of twenty days in issuing the order.[163] Although the order to testify may be issued before the witness's appearance,[164] it does not become legally effective until the witness has been asked a question, invoked his privilege, and been presented with the court order.[165] The court's role in issuing the order has been held to be ministerial and, thus, if the procedural requirements under the immunity statute have been met, the court may not refuse to issue the order or impose conditions on the grant of immunity.[166]

---

[156] *Id.; see also* Johnson v. Zerbst, 304 U.S. 458, 464 (1938).

[157] *See* Brown v. United States, 356 US 148 (1958); Mitchell v. United States, 526 U.S. 314 (1999).

[158] *But see* Presser v United States, 284 F.2d 233 (D.C. Cir 1960) (suggesting that the *Brown* rule applies in congressional proceedings).

[159] 18 U.S.C. §§6002, 6005.

[160] *See* "Congressional Immunity".

[161] The constitutionality of granting a witness only use immunity, rather than transactional immunity, was upheld in *Kastigar v. United States*, 406 U.S. 441 (1972). In *United States v. Romano*, 583 F.2d 1 (1st Cir. 1978), the defendant appealed from his conviction of several offenses on the ground, *inter alia*, that the prosecution's evidence had been derived, in part, from immunized testimony that he had given before a Senate subcommittee. Although the conviction was affirmed, the case illustrates the difficulty that the prosecutor may have in establishing that its evidence was not "tainted," but rather was derived from independent sources, especially in a case where a committee and the Justice Department cooperated on the investigation before immunity was granted. *See Kastigar*, 406 U.S. at 461-62.

[162] 18 U.S.C. §6005(a) (2012).

[163] However, the Justice Department may waive the notice requirement. Application of the Senate Permanent Subcommittee on Investigation*s*, 655 F.2d 1232, 1236 (D.C. Cir. 1980), *cert. denied*, 454 U.S. 1084 (1981).

[164] *Id.* at 1257.

[165] *See* In re McElreath, 248 F.2d 612 (D.C. Cir. 1957) (en banc).

[166] Application of the U.S. Senate Select Committee on Presidential Campaign Activities, 361 F. Supp. 1270 (D.D.C. 1973). In *dicta*, however, the court referred to the legislative history of the statutory procedure, which suggests that although a court lacks power to review the advisability of granting immunity, a court may consider the jurisdiction of Congress and the committee over the subject area and the relevance of the information that is sought to the committee's (continued...)

Fifth Amendment Due Process Rights

The due process clause of the Fifth Amendment requires that "the pertinency of the interrogation to the topic under the ... committee's inquiry must be brought home to the witness at the time the questions are put to him."[167] "Unless the subject matter has been made to appear with undisputable clarity, it is the duty of the investigative body, upon objection of the witness on grounds of pertinency, to state for the record the subject under inquiry at that time and the manner in which the propounded questions are pertinent thereto."[168] Additionally, in a contempt proceeding, to satisfy both the requirement of due process as well as the statutory requirement that a refusal to answer be "willful," a witness should be informed of the committee's ruling on any objections he raises or privileges that he asserts.[169]

Executive Privilege

The executive branch may respond to a congressional request or demand to testify or produce documents with an assertion of executive privilege. Executive privilege has two different dimensions—the deliberative process privilege, which relates to executive branch decision making processes and the presidential communications privilege, which relates to presidential decision making.

Presidential Communications Privilege

The seminal Supreme Court case discussing executive privilege in the context of presidential communications is *United States v. Nixon*. In *Nixon*, which arose out of a judicial subpoena issued to President Nixon at the request of the Watergate special prosecutor, the Court established executive privilege to be a constitutionally based privilege, rooted in "the supremacy of each branch within its own assigned area of constitution duties" and the separation of powers.[170] The privilege, when applied to presidential communications, is designed to protect direct presidential decision making processes. The Court considered presidential communications to be presumptively privileged, but concluded that the privilege was not absolute and could be overcome by an appropriate showing of need by the requesting party.[171]

While *Nixon* is the foundational executive privilege case, a later D.C. Circuit decision is the only case in which a court examines the application of executive privilege in the face of a congressional subpoena.[172] In *Senate Select Committee on Presidential Campaign Activities v. Nixon*, the court followed the analysis established in *Nixon* and held that presidential

---

(...continued)

inquiry. *See id.* at 1278-79.

[167] Deutch v. United States, 367 U.S. 456, 467-68 (1961). As the court explained in that case, there is a separate statutory requirement of pertinency.

[168] Watkins v. United States, 354 U.S. 178, 214-15 (1957).

[169] *Deutch*, 367 U.S. at 467-68.

[170] United States v. Nixon, 418 U.S. 683, 705 (1974).

[171] *See id.* at 713.

[172] Senate Select Comm. on Presidential Campaign Activities v. Nixon, 498 F. 2d 725 (D.C. Cir. 1974)

---

communications were presumptively privileged but could be overcome by a sufficient showing of need from the requesting congressional committee.[173]

Later cases relating to congressional investigations have provided little guidance on how to evaluate claims of executive privilege made in response to congressional subpoenas. In the absence of these clarifying decisions, information access cases in similar contexts, such as grand jury subpoenas and Freedom of Information Act (FOIA) requests, may provide some guidance.[174] Two cases from the D.C. Circuit discuss the differences between two aspects of executive privilege, the presidential communications privilege and the deliberative process privilege, discussed below. Based on these cases, it appears that the presidential communications privilege may only be asserted with regard to documents or communications that are authored by or solicited and received by the President or presidential advisers with "operational proximity" to the President. The courts determined that "operational proximity" included advisers within the White House, but did not include cabinet secretaries or cabinet employees.[175] Under the reasoning in these cases, the presidential communications privilege would not apply to documents that were created and distributed solely within an executive department. Additionally, these courts suggested that the privilege may only apply to documents relating to a quintessential and non-delegable presidential power.[176]

The privilege applies to both pre- and post-decisional documents and communications, in their entirety, regarding direct decision-making by the President.[177] Finally, the presidential communications privilege remains a qualified privilege that may be overcome by a requisite showing of need.

Deliberative Process Privilege

The deliberative process privilege may often be invoked in response to requests for documents and communications created during the decision making process, such as internal executive branch advisory opinions, recommendations, and related communications. The deliberative process privilege *may* shield the disclosure of executive branch documents and communications that are *predecisional*, meaning they are created prior to reaching the agency's final decision, and *deliberative*, meaning they relate to the thought process of executive officials and are not purely factual.[178] Additionally, the privilege does not protect entire documents; rather, the executive

---

[173] *Id.* at 730.

[174] *See* Judicial Watch v. Dept. of Justice, 365 F.3d 1108 (D.C. Cir. 2004) (FOIA request); In re: Sealed Case (Espy), 121 F.3d 729, 737 (D.C. Cir. 1997) (grand jury subpoena) [hereinafter *Espy*].

[175] *See Espy*, 121 F.3d at 752; Judicial *Watch*, 365 F.3d at 1120-21.

[176] *See Espy*, 121 F.3d at 752-53; *Judicial Watch*, 365 F.3d at 1119-21.

[177] *Espy*, 121 F.3d at 752.

[178] *Espy*, 121 F.3d at 737. *Espy* involved documents relating to the President's appointment and removal power, which the court characterized as a "quintessential and non-delegable Presidential power." The court continued to say:

> In many instances, presidential powers and responsibilities... can be exercised or performed without the President's direct involvement, pursuant to a presidential delegation of power or statutory framework. But the President himself must directly exercise the presidential power of appointment or removal. As a result, in this case there is assurance that even if the President were not a party to the communications over which the government is asserting presidential privilege, these communications nonetheless are intimately connected to his presidential decisionmaking.

Id. (internal citations omitted). Therefore, while the court did not hold that the presidential communications privilege may only be applied to communications and documents relating to quintessential and non-delegable presidential (continued...)

branch is required disclose non-privileged factual information that is reasonably segregable from privileged information in the requested documents. The deliberative process privilege is qualified, not absolute; it can be overcome by an adequate showing of need.[179]

The purpose underlying the deliberative process privilege is to protect the "'quality of agency decisions' by allowing government officials freedom to debate alternative approaches in private."[180] The executive branch also may contend that the privilege protects against disclosure of proposed policies before they are fully considered or adopted, preventing public confusion about the difference between preliminary discussions and final decisions.

No court has examined the scope of the deliberative process privilege in the context of a congressional subpoena. However, a D.C. Circuit case which arose in the context of a grand jury subpoena found that while the deliberative process privilege "originated as a common law privilege," some aspects of it may also "have roots in the constitutional separation of powers."[181] Whether the deliberative process privilege is a pure common law privilege, similar to common law privileges discussed below, or a hybrid common law and constitutional privilege may impact how successful an assertion of the privilege would be to shield disclosure of information to Congress. Congress's oversight authority is limited by constitutional privileges, but Congress is generally not required to recognize common law privileges.

This question may be addressed in the ongoing litigation regarding enforcement of a subpoena issued to the Attorney General as part of a congressional investigation of Operation Fast and Furious.[182] In that case, the House Committee on Oversight and Government Reform argues that the deliberative process privilege, which was asserted by the President with regard to DOJ documents subpoenaed by the Committee, is a wholly common law privilege that must be distinguished from other, constitutionally-based privileges. Therefore, the Committee contends, the common law privilege cannot shield the disclosure of documents that are subject to a constitutionally-rooted subpoena. The district court judge in the case appears to have questioned the Committee's argument and in an order rejected the Committee's argument that only constitutionally based privileges could be invoked in response to a subpoena.[183] However, the judge has yet to reach the merits regarding the dispute over the assertion of executive privilege.[184]

(...continued)

powers, this may serve as a limit on the privilege.

[179] *Id.*

[180] *Id.*

[181] *Id.*

[182] *See* Comm. on Oversight & Gov't Reform v. Holder, 979 F. Supp. 2d 1 (D.D.C. 2013). For more information on the investigation of Operation Fast and Furious, *see* CRS Report RL34097, *Congress's Contempt Power and the Enforcement of Congressional Subpoenas: Law, History, Practice, and Procedure*, by Todd Garvey and Alissa M. Dolan.

[183] For a detail discussion of recent developments in this case, *see* CRS Report WSLG1109, *Three Parties, Two Cases, One Set of Documents; Not a Fast and Furious Resolution*, by Alissa M. Dolan and Todd Garvey.

[184] For more information on this litigation, *see* CRS Report RL34097, *Congress's Contempt Power and the Enforcement of Congressional Subpoenas: Law, History, Practice, and Procedure*, by Todd Garvey and Alissa M. Dolan.

Common Law Privileges

Attorney-Client Privilege

Although there is limited case law with respect to attorney-client privilege claims before congressional committees,[185] appellate court rulings on the privilege in cases involving other investigative contexts (e.g., grand jury) have raised questions as to whether executive branch officials may claim attorney-client or other common law privileges in the face of investigative demands.[186] Congress's implicit constitutional prerogative to investigate is the legal basis for Congress's practice in this area, which has long been recognized by the Supreme Court as extremely broad and encompassing, and is at its peak when the subject is waste, fraud, abuse, or maladministration within a government department.[187] The attorney-client privilege is, on the other hand, not a constitutionally based privilege; rather it is a judge-made exception to the normal principle of full disclosure in the adversary process that is to be narrowly construed and has been confined to the judicial forum.[188]

In practice, the exercise of committee discretion in accepting a claim of attorney-client privilege has turned on a "weighing [of] the legislative need for disclosure against any possible resulting injury"[189] to the witness.[190] On a case-by-case basis, a committee can consider, amongst other factors:

- the strength of a claimant's assertion in light of the pertinency of the documents or information sought to the subject of the investigation;

---

[185] *See* In the Matter of Provident Life and Accident Co., E.D. Tenn., S.D., CIV-1-90-219, June 13, 1990 (noting that the court's earlier ruling on an attorney-client privilege claim was "not of constitutional dimensions, and is certainly not binding on the Congress of the United States.").

[186] In re Grand Jury Subpoena Duces Tecum, 112 F. 3d 910 (8th Cir. 1997), *cert. denied sub. nom.,* Office of the President v. Office of the Independent Counsel, 521 U.S. 1105 (1997) (rejecting claims by the First Lady of attorney-client and work-product privilege with respect to notes taken by White House Counsel Office attorneys); In re Bruce R. Lindsey (Grand Jury Testimony), 158 F. 3d 1263 (D.C. Cir. 1998), *cert. denied,* 525 U.S. 996 (1998) (holding that a White House attorney may not invoke attorney-client privilege in response to a grand jury subpoena seeking information on possible commission of federal crimes); In re Sealed Case (Espy), 121 F.3d 729 (D.C. Cir. 1997) (deciding that the deliberative process privilege is a common law agency privilege which can be overcome by a showing of need by an investigating body); In re: A Witness Before the Special Grand Jury, 288 F.3d 289 (7th Cir. 2002) (holding that the attorney-client privilege is not applicable to communications between state government counsel and state office holder); *But see* In re Grand Jury Investigation, 399 F.3d 527 (2d Cir. 2005) (upholding a claim of attorney-client privilege with respect to communications between a former chief legal counsel to the Governor of Connecticut who was under grand jury investigation. It is worth noting that the Second Circuit recognized its apparent conflict with the afore-cited cases, however, the ruling is arguably distinguishable on its facts. *See* Kerri R. Blumenauer, *Privileged or Not? How the Current Application of the Government Attorney-Client Privilege Leaves the Government Feeling Unprivileged,* 75 FORDHAM L. REV. 75 (2006)).

[187] McGrain v. Daugherty, 272 U.S. 135, 177 (1926); Watkins v. United States, 354 U.S. 178, 187 (1957); Eastland v. United States Servicemen's Fund, 421 U.S. 491, 504 n.15 (1975).

[188] Westinghouse Electric Corp. v. Republic of the Philippines, 951 F.2d 1414, 1423 (3d Cir. 1991).

[189] Hearings, "International Uranium Cartel," Subcomm. on Oversight and Investigations, House Comm. on Interstate and Foreign Commerce, 95th Cong., Vol. 1, 123 (1977).

[190] Committees may also consider their statutory duty to engage in continuous oversight of the application, administration, and execution of laws that fall within their jurisdiction. *See* 2 U.S.C. §190d.

- the practical unavailability of the documents or information from any other source; the possible unavailability of the privilege to the claimant if it had been raised in a judicial forum; and

- the committee's assessment of the cooperation of the witness in the matter.

A valid claim of attorney-client privilege, free of any taint of waiver, exception, or other mitigating circumstance, would merit substantial weight. Any serious doubt, however, as to the validity of the asserted claim would diminish its compelling character.[191] Moreover, the conclusion that recognition of non-constitutionally based privileges, such as attorney-client privilege, is a matter of congressional discretion is consistent with both traditional British parliamentary and Congress's historical practice.[192]

Although no court has recognized the inapplicability of the attorney-client privilege in congressional proceedings in a decision directly addressing the issue,[193] an opinion issued by the Legal Ethics Committee of the District of Columbia Bar in February 1999 clearly acknowledges the long-standing congressional practice.[194] The ruling arose out of a House Commerce Committee subcommittee investigation of the planned relocation of the Federal Communications Commission offices to the Portals complex.[195] The subcommittee sought certain documents from the Portals developer, Mr. Franklin L. Haney. Mr. Haney's refusal to cooperate resulted in the issuance of subpoenas for production of documents to him and his attorneys. Both Mr. Haney and the attorneys asserted attorney-client privilege in their continued refusal to comply. The law firm also sought an opinion from the D.C. Bar's Ethics Committee as to its obligations in the face of the subpoena and a possible contempt citation. While awaiting an opinion from the Ethics Committee, the subcommittee cited the firm for contempt for their continued refusal to comply.

---

[191] *See, e.g., Contempt of Congress Against Franklin L. Haney*, H.Rept. 105-792, 105th Cong., 11-15 (1998); *Proceedings Against John M. Quinn, David Watkins, and Matthew Moore (Pursuant to Title 2, United States Code, Sections 192 and 194)*, H.Rept. 104-598, 104th Cong., 40-54 (1996); *Refusal of William H. Kennedy, III, To Produce Notes Subpoenaed by the Special Committee to Investigate Whitewater Development Corporation and Related Matters*, S.Rept. 104-191, 104th Cong., 9-19 (1995); *Proceedings Against Ralph Bernstein and Joseph Bernstein*, H.Rept. 99-462, 99th Cong., 13, 14 (1986); *Hearings, International Uranium Control, before the Subcommittee on Oversight and Investigations, House Committee on Interstate and Foreign Commerce*, 95th Cong., 60, 123 (1977).

[192] *See* CRS Report 95-464, *Investigative Oversight: An Introduction to the Law, Practice and Procedure of Congressional Inquiry*, pp. 43-55 (out of print; available from the authors). *See also* Glenn A. Beard, *Congress v. the Attorney-Client Privilege: A "Full and Frank Discussion,"* 35 AMER. CRIM. L. REV. 119, 122-27 (1997) ("[C]ongressional witnesses are not legally entitled to the protection of the attorney-client privilege, and investigating committees therefore have discretionary authority to respect or overrule such claims as they see fit."); Thomas Millett, *The Applicability of Evidentiary Privileges for Confidential Communications Before Congress*, 21 JOHN MARSHALL L. REV. 309 (1988).

[193] The Supreme Court has recognized that "only infrequently have witnesses ... [in congressional hearings] been afforded the procedural rights normally associated with an adjudicative proceeding." Hannah v. Larche, 363 U.S. 420, 425 (1960); *see also* United States v. Fort, 443 F. 2d 670 (D.C. Cir. 1970), *cert. denied*, 403 U.S. 932 (1971) (rejecting the contention that the constitutional right to cross-examine witnesses applied to a congressional investigation); In the Matter of Provident Life and Accident Co., E.D. Tenn., S.D., CIV-1-90-219, June 13, 1990 (noting that the court's earlier ruling on an attorney-client privilege claim was "not of constitutional dimensions, and is certainly not binding on the Congress of the United States.").

[194] Opinion No. 288, *Compliance With Subpoena from Congressional Committee to Produce Lawyers' Files Containing Client Confidences or Secrets*, Legal Ethics Committee, District of Columbia Bar, February 16, 1999 *available at* http://www.dcbar.org/for_lawyers/ethics/legal_ethics/opinions/opinion288.cfm [hereinafter D.C Ethics Committee Opinion].

[195] *See* H. Rep. No. 105-792, 105th Cong., 1-6, 7-8, 15-16 (1997).

The firm then proposed to turn over the documents if the contempt citation was withdrawn, to which the subcommittee agreed.[196]

Subsequently, the D.C. Bar's Ethics Committee issued an opinion vindicating the action taken by the firm. The Ethics Committee determined that an attorney faced with a congressional subpoena that would reveal client confidences or secrets:

> has a professional responsibility to seek to quash or limit the subpoena on all available, legitimate grounds to protect confidential documents and client secrets. If, thereafter, the Congressional subcommittee overrules these objections, orders production of the documents and threatens to hold the lawyer in contempt absent compliance with the subpoena, then, in the absence of a judicial order forbidding the production, the lawyer is permitted, but not required, by the D.C. Rules of Professional Conduct to produce the subpoenaed documents.[197]

The D.C. Bar opinion urges attorneys to press every appropriate objection to the subpoena until no further avenues of appeal are available, and even suggests that clients might be advised to retain other counsel to institute a third-party action to enjoin compliance,[198] but allows the attorney to relent at the earliest point when he is put in legal jeopardy. The opinion represents the first, and thus far the only, bar association in the nation to directly and definitively address the merits of the issue.

In the end, it is the congressional committee alone that determines whether to accept a claim of attorney-client privilege.

Work Product Immunity and Other Common Law Testimonial Privileges

The Federal Rules of Evidence recognize testimonial privileges for witnesses in judicial proceedings so that they need not reveal confidential communications between doctor and patient, husband and wife, or clergyman and parishioner.[199] Although there is no court case directly on point, it appears that, like the attorney-client privilege, congressional committees are not legally required to allow a witness to decline to testify on the basis of these other, similar testimonial privileges.[200] In addition, court decisions indicate that various rules of procedure generally

---

[196] *See* H. Comm. on Commerce, *Meeting on Portal Investigation (Authorization of Subpoenas; Receipt of Subpoenaed Documents and Consideration of Objections); and Contempt of Congress Proceedings Against Franklin L. Haney*, H. Comm. on Commerce, Comm. Print 105-V, 105th Cong. (1998).

[197] D.C. Ethics Committee Opinion, *supra* note 194. This opinion interpreted the phrase "required by law" as used in Rule 1.6(d)(2)(A), which states that a lawyer may reveal client confidences or secrets only when expressly permitted by the D.C. Bar rules or when "required by law or court order."

[198] A direct suit to enjoin a committee from enforcing a subpoena has been foreclosed by the Supreme Court's decision in *Eastland* v. *United States Servicemen's Fund*, 421 U.S. 491, 501 (1975), but that ruling does not appear to foreclose an action against a "third party," such as the client's attorney, to test the validity of the subpoena or the power of a committee to refuse to recognize the privilege. *See, e.g.,* United States v. AT&T, 567 F. 2d 121 (D.C. Cir. 1977) (entertaining an action by the Justice Department to enjoin AT&T from complying with a subpoena to provide telephone records that might compromise national security matters).

[199] FED. R. EVID. 501.

[200] *See generally* House Comm. on Energy & Commerce, Subcomm. on Oversight & Investigations, *Attorney-Client Privilege: Memoranda Opinions of the American Law Division, Library of Congress*, Comm. Print 98-I, 98th Cong. (1983) [hereinafter Attorney-Client Privilege Comm. Print]. *But see Moreland, supra* note 34, at 265-67. It should be noted that courts have refused to grant claims of work-product immunity, in response to a grand jury subpoena, over documents prepared by the White House Counsel's Office in anticipation of possible congressional hearings. *See, e.g.,* (continued...)

---

applicable to judicial proceedings, such as the right to cross-examine and call other witnesses, need not be accorded to a witness in a congressional hearing.[201] The basis for these determinations is rooted in Congress's Article I, § 5 rulemaking powers,[202] under which each house is the exclusive decision maker regarding the rules of its own proceedings. This rulemaking authority and general separation of powers considerations suggest that Congress and its committees are not obliged to abide by rules established by the courts to govern their own proceedings.[203]

Though congressional committees may not be legally obligated to recognize privileges for confidential communications, they may do so at their discretion. Historical precedent suggests that committees often have recognized such privileges.[204] The decision as to whether or not to allow such claims of privilege turns on a "weighing [of] the legislative need for disclosure against any possible resulting injury."[205]

Statutory Limitations on Congressional Access to Information

In certain circumstances, Congress has chosen to enact laws that limit its own ability to access specific types of information. Arguably, the quintessential example of such self-limiting action is 26 U.S.C. § 6103(f), under which only the House Committee on Ways and Means, Senate Committee on Finance, and the Joint Committee on Taxation are permitted access to individual's tax returns.[206] Should any other committee require such information, it must first obtain a House or Senate resolution[207] specifying the purpose for which the information is to be furnished and that the requested information cannot be reasonably obtained from any other source.[208] The information is to be provided only when the requesting committee is sitting in closed executive session.[209]

Other commonly cited statutory restrictions on oversight are 50 U.S.C. §§ 3091-3093, relating to foreign intelligence activities. Section 3091 governs congressional oversight of "intelligence

---

(...continued)

In re Grand Jury Subpoena Duces Tecum, 112 F.3d 907, 924-25 (8th Cir. 1997); In re Grand Jury Proceedings, 5 F. Supp. 2d 21, 39 (D.D.C. 1998).

[201] United States v. Fort, 443 F.2d 670 (D.C. Cir. 1970), *cert. denied*, 403 U.S. 932 (1971), (citing Hannah v. Larche, 363 U.S. 420 (1960)).

[202] U.S. CONST. art. 1, §5, cl. 2.

[203] *See generally* Telford Taylor, GRAND INQUEST: THE STORY OF CONGRESSIONAL INVESTIGATIONS 227-28 (1974).

[204] *See* Hamilton, *supra* note 124, at 244; *see also* S. Rept. No. 2, 84th Cong. (1955). Hamilton notes that John Dean, the former counsel to the President, testified before the Senate Watergate Committee after President Nixon had "waived any attorney-client privilege he might have had because of their relationship." Hamilton, *supra* note 124, at 244.

[205] Attorney-Client Privilege Comm. Print, *supra* note 200, at 27 (citing *Hearings on an International Uranium Cartel before the Subcommittee on Oversight and Investigations, House Committee on Interstate and Foreign Commerce*, 95th Cong., 60, 123 (1977)).

[206] 26 U.S.C. §6103(f)(1). Returns are to be submitted to the requesting Committee in a manner that protects the privacy of the individual. In the event that information identifying, either directly or indirectly, any tax filer is requested, it may only be furnished to the committee "when sitting in closed executive session unless such taxpayer otherwise consents in writing to such disclosure." *Id.*

[207] In the case of other joint or special committees, a concurrent resolution is required. *Id.*

[208] *Id.* at §6103(f)(3).

[209] *Id.*

---

activities"[210] generally. It requires that the President ensure that congressional intelligence committees are "fully and currently informed" of intelligence activities[211] and "promptly" notified of illegal intelligence activities.[212] Section 3092 governs oversight of intelligence activities that are not covert actions and § 3093 governs oversight of covert actions. Each section imposes a duty on the Director of National Intelligence (DNI) and the heads of other entities involved in intelligence activities to:

> with due regard for the protection from unauthorized disclosure of classified information relating to sensitive intelligence sources and methods or other exceptionally sensitive matters... keep the congressional intelligence committees fully and currently informed of all intelligence activities, other than a covert action... which are the responsibility of, are engaged in by, or are carried out for or on behalf of, any department, agency, or entity of the United States Government....[213]

Self-imposed limits on congressional oversight powers raise the question of whether statutes that generally prohibit public disclosure of information also restrict congressional access. Federal courts have held that the executive branch and private parties may not withhold documents from Congress based on a law that restricts public disclosure, because the release of information to a congressional requestor is not considered to be a disclosure to the general public.[214] Accordingly, it appears unlikely that a reviewing court would interpret a statute as restricting Congress's access to information unless the statute is express and unambiguous. Once documents are in congressional control, the courts will presume that committees "will exercise their powers responsibly and with proper regard for rights of affected parties."[215] Additionally, it appears that the courts may not prevent congressional disclosure of confidential information if such disclosure falls within the scope of the Speech or Debate Clause privilege.[216]

From time to time the President, the executive branch, and private parties have argued that certain statutes of general applicability prevent the disclosure of confidential or sensitive information to congressional committees. For example, a frequently cited statute to justify such non-disclosure is the Trade Secrets Act, a criminal provision that generally prohibits the disclosure of trade secrets and other confidential business information by a federal officer or employee "unless otherwise

---

[210] "Intelligence activities" is defined to include "cover actions" and "financial intelligence activities," but is not further defined in law. 50 U.S.C. § 3091(f). "Cover action" is also defined in statute. 50 U.S.C. § 3093(e). "Intelligence activities" is defined by Executive Order 12333 (as amended) as "all activities that agencies within the Intelligence Community are authorized to conduct pursuant to this Order." Exec. Order 12333, §3.4(e), 46 Fed. Reg. 59941 (Dec. 4, 1981). Additionally, detailed definitions of intelligence activities and "intelligence-related activities" are contained in the Senate resolution establishing the Senate Select Committee on Intelligence and the House Rule establishing the House Permanent Select Committee on Intelligence (HPSCI). *See* S. Res. 400, 94th Cong., §14(a); House Rule X(11).

[211] This requirement includes reporting on "significant anticipated intelligence activity as required by this subchapter." 50 U.S.C. § 3091(a).

[212] 50 U.S.C. § 3091(a).

[213] 50 U.S.C. §§ 3092(a), 3093(b).

[214] *See, e.g.,* F.T.C. v. Owens-Corning Fiberglass Corp., 626 F.2d 966, 970, 974 (D.C. Cir. 1980); Exxon Corp. v. F.T.C., 589 F.2d 582, 585-89 (D.C. Cir. 1978), *cert. denied,* 441 U.S. 943 (1979); Ashland Oil Co., Inc. v. F.T.C., 548 F.2d 977, 979 (D.C. Cir. 1976).

[215] *Exxon Corp.,* 589 F.2d at 589; *see also Owens-Corning Fiberglass Corp.,* 626 F.2d at 974; *Ashland Oil,* 548 F.2d at 979; Moon v. CIA, 514 F. Supp. 836, 849-51 (S.D.N.Y. 1981).

[216] *See* Doe v. McMillan, 412 U.S. 306 (1973); *see also Owens-Corning Fiberglass Corp.,* 626 F.2d at 970. For more information on the Speech or Debate Clause, *see* CRS Report R42648, *The Speech or Debate Clause: Constitutional Background and Recent Developments,* by Alissa M. Dolan and Todd Garvey.

authorized by law."[217] A review of the Trade Secrets Act's legislative history, however, provides no indication that it was ever intended to apply to Congress, its employees, or any legislative branch agency or its employees.[218] Moreover, as a matter of statutory construction it would appear to be unusual for Congress to subject, *sub silentio*, its staff to criminal sanctions for such disclosures, especially given its well-established oversight and investigative prerogatives, and its constitutional privilege with respect to Speech or Debate.[219] As such, there appears to be little doubt that disclosure to Congress of confidential information covered by the Trade Secrets Act would be deemed to be "authorized by law."

In instances in which the target of a congressional inquiry attempt to withhold information based on a general nondisclosure statute that is silent with respect to congressional disclosure, the committee may have to take additional steps to access the information. Potential solutions include: negotiations with the target; accommodations in the form of accepted redactions or other means of providing the information; or a so-called "friendly subpoena," which may provide the targeted entity or individual with the necessary legal cover to assist the committee with its inquiry. Each of these and many other prospective solutions can be employed at the committee's discretion.

Limitations Relating to Global Investigations

Options for Obtaining Materials From Overseas

If a congressional demand for information has been enforced in U.S. courts, through, for example, a criminal contempt conviction or the civil enforcement of a subpoena, U.S. courts may be able to seek assistance from foreign countries to enforce a court order. There are two ways for U.S. courts to request assistance from foreign countries in obtaining evidence (including witness testimony) located outside the United States: mutual legal assistance treaties and letters rogatory. Mutual legal assistance treaties provide for two countries' mutual assistance in criminal proceedings. Letters rogatory are formal requests made by a court in one country to a competent body in another country to serve process or order testimony of a witness or the production of evidence.[220] U.S. courts are statutorily authorized to issue such letters.[221] However, letters rogatory are generally considered a measure of last resort and are generally used only when no mutual legal assistance treaty exists.[222]

The existence of a mutual legal assistance treaty, however, does not guarantee that a congressional subpoena will be enforced in a foreign jurisdiction. Rather, the specific wording of the treaty must be consulted. For example, the United States and the United Kingdom (U.K.) have

---

[217] 18 U.S.C. §1905 (2006).

[218] *See* CNA Financial Corp. v. Donovan, 830 F.2d 1132, 1144-52 (D.C. Cir. 1987) (discussing, in depth, the legislative history of the Trade Secrets Act).

[219] U.S. Const. art. 1, §6, cl. 1.

[220] *See* 22 C.F.R. §92.54.

[221] 28 U.S.C. §§1781, 1782.

[222] *See* U.S. Department of State, "Preparation of Letters Rogatory," *available at* http://travel.state.gov/content/travel/english/legal-considerations/judicial/obtaining-evidence/preparation-letters-rogatory.html ("Letters rogatory may be used in countries where multi-lateral or bilateral treaties on judicial assistance are not in force to effect service of process or to obtain evidence if permitted by the laws of the foreign country").

a mutual legal assistance treaty that provides for various forms of assistance in criminal investigations and prosecutions, including serving documents, transferring persons in custody for testimony, and, in some cases, compelling testimony.[223] A U.S. court would likely invoke the treaty when seeking assistance from the U.K. in obtaining evidence.[224] Article 19 states that the treaty applies to any proceeding "related to criminal matters," including "any measure or step taken in connection with the investigation or prosecution of criminal offenses."[225] In addition, it allows relevant officials, in their discretion, to "treat as proceedings for the purpose of this treaty such hearings before or investigations by any court, administrative agency or administrative tribunal with respect to the imposition of civil or administrative sanctions."[226] Although this language might appear on its face to apply to civil or criminal contempt proceedings, the relevant proceeding would likely be considered the underlying congressional testimony, rather than the court contempt proceeding.[227] Because it would not result in criminal or civil sanctions, British officials may not view a congressional committee hearing as a "proceeding" under the treaty.

If a letter rogatory were found to be an appropriate vehicle despite the U.S.-U.K. mutual legal assistance treaty, it appears that the U.K. might nevertheless decline to enforce such a letter. Principles of international comity—"friendly dealing between nations at peace"[228]—undergird countries' mutual compliance with letters rogatory. Although reciprocity is not coterminous with international comity and the Supreme Court has held that judicial assistance by U.S. courts need not depend on reciprocity,[229] many countries use reciprocity as a guide to determine compliance with letters rogatory. Thus, it is important to examine U.S. compliance with other countries' letters rogatory to determine the likely extent of reciprocal compliance abroad. The applicable statute authorizes a U.S. district court to assist a foreign court if:

- the person from whom discovery is sought resides (or may be found) in the district of the court to which the application is made;

- the discovery is for use in a proceeding before a foreign tribunal; and

- the application is made directly by a foreign tribunal rather than by any other "interested person."[230]

With regard to a congressional investigation, the requirement that the evidence be for use in a "proceeding before a foreign tribunal" is the only requirement that might present a hardship for a

---

[223] Treaty with the United Kingdom on Mutual Legal Assistance on Criminal Matters, U.S.-U.K., S. Treaty Doc. 104-2 (1996).

[224] However, the U.S.-U.K. mutual assistance treaty does not expressly prohibit assistance requested outside the scope of the treaty. *See id.* at art. 17 ("Assistance and procedures set forth in this treaty shall not prevent either of the parties from granting assistance to the other party through the provisions of other internal agreements to which it is a party or through the provisions of its national laws).

[225] *Id.* at art. 19.

[226] *Id.*

[227] *See, e.g.,* In re Letters of Request to Examine Witnesses from the Court of Queens Bench for Manitoba, 488 F.2d 511 (9th Cir. 1973) (denying assistance on ground that the entity issuing the subpoena was not a tribunal, despite the fact that the request was sent by the Chief Justice of the Court of Queen's Bench for Manitoba).

[228] Hilton v. Guyot, 159 U.S. 113, 162 (1895).

[229] *See* Intel Corp. v. Advanced Micro Devices, Inc., 542 U.S. 241, 263 ("Section 1782 is a provision for assistance to tribunals abroad. It does not direct United States courts to engage in comparative analysis to determine whether analogous proceedings exist here. Comparisons of that order can be fraught with danger.").

[230] 28 U.S.C. §1782 (2006).

foreign governmental body in an analogous situation. Domestic courts have generally interpreted the word "tribunal" as including only entities with the capacity to make a binding adjudication.[231] Following this interpretation, a foreign country following a reciprocal approach may elect to decline to assist when requests originate from congressional committees, which are not commonly considered "tribunals" since they lack the legal authority to render binding adjudications.

Ability to Serve Congressional Subpoenas Overseas

There appear to be very few examples of congressional attempts to issue, serve, and enforce subpoenas abroad.[232] Congress's experiences during the Iran-Contra investigations demonstrate both of the potential difficulties of securing judicial assistance abroad and the need for imaginative improvisation.[233] The House and Senate Select Committees investigating the Iran-Contra matter were faced with formidable obstacles from the outset, including, but not limited to: a relatively short deadline to complete their investigation; a parallel Independent Counsel investigation competing for the same evidence; witnesses and evidence in foreign countries with strict secrecy laws; and an Administration that would not cooperate in facilitating any possible diplomatic accommodations.

These challenges were evident in the Committees' attempts to obtain information contained in Swiss bank accounts. The Committees sought a sharing agreement with the Independent Counsel, who was authorized by federal law and a Swiss treaty to seek Swiss judicial assistance, but he was reluctant to jeopardize his relationship with the Swiss government.[234] Instead, in 1987, the Committees issued an order requiring that former Major Richard V. Secord execute a consent directive authorizing the release of his offshore bank records and accounts to the Committee.[235] When Mr. Secord refused to sign the consent directive, the Committee sought a court order directing him to comply.[236] The court ruled that there was a testimonial aspect to requiring the signing of the consent directive and, thus, a court order would violate Mr. Secord's Fifth Amendment right against self-incrimination.[237] The court did not otherwise challenge the Committees' ability to seek such an order.

---

[231] *See, e.g.*, In re Letters Rogatory Issued By Director of Inspection of Government of India, 285 F.2d 1017 (2d Cir. 1967) (denying judicial assistance for an Indian tax collection entity because the tax assessment process did not result in any adjudicative proceeding); In re Letters of Request to Examine Witnesses from the Court of Queens Bench for Manitoba, Canada, 488 F.2d 511 (9th Cir. 1973) (holding that assistance to the Canadian Commission of Inquiry was not contemplated by the statute because the body's purpose is to conduct investigations unrelated to judicial or quasi-judicial controversies).

[232] *See* John C. Grabow, Congressional Investigations: Law and Practice, §3.2[b] (1988) (noting a 1985 attempt by a Senate committee to serve a member of the Soviet Navy while on a Soviet freighter located temporarily in American waters, and a 1986 attempt by various House committees to serve Ferdinand Marcos, the exiled former president of the Philippines.) However, the author does not provide any supporting authority documenting these attempts or any explanation for why they were unsuccessful.

[233] *See generally* George W. Van Cleve & Charles Tiefer, *Navigating the Shoals of "Use" Immunity and Secret International Enterprises in Major Congressional Investigations: Lessons of the Iran-Contra Affair*, 55 Mo. L. Rev. 43 (1990) [hereinafter Van Cleve & Tiefer].

[234] *See* 28 U.S.C. § 1782.

[235] Senate Select Comm. on Secret Military Assistance to Iran and the Nicaraguan Opposition v. Secord, 664 F. Supp. 562, 563 (D.D.C. 1987).

[236] *Id.*

[237] *Id.* at 564-66. In 1988 the Supreme Court adopted the Senate's argument in a different case, holding that such a (continued...)

As a last resort, the Committees concluded that to obtain the critical financial records they had to grant use immunity to a principal target of the investigation, who was living in Paris and would not subject himself to U.S. jurisdiction, in return for the records. To establish its own investigative legitimacy and allay concerns about the force of the immunity grant, the Committees obtained an order (a "commission") from a district court, under Rule 28 of the Federal Rules of Civil Procedure, empowering him (the "commissioner") to obtain evidence in another country and to bring it back.[238] Finally, the House Committee issued the chief counsel a commission, much like a subpoena in format, to further document his official status. The witness turned over the financial documents and aided in deciphering and understanding them.[239] The legal sufficiency of the tactic was never tested in court but proved effective in obtaining the documents.

Frequently Encountered Information Access Issues

Congressional oversight and investigations can often, though not always, become adversarial, especially if the target of an investigation refuses to disclose requested information. In those situations, the targeted entity may attempt to argue that disclosure of the information is prohibited by a specific law, rule, or executive decision. Another common tactic is to assert that the information is so sensitive that Congress is not among those entitled or authorized to have the information. This section will address some of the most common laws, rules, and orders that have been cited as the basis for targeted entities withholding information from Congress.

The Privacy Act

The Privacy Act prohibits, with certain exceptions, the disclosure by a federal agency of "any record which is contained in a system of records" to any person or to another agency, except pursuant to a written request by, or with the prior written consent of, the subject of the record.[240] While the Privacy Act restricts disclosures by federal departments, Congress has expressly reserved its constitutional right of access to covered information.[241] The statutory limitations do not apply to disclosure of records by the executive "to either House of Congress, or, to the extent of matter within its jurisdiction, any committee or subcommittee thereof, any joint committee of Congress or subcommittee of any such joint committee...."[242] This exemption applies, by its

---

(...continued)

directive is not testimonial in nature. *See* Doe v. United States, 487 U.S. 201 (1988).

[238] This tool contrasts with a letter rogatory, which goes to a foreign court, and with domestic deposition practice, which occurs on notice without going to or from any court.

[239] *Id.* at 79-80.

[240] 5 U.S.C. §552a. The term "record" is defined as "any item, collection, or grouping of information about an individual that is maintained by an agency, including, but not limited to, his education, financial transactions, medical history, and criminal or employment history and that contains his name, or the identifying number, symbol, or other identifying particular assigned to the individual, such as a finger or voice print or a photograph...." 5 U.S.C. § 552a(a)(4). The phrase "system of records" means "a group of any records under the control of any agency from which information is retrieved by the name of the individual or by some identifying number, symbol, or other identifying particular assigned to the individual...." 5 U.S.C. § 552a(a)(5).

[241] *See, e.g.,* Watkins v. United States, 354 U.S. 178, 200 n.33 (1957); McGrain v. Daugherty, 273 U.S. 135 (1927).

[242] 5 U.S.C. §552a(b)(9). The House Report on the act explained that the congressional exemption "relates to personal information needed by the Congress and its committees and subcommittees. Occasionally, it is necessary to inquire into such subjects for legislative and investigative reasons." *See* H. Rept. 93-1416, 93rd Cong., 13 (1974). The legislative history of the act is sketched in *Devine v. United States*, 202 F.3d 547, 552 (2nd Cir. 2000).

---

terms, to a disclosure to the House or Senate, or to a committee or subcommittee that has jurisdiction over the subject of the disclosure. The exemption does not, however, permit disclosures to committees without jurisdiction, minority Members of committees, or to individual Members of Congress.

Furthermore, the original guidelines adopted by the Office of Management and Budget (OMB)[243] state that the congressional exemption "does not authorize the disclosure of a record to Members of Congress acting in their individual capacities without the consent of the individual."[244] Similarly, some court rulings have found that the exemption applies "only to a House of Congress or a committee or subcommittee, not to individual congressmen."[245] One case construed the exemption somewhat more broadly and held that it applies to a disclosure to an individual Member "in his official capacity as a member of ... [a] subcommittee, not as an individual Member of Congress."[246]

The Freedom of Information Act

The Freedom of Information Act (FOIA) requires publication in the *Federal Register* of various information, such as descriptions of an agency's organization and procedures. It also requires that certain materials, such as statements of policy that have not been published in the *Federal Register* and certain staff manuals, be made available for public inspection.[247] In addition, FOIA provides that all other records are to be disclosed in response to a specific request by any person, except records that fall under one of the nine exemptions from the disclosure requirements.[248] FOIA also provides for both administrative and judicial appeals when access to information is thought to be improperly denied by an agency.

FOIA applies to "agencies,"[249] which are defined to include "any executive department, military department, Government corporation, Government controlled corporation, or other establishment in the executive branch of the Government (including the Executive Office of the President), or any independent regulatory agency."[250] Congress is not included within the scope of the definition of agency. Therefore, records of the House, Senate, congressional committees, and Members are not subject to disclosure under FOIA.[251]

---

[243] OMB is required to prescribe guidelines and regulations for the use of agencies in implementing the act. *See* 5 U.S.C. §552a(v).

[244] Office of Management and Budget, *Privacy Act Guidelines*, 40 FED. REG. 28949, 28955 (1975).

[245] Swenson v. United States Postal Service, 890 F.2d 1075, 1077 (9th Cir. 1989); *accord* Williams v. Stovall, 1993 WL 431149 (D.C. Cir. Oct. 14, 1993) (per curiam) (stating that the "Privacy Act's exception for information disclosed to Congress or its committees does not expressly provide for disclosure to individual members of Congress"); *cf.* Exxon Corp. v. FTC, 589 F.2d 582, 592-94 (D.C. Cir. 1978), *cert. denied*, 441 U.S. 943 (1979). On remand, the district court in *Swenson* held that the defendant had violated the Privacy Act by disclosing private facts about plaintiff's status as a Postal Service employee to two Members of Congress who contacted the Service following allegations by the plaintiff that the Service had undercounted certain routes. *See* 1994 U.S. Dist. LEXIS 16524 (E.D. Cal. Mar. 10, 1994).

[246] *Devine*, 202 F.3d at 549, 551 (letter from agency Inspector General, concerning investigation, to chairman and member of subcommittee with jurisdiction over subject of letter, was within scope of congressional exemption).

[247] 5 U.S.C. §552.

[248] 5 U.S.C. §552(b).

[249] 5 U.S.C. §552(a).

[250] 5 U.S.C. §552(f)(1).

[251] *See, e.g.*, United We Stand Am. v. IRS, 359 F.3d 595, 597 (D.C. Cir. 2004) (stating that "The Freedom of (continued...)

Additionally, FOIA specifically provides that the statute "is not authority to withhold information from Congress."[252] The D.C. Circuit, in *Murphy v. Department of the Army*,[253] explained that FOIA exemptions were no basis for withholding information from Congress because of:

> the obvious purpose of the Congress to carve out for itself a special right of access to privileged information not shared by others.... Congress, whether as a body, through committees, or otherwise, must have the widest possible access to executive branch information if it is to perform its manifold responsibilities effectively. If one consequence of the facilitation of such access is that some information will be disclosed to congressional authorities but not to private persons, that is but an incidental consequence of the need for informed and effective lawmakers.[254]

When a congressional committee of jurisdiction is seeking information from an agency for legislative or oversight purposes, it does not act pursuant to FOIA, but rather pursuant to Congress's constitutional oversight authority.[255] Therefore, an agency may not cite a FOIA exemption as the reason for withholding disclosure.

Individual Members, Members not on a committee of jurisdiction, or minority Members of a jurisdictional committee, may, like any person, request agency records.[256] When they do, however, they are not acting pursuant to Congress's constitutional authority to conduct oversight and investigations. Therefore, the DOJ has interpreted the congressional exemption not to apply to such requests.[257] Thus, the standard FOIA exemptions that an agency could invoke to prevent disclosure to the general public can also be cited to prevent disclosure to these categories of Members.

Grand Jury Materials

In the course of an investigation, Congress may seek access to evidence that was presented before a grand jury. As a general matter, Federal Rule of Criminal Procedure 6(e) provides for the secrecy of "matters occurring before the grand jury," unless a court authorizes disclosure for the purposes of a judicial proceeding, or at the request and showing by a defendant that he needs the information to justify dismissal of an indictment. Although the rule codifies the traditional policies underlying grand jury secrecy, it remains subject to recognized exceptions.[258] The rule,

---

(...continued)

Information Act does not cover congressional documents."); Dow Jones & Co. v. DOJ, 917 F.2d 571, 574 (D.C. Cir. 1990) (holding that Congress is not an agency for any purpose under FOIA); Dunnington v. DOD, No. 06-0925, 2007 WL 60902, at *1 (D.D.C. Jan. 8, 2007) (ruling that Senate and House are not agencies under FOIA).

[252] 5 U.S. C. §552(d).

[253] 613 F.2d 1151 (D.C. Cir. 1979).

[254] *Id.* at 1155-56, 1158.

[255] See, *e.g.*, McGrain v. Daugherty, 273 U.S. 135 (1927). When a committee seeks information from the executive, it may do so by means of an informal request from committee staff, a letter signed by the committee chair, or by exercise of the subpoena authority, which is vested in standing committees by both bodies. House Rule XI, cl. 2(m); Senate Rule XXVI.

[256] H. Rept. 1497, 89th Cong., 11-12 (1966).

[257] *See* Department of Justice, Office of Information and Privacy, Freedom of Information Act Guide, 41-42, (Spring 2010), *available at* http://www.justice.gov/oip/foia_guide09/procedural-requirements.pdf (stating that "individual Members of Congress possess the same rights of access as 'any person'").

[258] *See* In re Report & Recommendation of Grand Jury, 370 F. Supp. 1219, 1229 (D.D.C. 1974).

however, was arguably not intended to insulate from disclosure all information once it is presented to a grand jury.[259] Rather, according to the courts, the aim of the rule is to "prevent disclosure of the way in which information was presented to the grand jury, the specific questions and inquiries of the grand jury, the deliberations and vote of the grand jury, the targets upon which the grand jury's suspicion focuses, and specific details of what took place before the grand jury."[260]

Court approved disclosures of grand jury material require "a strong showing of particularized need."[261] Persons or entities seeking disclosure "must show that the material they seek is needed to avoid a possible injustice in another judicial proceeding, that the need for disclosure is greater than the need for continued secrecy, and that their request is structured to cover only material so needed."[262] Since any examination begins with a preference for preservation of the grand jury's secrets, the particularized need requirement cannot be satisfied simply by demonstrating that the information sought would be relevant or useful or that acquiring it from the grand jury rather than from some other available source would be more convenient.[263]

There are numerous examples in which entities of the legislative branch have sought and received material that was covered by Rule 6(e). For example, in 1952, the Senate Banking Committee filed a motion requesting access to documents in the custody of the United States Attorney that had been shown to a federal grand jury.[264] The court ordered the documents disclosed, over the

---

[259] United States v. Saks & Co., 426 F. Supp. 812, 814 (S.D.N.Y. 1976).

[260] In re Grand Jury Investigation of Ven-Fuel, 441 F. Supp. 1299, 1302-03 (D. Fla. 1977) (citing United States v. Interstate Dress Carriers, Inc., 280 F.2d 52, 54 (2d Cir. 1960); United States v. Saks & Co., 426 F. Supp. at 815; In re Senate Banking Committee Hearings, 19 F.R.D. 410, 412-13 (N.D.Ill.1956)).

[261] United States v. Sells Engineering, Inc., 463 U.S. 418, 443 (1983); *see also Right of Party in Civil Action to Obtain Disclosure, Under Rule 6(e)(3)(C)(i) of the Federal Rules of Criminal Procedure, of Matters Occurring Before Grand Jury,* 71 A.L.R. Fed. 10.

[262] *Douglas Oil Co.,* 441 U.S. at 222; *see also* United States v. Moussaoui, 483 F.3d 220, 235 (4th Cir. 2007); McAninch v. Wintermute, 491 F.3d 759, 767 (8th Cir. 2007); United States v. Aisenberg, 358 F.3d 1327, 1348 (11th Cir. 2004); United States v. Campbell, 324 F.3d 497, 498-99 (7th Cir. 2003); In re Special Grand Jury 89-2, 143 F.3d 565, 569-70 (10th Cir. 1998); In re Grand Jury Proceedings (Ballas), 62 F.3d 1175, 1179 (9th Cir. 1995); United States v. Miramontex, 995 F.2d 56, 59 (5th Cir. 1993).

[263] In re Grand Jury 95-1, 118 F.3d 1433, 1437 (10th Cir. 1997); *see also* In re Grand Jury Investigation (Missouri), 55 F.3d 350, 354-55 (8th Cir. 1995); Cullen v. Margiotta, 811 F.2d 698, 715 (2d Cir. 1987); Hernly v. United States, 832 F.2d 980, 883-85 (7th Cir. 1987); In re Grand Jury Proceedings GJ-76-4 & GJ-75-3, 800 F.2d 1293, 1302 (4th Cir. 1986). The need to shield the grand jury's activities from public display is less compelling once it has completed its inquiries and been discharged, especially if the resulting criminal proceedings have also been concluded. United States v. Socony-Vacuum Oil Co., 310 U.S. 150, 234 (1940); United States v. Blackwell, 954 F. Supp. 944, 966 (D.N.J. 1997). *See also In re Grand Jury Investigation (Missouri),* 55 F.3d at 354; In re Grand Jury Proceeding Relative to Perl, 838 F.2d 304, 307 (8th Cir. 1988); *In re Grand Jury Proceedings GJ-76-4 & GJ-75-3,* 800 F.2d at 1301; In re Shopping Cart Antitrust Litigation, 95 F.R.D. 309, 312-13 (S.D.N.Y. 1982). Of course, there must still be a counterbalancing demonstration of need, a requirement that becomes more difficult if the grand jury witnesses whose testimony is to be disclosed still run the risk of retaliation. United States v. Aisenberg, 358 F.3d 1327, 1348 (11th Cir. 2004); *Cullen,* 811 F.2d 698. *See also Hernly,* 832 F.2d at 985; In re Grand Jury Testimony, 832 F.2d 60, 64 (5th Cir. 1987); *In re Grand Jury Investigation (Missouri),* 55 F.3d at 355. Moreover, the courts seem responsive to requests to disclose matters occurring before the grand jury for the purpose of resolving some specific inconsistency in the testimony of a witness, or to refresh a witness's recollection during the course of a trial. *Douglas Oil,* 441 U.S. at 222 n.12; *see also* United States v. Rockwell International Corp., 173 F.3d 757, 759 (10th Cir. 1999); *In re Grand Jury,* 832 F.2d at 63; Lucas v. Turner, 725 F.2d 1095, 1105 (7th Cir. 1984); United States v. Fischbach and Moore, Inc., 776 F.2d 839, 845 (9th Cir. 1985). Under much the same logic, a court may afford a grand jury witness access to his or her earlier testimony prior to a subsequent appearance. In re Grand Jury, 490 F.3d 978, 986-90 (D.C. Cir. 2007).

[264] In re Senate Banking Committee Hearings, 19 F.R.D. 410 (N.D. Ill. 1956).

---

objections of the United States Attorney, concluding that "when the fact or document is sought for itself, independently, rather than because it was stated before or displayed to the grand jury, there is no bar of secrecy."[265]

Similarly, in *In re Grand Jury Investigation of Ven-Fuel et al.*,[266] a federal district court held that a subcommittee request for documents presented to a grand jury was not prohibited by Rule 6(e). The court held that when Congress is acting within the "legitimate sphere of legislative activity" it is legally entitled to Rule 6(e) information.[267] The court thus ordered that the Chair and Members of the Subcommittee "be permitted to examine all of the documents, without segregation and identification of those upon which the criminal indictment was based, in order to determine what specific documents they wish produced for their use."[268]

When information sought by a congressional committee seeks to reveal what actually occurred before the grand jury, however, the courts have been much more reluctant to order its disclosure. In *In Re Grand Jury Impaneled October 2, 1978 (79-2)*,[269] the District Court for the District of Columbia held that a subcommittee's request for an inventory of all documents subpoenaed by a grand jury fell within the scope of Rule 6(e) and, therefore, was not required to be disclosed.[270] The court was particularly concerned that such a disclosure would "set a dangerous precedent by revealing a great deal about the scope and focus of the grand jury's investigation."[271]

Documents Related to Pending Litigation

Often congressional committees decide to investigate matters in which federal litigation is currently pending, which may be met by resistance from the DOJ. These rationales have included: a desire to avoid prejudicial pre-trial publicity; protecting the rights of innocent third parties; protecting the identity of confidential informants; preventing disclosure of the government's strategy in anticipated or pending judicial proceedings; avoiding a potential chilling effect on the exercise of prosecutorial discretion by DOJ attorneys; and precluding interference with the President's constitutional duty to faithfully execute the laws.[272] Jackson's views were reiterated by Attorney General William French Smith in a 1982 congressional investigation of the EPA, in which DOJ argued that withholding EPA attorneys' memoranda and notes, regarding enforcement strategy, case preparation, and settlement consideration, prevented prejudice to the cause of effective law enforcement.[273] He additionally expressed concern that disclosure would

---

[265] *Id.* at 412.

[266] 441 F. Supp. 1299, 1302-03 (D. Fla. 1977).

[267] *Id.* at 1307 (stating that "[t]here is no question that Chairman Moss and the Subcommittee have demonstrated their constitutionally independent legal right to the documents that they seek for their legitimate legislative activity.").

[268] *Id.*

[269] 510 F. Supp. 112 (D.D.C. 1981).

[270] *Id.* at 114.

[271] *Id.* at 115 (citing S.E.C. v. Dresser Indus., 628 F.2d 1368, 1382 (D.C. Cir. 1980), *cert. denied*, 449 U.S. 993 (1980); United States v. Stanford, 589 F.2d 285, 291 n.6 (7th Cir. 1978), *cert. denied*, 440 U.S. 983 (1980); Davis v. Romney, 55 F.R.D. 337, 341-42 (E.D. Pa. 1972)).

[272] DOJ's views of this issue were most famously articulated by then Attorney General Robert Jackson in 1941. 40 Op. Atty. Gen. 45 (1941). The opinion argued that "congressional or public access to [internal DOJ documents] would not be in the public interest" because it would "seriously prejudice law enforcement." *Id.* at 46-47.

[273] *See* Letter to Hon. John D. Dingell Chairman, House Subcommittee on Oversight and Investigation, Committee on Energy and Commerce, from Attorney General William French Smith, dated November 30, 1982, *reprinted in* H.Rept. No. 97-968 at 37-38 [hereinafter Dingell Letter].

raise "a substantial danger that congressional pressures will influence the course of the investigation."[274]

In the 2001-2002 House Government Reform Committee investigation of the FBI misuse of informants, despite maintaining its historical position, DOJ ultimately disclosed internal deliberative prosecutorial documents following increased congressional pressure. In a February 1, 2002, letter to Chairman Burton, the DOJ Assistant Attorney General for Legislative Affairs explained:

> Our particular concern in the current controversy pertains to the narrow and especially sensitive categories of advice memoranda to the Attorney General and the deliberative documents making recommendations regarding whether or not to bring criminal charges against individuals. We believe that the public interest in avoiding the polarization of the criminal justice process required greater protection of those documents which, in turn, influences the accommodation process. This is not an "inflexible position," but rather a statement of a principled interest in ensuring the integrity of prosecutorial decision-making.[275]

A review of the case law in this area suggests that the courts have recognized the potentially prejudicial effect congressional hearings can have on pending cases.[276] While not questioning the prerogatives of Congress with respect to oversight and investigation, the cases pose a political choice for Congress. On one hand, congressionally generated publicity may harm the executive branch's prosecutorial effort. On the other hand, access to information under secure conditions can fulfill the congressional oversight objectives and need not be inconsistent with the executive's authority to pursue its case. Although powerful arguments may be made on both sides, the decision to pursue a congressional investigation of pending civil or criminal matters remains a choice that is solely within Congress' discretion to make. As the Iran-Contra Independent Counsel observed "[t]he legislative branch has the power to decide whether it is more important perhaps to destroy a prosecution than to hold back testimony they need. They make that decision. It is not a judicial decision, or a legal decision, but a political decision of the highest importance."[277]

Classified Material

How are materials classified?

The standards for classifying and declassifying information are contained in Executive Order 13526 and were adopted by President Obama on December 29, 2009.[278] These standards provide that the President, Vice President, agency heads, and any other officials designated by the

---

[274] *Id.* (quoting former Deputy Assistant General Thomas E. Kauper). This policy is said to be "premised in part on the fact that the Constitution vests in the President and his subordinates the responsibility to 'take Care that the Laws be faithfully executed.'" *Id.*

[275] *Investigation Into Allegations of Justice Department Misconduct In New England-Volume I, Hearings Before the H. Comm. on Government Reform*, 107th Cong. 520-56, 562-604 (May 3, Dec. 13, 2001; Feb. 6, 2002).

[276] *See* CRS Report R42811, *Congressional Investigations of the Department of Justice, 1920-2012: History, Law, and Practice*, by Alissa M. Dolan and Todd Garvey at 8-10.

[277] Lawrence E. Walsh, *The Independent Counsel and the Separation of Powers*, 25 HOUS. L. REV. 1, 9 (1988).

[278] Exec. Order No. 13526, 75 FED. REG. 707 (January 5, 2010).

President may classify information upon a determination that its unauthorized disclosure could reasonably be expected to damage national security.[279] Such information must be owned by, produced by, or under the control of the federal government, and must concern one of the areas delineated by the Executive Order.[280]

Information is classified at one of three levels based on the amount of danger that its unauthorized disclosure could reasonably be expected to cause to national security.[281] Information is classified as:

- "top secret" if its unauthorized disclosure could reasonably be expected to cause "exceptionally grave damage" to national security;

- "secret" if its unauthorized disclosure could reasonably be expected to cause "serious damage" to national security; and

- "confidential" if its unauthorized disclosure could reasonably be expected to cause "damage" to national security.

Significantly, for each level, the original classifying officer must identify or describe the specific danger potentially presented by the information's disclosure.[282] The officer who originally classifies the information establishes a date for declassification based upon the expected duration of the information's sensitivity. If the officer cannot set an earlier declassification date, then the information must be marked for declassification after 10 or 25 years, depending on the sensitivity of the information.[283] The deadline for declassification can be extended if the threat to national security still exists.[284]

Who can access classified materials?

Access to classified information is generally limited to those who:

- demonstrate their eligibility to the relevant agency head (for example, through a security clearance);

- sign a nondisclosure agreement; and

- have a need to know the information, which is satisfied upon "a determination within the executive branch... that a prospective recipient requires access to

---

[279] *Id.* at §1.3. The unauthorized disclosure of foreign government information is presumed to damage national security. *Id.* at §1.1(b).

[280] *Id.* at §1.4. The areas are as follows: military plans, weapons systems, or operations; foreign government information; intelligence activities, intelligence sources/methods, cryptology; foreign relations or foreign activities of the United States, including confidential sources; scientific, technological, or economic matters relating to national security; federal programs for safeguarding nuclear materials or facilities; vulnerabilities or capabilities of national security systems; or weapons of mass destruction. *Id.* In addition, when classified information that is incorporated, paraphrased, restated, or generated in a new form, that new form must be classified at the same level as the original. *Id.* at §§2.1-2.2.

[281] *Id.* at §1.2.

[282] *Id.* Classifying authorities are specifically prohibited from classifying information for reasons other than protecting national security, such as to conceal violations of law or avoid embarrassment. *Id.* at §1.7(a).

[283] *Id.* at §1.5.

[284] Exec. Order No. 13526 at §1.5(c).

---

specific classified information in order to perform or assist in a lawful and authorized governmental function."[285]

The information being accessed may not be removed from the controlling agency's premises without permission.[286] Each agency is required to establish systems for controlling the distribution of classified information.[287]

The Executive Order does not contain any instructions regarding disclosures to Congress or its committees of jurisdiction. "Members of Congress, as constitutionally elected officers, do not receive security clearances as such, but are instead presumed to be trustworthy," thereby fulfilling the first requirement to access classified materials.[288] Members of Congress must still satisfy the "need to know" requirement. A Member could assert that he fulfills this requirement based on the constitutional duties and responsibilities of his office. However, it should be noted that the executive branch may disagree with this interpretation and has previously stated that it retains the final authority to determine if a Member has a need to know.[289] For example, a 1996 Office of Legal Counsel Opinion stated that "the longstanding practice under Executive Order 12356 (and its successor) has been that the 'need-to-know' determination for disclosures of classified information to Congress is made through established decisionmaking channels at each agency."[290]

Congressional aides, support staff, and other legislative branch employees do not automatically have access to classified information and, therefore, must go through the necessary security clearance process prior to being permitted to review such information.

The Executive Order's silence with respect to disclosure to Congress, combined with the absence of any other law restricting congressional access to classified material, suggests that mere classification likely cannot be used as a legal basis to withhold information from Congress. That said, practical and political concerns with respect to controlled access, secure storage, and public disclosure may provide persuasive rationales for withholding or limiting congressional access. Committees and subcommittees have wide discretion to negotiate with the Administration regarding these issues. For example, an investigating committee or subcommittee could choose to review documents at an executive branch secure facility, permit redactions of certain information, limit the ability of staff to review certain material, and/or opt to hold non-public meetings, briefings, and hearings where classified information will be discussed. None of these measures are legally required, but all are within the investigating entity's discretion and may assist in facilitating the disclosure of materials sought during the investigation.

---

[285] *Id.* at §§ 4.1, 6.1(dd). The need-to-know requirement can be waived, however, for former Presidents and Vice Presidents, historical researchers, and former policy-making officials who were appointed by the President or Vice President. *Id.* at § 4.4.

[286] *Id.* at §4.1.

[287] *Id.* at §4.2.

[288] Christopher H. Schroeder, *Access to Classified Information*, 20 Op. Off. Legal Counsel 402, *11 (1996).

[289] *See, e.g., id.*

[290] *Id.* at *13.

Judicial Precedent Involving Congressional Access to Classified Materials

Though there have been numerous notable congressional investigations of programs and activities involving classified information,[291] it appears that only one information access dispute reached the courts. The House Interstate and Foreign Commerce Committee subcommittee investigation involved allegations of improper domestic and foreign intelligence gathering and warrantless wiretapping. In 1976, the subcommittee issued subpoenas to the American Telephone and Telegraph Company (AT&T)seeking copies of "all national security request letters sent to AT&T and its subsidiaries by the FBI as well as records of such taps prior to the time when the practice of sending such letters was initiated."[292] Before AT&T could comply with the request, the DOJ and the Subcommittee's Chairman, Representative John Moss, entered into negotiations to reach an alternate agreement that would prevent AT&T from turning over all of its records.[293] When these negotiations broke down, the DOJ sought an injunction prohibiting AT&T from complying with the Subcommittee's subpoenas, arguing that the potential for disclosure of the information outside of Congress would damage "the national interest." [294] After the district court deferred to the President's "final determination" regarding the potential damage of complying with the subpoena and issued the injunction, [295] the Court of Appeals for the District of Columbia Circuit (D.C. Circuit) heard the case. [296]

The court carefully addressed the claims of absolute rights asserted by both Congress and the executive branch. Congress, based on the Speech or Debate Clause,[297] asserted that judicial interference with its investigations was constitutionally prohibited. Relying on both *Eastland v. United States Servicemen's Fund*[298] and *United States v. Nixon*,[299] the court concluded that while generally congressional subpoena power cannot be interfered with by the courts, the "*Eastland* immunity is not absolute in the context of a conflicting constitutional interest asserted by a coordinate branch of government."[300] The Executive Branch asserted absolute discretion with respect to national security materials. In response, the court noted that Supreme Court precedent does "not establish judicial deference to executive determinations in the area of national security when the result of that deference would be to impede Congress in exercising its legislative powers."[301] Given the sensitivity of the constitutional balancing required to resolve the claim and the fact that the parties had nearly reached an out-of-court settlement, the court declined to rule

---

[291] *See, e.g.,* S. Rep. No.755, Books 1-3, 94th Cong. (1976); Intelligence Activities, S. Res. 21: Hearings Before the Senate Select Comm. to Study Governmental Operations with Respect to Intelligence Activities, vols. 1-6, 94th Cong. (1975); FBI Oversight: Hearings Before the Subcomm. on Civil and Constitutional Rights of the House Comm. of the Judiciary, parts 1-3, 94th Cong. (1975-1976), parts 1-2, 95th Cong. (1978).

[292] United States v. AT&T, 551 F.2d 384, 385 (D.C. Cir. 1976) [hereinafter *AT&T I*].

[293] *Id.* at 386. The precise details of the delicate negotiations between the DOJ and the Subcommittee are explained by the court, and, therefore, will not be recounted here. *See id.* at 386-88.

[294] *Id.* at 388.

[295] United States v. AT&T, 419 F. Supp. 454, 458-61 (D.D.C. 1976).

[296] *See AT&T I,* 551 F.2d 384. The appeals court first disposed of several prudential concerns, specifically considering the doctrines of mootness, political question, and standing, determining that none of them prevented the court from reaching the merits of the injunction. *See AT&T I,* 551 F.3d at 390-91.

[297] U.S. CONST. art. 1, §6, cl. 1.

[298] 421 U.S. 491 (1975).

[299] 418 U.S. 683 (1974).

[300] *Id.* at 392 (citing *United States v. Nixon,* 418 U.S. 683, 706 (1974)).

[301] *Id.* (citing United States v. Curtiss-Wright Export Corp., 299 U.S. 304 (1936); Chicago & Southern Air Lines v. Waterman Steamship Corp., 333 U.S. 103 (1948)).

---

on the merits of the claim.[302] The court directed the parties to continue negotiations and report to the district court on their progress.[303]

After continued negotiations, the parties reached an impasse and found themselves back before the D.C. Circuit.[304] Again, the court was faced with a dispute between two assertions of absolute constitutional authority. It rejected the executive branch's claim stating:

> the executive would have it that the Constitution confers on the executive absolute discretion in the area of national security. This does not stand up. While the Constitution assigns to the President a number of powers relating to national security ... it confers upon Congress other powers equally inseparable from the national security...[305]

The appeals court also rejected Congress's argument about judicial interference with congressional investigations, stating that:

> the [Speech or Debate] Clause does not and was not intended to immunize congressional investigatory actions from judicial review. Congress'[s] investigatory power is not, itself, absolute. And the fortuity that documents sought by a congressional subpoena are not in the hands of a party claiming injury from the subpoena should not immunize that subpoena from challenge by that party.[306]

Like its previous decision, rather than ruling on the merits of the constitutional conflict the court attempted to fashion a compromise that would force the parties back into negotiations. DOJ was allowed to limit the sample size of the unedited memoranda and prohibit committee staff from removing their notes from the FBI's possession.[307] If the Subcommittee alleged inaccuracy or deception, the materials were to be forwarded to the district court for *in camera* review and any remedial action the court found necessary.[308] In addition, the Attorney General was permitted to employ a substitution procedure for the most sensitive documents; however, the substitutions had to be approved by the district court based on a showing of "the accuracy and fairness of the edited memorandum, and the extraordinary sensitivity of the contents of the original memorandum to the national security."[309]

In the end, the *AT&T* court never ruled on the merits of the dispute and never resolved the constitutional conflict between the branches. At most, *AT&T* stands for the proposition that neither claims of executive control over national security documents, nor congressional assertions

---

[302] Rather, it remanded the case to the district court to modify the injunction to exclude information for which no claim of national security had been made. *Id.* at 395 (stating that "[w]e direct the District Court to modify the injunction to exclude request letters pertaining to taps classified by the FBI as domestic, since there was no contention by the Executive, nor finding by the District Court, of undue risk to the national security from transmission of these letters to the Subcommittee.").

[303] *Id.*

[304] *See* United States v. AT&T, 567 F.2d 121, 124-25 (D.C. Cir. 1977) (detailing the extensive negotiations between the DOJ and the Subcommittee since the court last heard from the parties) [hereinafter *AT&T II*]. Earlier negotiations focused on access to unredacted DOJ memoranda.

[305] *Id.* at 128.

[306] *AT&T II*, 567 F.2d at 129 (citing Barenblatt v. United States, 360 U.S. 109, 111-12 (1959); *Eastland*, 421 U.S. 491, 513 (1975)).

[307] *Id.* at 131-32.

[308] *Id.*

[309] *Id.* at 132.

---

of access are absolute. Instead, both claims are qualified and, therefore, subject to potential judicial review, but only after every attempt to resolve the differences between the branches themselves has been exhausted. In addition, *AT&T* provides support for the proposition that third-party subpoenas—such as ones to telecommunications companies—can be challenged in federal court and are not subject to the constitutional protection provided by the Speech or Debate Clause.[310]

Sensitive But Unclassified Materials

Committees conducting investigations and oversight of executive branch agencies may require access to information and documents that are "sensitive" but do not rise to the level of being classified. This general category of "sensitive but unclassified" (SBU) information can present access issues for congressional committees. The fact that information is "sensitive" does not provide a *legal* basis for withholding it from duly authorized jurisdictional committees of Congress. However, there may be legitimate political and policy reasons why an agency's classification of information as "sensitive" should be afforded due deference.

SBU material can take numerous forms; some categories are statutorily authorized, while others are creations of the agency that authored or is holding the requested information. One example of a statutorily authorized SBU category is found in the statute creating the Transportation Security Administration (TSA). The statute requires the TSA Director to:

> prescribe regulations prohibiting the disclosure of information obtained or developed in carrying out security... if the [he] decides that disclosing the information would– (A) be an unwarranted invasion of personal privacy; (B) reveal a trade secret or privileged or confidential commercial or financial information; or (C) be detrimental to the security of transportation.[311]

The statute also expressly states that the general authority provided to withhold information from the public "does not authorize information to be withheld from a committee of Congress authorized to have the information."[312] Pursuant to this statute, TSA promulgated regulations defining "sensitive security information" (SSI) and restrictions on its disclosure.[313] In addition, the SSI regulations also appear to insulate congressional committees and their staffs from any sanctions or penalty from the receipt and disclosure of SSI. The definition of "covered persons," those subject to the SSI regulations, does not appear to include Members of Congress, committees, or congressional staff.[314] Moreover, the regulations specifically state, as directed by the statute, that "[n]othing in this part precludes TSA or the Coast Guard from disclosing SSI to a committee of Congress authorized to have the information...."[315]

---

[310] *See generally* CRS Report R42648, *The Speech or Debate Clause: Constitutional Background and Recent Developments*, by Alissa M. Dolan and Todd Garvey.

[311] 49 U.S.C. §114(r)(1); *see also* CRS Report RL33670, *Protection of Security-Related Information*, by Gina Stevens and Todd B. Tatelman.

[312] 49 U.S.C. §114(r)(2).

[313] 49 C.F.R. Part 1520.

[314] *See* 49 C.F.R. §1520.7 (providing 13 specific categories of "covered persons").

[315] 49 C.F.R. §1520.15(c).

Many agencies have developed their own internal information protection regimes that may be cited in response to congressional requests. One example of such an agency created regime is "for official use only" (FOUO). According to a DHS Management Directive, the FOUO classification[316] distinguishes between documents marked FOUO and other information that may be protected from public disclosure under different designations. Specifically, the Directive defines FOUO as "not to be considered classified information"[317] and "is not automatically exempt from disclosure under the provisions of [FOIA]."[318] The Directive makes clear that FOUO information is not intended to be withheld from other governmental entities, stating that such information "may be shared with other agencies, federal, state, tribal, or local government and law enforcement officials."[319] Such a definition appears to include Congress (and, thus, authorized committees and subcommittees) among the entities to which the information can be disclosed. Such inclusion is consistent with Congress's broad constitutionally-based authority to obtain information from executive agencies.

Individual Member and Minority Party Authority to Conduct Oversight and Investigations

The role of Members of the minority in the investigatory oversight process is governed by the rules of each house and its committees. While minority Members are specifically accorded some rights,[320] no House or committee rules authorize either ranking minority Members or individual Members on their own to institute official committee investigations, hold hearings, or issue subpoenas. Although individual Members may seek the voluntary cooperation of agency officials or private persons, no judicial precedent has directly recognized an individual Member's right, other than a committee chair,[321] to exercise the committee's oversight authority without the permission of a majority of the committee or its chair. Moreover, in *Leach v. Resolution Trust Corporation*,[322] a federal district court dismissed the attempt of the then-ranking minority member of the House Banking [now Financial Services] Committee to compel disclosure of documents from two agencies under the FOIA and the Administrative Procedure Act. The court held that the case was one "in which a congressional plaintiff's dispute is primarily with his or her fellow legislators," since the ranking minority Member's "complaint derives solely from his

---

[316] Department of Homeland Security, Management Directive System MD No. 11042.1, Safeguarding Sensitive but Unclassified (For Official Use Only) Information (2005).

[317] *Id.* at ¶ 4.

[318] *Id.* at ¶ 6(a)(4).

[319] *Id.* at ¶ 6(h)(6).

[320] For example, in the House of Representatives, whenever a hearing is conducted on any measure or matter, the minority may, upon the written request of a majority of the minority members to the chairman before the completion of the hearing, call witnesses selected by the minority, and presumably request documents. House Rule XI 2(j)(1); *see also* House Banking Committee Rule IV(4)

[321] Ashland Oil Co., Inc. v. FTC, 548 F. 2d 977, 979-80 (D.C. Cir. 1976), *affirming* 409 F. Supp. 297 (D.D. C. 1976); *see also* Exxon v. FTC, 589 F.2d 582, 592-93 (D.C. Cir. 1978) (acknowledging that the "principle is important that disclosure of information can only be compelled by authority of Congress, its committees and subcommittees, not solely by individual members..."); In re Beef Industry Antitrust Litigation, 589 F.2d 786, 791 (5th Cir. 1979) (refusing to permit two Congressmen from intervening in private litigation because they "failed to obtain a House Resolution or any similar authority before they sought to intervene.")

[322] 860 F. Supp. 868 (D.D.C. 1994).

---

failure to persuade his colleagues to authorize his request for the documents in question..."[323] Therefore, the plaintiffs had a clear "collegial remedy" to the problem.[324]

Senate rules provide substantially more effective means for individual minority-party Members to engage in "self-help" to support oversight objectives than afforded their House counterparts. Senate rules emphasize the rights and prerogatives of individual Senators and, therefore, minority groups of Senators.[325] The most important of these rules are those that effectively allow unlimited debate on a bill or amendment unless an extraordinary majority votes to invoke cloture.[326] Senators can use their right to filibuster, or simply the threat of filibuster, to delay or prevent the Senate from engaging in legislative business. Other Senate rules can also directly or indirectly aid the minority in gaining investigatory rights. For example, the right of extended debate also applies in committee and, unlike on the floor, the cloture rule may not be invoked in committee. Each Senate committee decides for itself how it will control debate, and therefore a Member may have great opportunities to filibuster in committee. Also, Senate Rule XXVI prohibits the reporting of any measure or matter from a committee unless a majority of the committee is present, another point of possible tactical leverage. Even beyond the potent power to delay, Senators can promote their goals by taking advantage of other parliamentary rights and opportunities that are provided by the Senate's formal procedures and customary practices, such as are afforded by the processes dealing with floor recognition, committee referrals, and the amending process.

5 U.S.C. § 2954: The "Rule of Seven" Statute

Another potential tool for minority participation in oversight is 5 U.S.C. § 2954, commonly known as the "rule of seven."[327] Under the statute, seven Members of the House Oversight and Government Reform Committee or five Members of the Senate Committee on Homeland Security and Governmental Affairs can request information from executive agencies on matters within their committee jurisdiction, which the agencies "shall" provide.[328] While the statute appears to confer a right upon these Members, a judicially recognized right of action to enforce the statute when an agency refuses to disclose information has not been established, as illustrated by relevant district court opinions.

The rule of seven statute is derived from a 1928 Act that repealed legislation requiring the submission to Congress of some 128 reports.[329] Many of these reports had become obsolete and were deemed at the time to have no value, serve no useful purpose, and were not printed by the

---

[323] *Id.* at 874-76.

[324] *Id.*

[325] *See* CRS Report RL30850, *Minority Rights and Senate Procedures*, by Judy Schneider.

[326] Senate Rules XIX and XXII.

[327] *Id.* at 876 n.7. 5 U.S.C. §2954 provides: "An Executive agency, on request of the Committee on [Oversight and] Government [Reform] of the House of Representatives, or of any seven members thereof, or on request of the Committee on Government Operations of the Senate, or any five members thereof, shall submit any information requested of it relating to any matter within the jurisdiction of the committee."

[328] The text of the statute refers to the House Committee on Government Operations, a predecessor to the House Committee on Oversight and Government Reform, and the Senate Committee on Governmental Affairs, a predecessor to the Senate Committee on Homeland Security and Governmental Affairs.

[329] Act of May, 29, 1928 at §2, 45 Stat. 996.

House of Representatives.[330] The legislative history of the provision does not unambiguously state the statute's purpose. The Senate report indicated a limited purpose: to make "it possible to require any report discontinued by the language of this bill to be resubmitted to either House upon its necessity becoming evident to the membership of either body."[331] The House report agreed on that point, but added the following: "If any information is desired by any Member or Committee upon a particular subject that information can be better secured by a request made by an individual Member or Committee, so framed as to bring out the special information desired."[332] It is uncertain, then, how closely 5 U.S.C. § 2954 is tied to the 128 reports abolished by the original 1928 legislation.[333]

Moreover, the provision only empowers the two named committees and lacks an explicit enforcement mechanism. Agency refusals to comply with information requests would not be subject to the existing criminal contempt process, and the outcome of a civil suit to compel production on the basis of the provision is problematic.

Waxman v. Evans was the first attempt to secure court enforcement of a document demand under § 2954.[334] The 2001 case involved a request of 16 minority party members of the House Government Reform Committee for 2000 Census data from the Secretary of Commerce. The congressional plaintiffs sought declaratory and injunctive relief, arguing that the plain language of § 2954 unambiguously directs agency compliance with information requests.[335] In addition, the plaintiffs argued that they were entitled to judicial relief because of the agency's direct and particularized rejection of an entitlement specifically granted to them by law. The government argued that because the case had arisen out of a political information access dispute between Congress and the Executive, the court should refrain from hearing the case in accordance with the doctrine of equitable discretion. Alternatively, the government argued that § 2954 should be construed narrowly to avoid doubts of its constitutionality and accord with its legislative history. Under its interpretation, the statute only preserved Congress' access to the information formerly contained in the reports abolished by the 1928 Act, but did not guarantee an unqualified right of access to information possessed by the executive branch.

After the Members prevailed in the district court, the government moved for reconsideration based on a new argument: the Members did not have standing to sue or a cause of action. The district court declined to consider these arguments on the ground that the government could have presented them in support of its original motion to dismiss but did not do so. On appeal to the Ninth Circuit, the case was ultimately deemed moot, because a parallel FOIA suit led to the release of the information.[336] The district court's opinion was reversed, vacated, and dismissed.[337]

---

[330] H.Rpt. 1757, 70th Cong. (1928); S.Rpt. 1320, 70th Cong. (1928). A study of the Bureau of Efficiency had recommended their elimination.

[331] S.Rpt. 1320, 70th Cong., at 4.

[332] H.Rpt. 1757, 70th Cong., at 258; *see also* 69 CONG. REC. 9413-17, 10613-16 (1928) (House and Senate floor debates).

[333] In codifying Title 5 in 1966, Congress made it clear that it was effecting no substantive changes in existing laws: "The legislative purpose in enacting sections 1-6 of this act is to restate, without substantive change, the laws replaced by those sections on the effective date of this Act." P.L. 89-544, §7(a).

[334] Waxman, et al. v. Evans, 2002 U.S. Dist. LEXIS 25975 (C.D. Cali. 2001).

[335] Additionally, although resort to the provision's legislative history is unnecessary when the text is clear, the plaintiffs also argued that the legislative history was supportive.

[336] *See* Carter v. U.S. Dept. of Commerce, 307 F.3d 1084 (9th Cir. 2002).

In 2006, a second attempt to secure judicial enforcement of a § 2954 document demand in the same district court was rejected. In *Waxman v. Thompson*,[338] 19 members of the House Government Reform Committee brought suit to compel release by the Department of Health and Human Services (HHS) of cost estimates prepared by its Office of Actuary during congressional consideration of Medicare reform legislation in 2003. In addition to asserting a right of access under § 2954, the congressional plaintiffs alleged a violation of another federal statute stating that "[t]he right of employees ... to furnish information to either House of Congress, or to a committee or member thereof, may not be interfered with or denied."[339] The government opposed the claims, arguing that the congressional plaintiffs did not have standing to sue and that the court did not have jurisdiction to hear the claim.

The district court, applying the guiding principles established by the Supreme Court in the 1997 decision in *Raines v. Byrd*,[340] ruled that the congressional plaintiffs did not have standing to sue. In *Raines*, the Supreme Court held that a congressional plaintiff may have standing in a suit against the executive branch if the plaintiff(s) alleges either (1) a personal injury (e.g., loss of Member's seat) or (2) an institutional injury that is not "abstract and widely dispersed" and amounts to vote nullification.[341] Bound by the Supreme Court's precedent, the district court concluded that the Members only potential injury was institutional, rather than personal in nature, and necessarily damaged all Members and both houses equally. However, the court concluded that the plaintiffs had not shown that the government's actions had nullified their votes. Therefore, under *Raines*, the Members did not have standing to sue and the suit was dismissed.

Specialized Investigations

Oversight at times occurs through specialized, temporary investigations of a specific event or development. These are often dramatic, high profile endeavors, focusing on scandals, alleged abuses of authority, suspected illegal conduct, or other unethical behavior. The stakes are high, possibly even leading to the end of individual careers of high ranking executive officials. Congressional investigations can induce resignations, firings, and impeachment proceedings and question major policy actions of the executive, as with these notable occasions: the Senate Watergate Committee investigation into the Nixon Administration in the early 1970s; the Church and Pike select committees' inquiries in the mid-1970s into intelligence agency abuses; the 1981 select committee inquiry into the ABSCAM scandal; the 1987 Iran-contra investigation during the Reagan Administration; the multiple investigations of scandals and alleged misconduct during the Clinton Administration; and the Hurricane Katrina probe in 2005 during the Bush Administration. As a consequence, interest—in Congress, the executive, and the public—is frequently intense and impassioned.

(...continued)

[337] Waxman v. Evans, 52 Fed. Appx. 84, 2002 US App. LEXIS 25306 (9th Cir. 2002). On motion of the plaintiffs, the court of appeals modified this order on January 9, 2003, striking its reversal of the district court's ruling, but leaving in effect its order to vacate and dismiss.

[338] No. CV-04-3467 MMM (Manx) (C.D. Calif., May 17, 2004).

[339] 5 U.S.C. § 7211.

[340] 521 U.S. 811 (1997).

[341] *Id.* at 824-26. *See* CRS Report R42454, *Congressional Participation in Article III Courts: Standing to Sue*, by Alissa M. Dolan and Todd Garvey.

Prominent Select Investigative Committees

Senate Watergate Committee (1973-74), S.Res. 60, 93rd Congress, 1st session.

"To establish a select committee of the Senate to conduct an investigation and study of the extent, if any, to which illegal, improper, or unethical activities were engaged in by any persons, acting individually or in combination with others, in the presidential election of 1972, or any campaign, canvass, or other activity related to it."

House Select Committee on the Iran-Contra Affair (1987), H.Res. 12, 100th Congress, 1st session.

"The select committee is authorized and directed to conduct a full and complete investigation and study, and to make such findings and recommendations to the House as the select committee deems appropriate," regarding the sale or transfer of arms, technology, or intelligence to Iran or Iraq; the diversion of funds realized in connection with such sales and otherwise, to the anti-government forces in Nicaragua; the violation of any law, agreement, promise, or understanding regarding the reporting to and informing of Congress; operational activities and the conduct of foreign and national security policy by the staff of the National Security Council; authorization and supervision or lack thereof of such matters by the President and other White House personnel; the role of individuals and entities outside the government; other inquiries regarding such matters, by the Attorney General, White House, intelligence community, and Departments of Defense, Justice, and State; and the impact of such matters on public and international confidence in the United States Government.

---

1. These investigative hearings may be *televised* or *webcast* and often result in *extensive news media coverage*.

2. Such investigations may be undertaken by *different organizational arrangements*. These include temporary select committees, standing committees and their subcommittees, specially created subcommittees, or specially commissioned task forces within an existing standing committee.

3. Specially created investigative committees usually have a *short life span* (e.g., six months, one year, or at the longest until the end of a Congress, at which point the panel would have to be reapproved if the inquiry were to continue).

4. The investigative panel often has to *employ additional and special staff*— including investigators, attorneys, auditors, and researchers—because of the added work load and need for specialized expertise in conducting such investigations and in the subject matter. Such staff can be hired under contract from the private sector, transferred from existing congressional offices or committees, transferred from the congressional support agencies, or loaned by executive agencies, including the Federal Bureau of Investigation. The staff would require appropriate security clearances if the inquiry looked into matters of national security.

5. Such special panels have often been vested with investigative authorities not ordinarily available to standing committees. Staff deposition authority is the most commonly given, but given the particular circumstances, special panels have been vested with the authority to obtain tax information, to seek international assistance in information gathering efforts abroad, and to participate in judicial proceedings.

Table 1. Special Investigative Authorities of Selected Investigating Committees

Investigation	Authority Citation	Deposition Authority	International Information Gathering Authority	Tax Information Access Authority	Authority to Participate In Judicial Proceedings
Sen. Select Committee on Watergate	S.Res. 60 and S.Res. 194, 93rd Cong., (1973).	Member/ Staff	No	No	Yes
Nixon Impeachment Proceedings	H.Res. 803, 93rd Cong., (1974).	Member/ Staff	Yes	No	No
Billy Carter Investigation	126 Cong. Rec. 19544-46 (1980) (unanimous consent agreement); S.Res. 495, 96th Cong., (1980) (staff deposition authority); S.Res. 496, 96th Cong., (1980) (tax access authority).	Staff	No	Yes	No
House Assassinations Inquiry	H.Res. 222, 95th Cong., (1974).	Member/ Staff	Yes	No	No
Church Committee	S.Res. 21, 94th Cong., (1974).	Member/ Staff	Yes	No	No
Koreagate	H.Res. 252 and H.Res. 752, 95th Cong., (1977).	Member/ Staff	Letters Rogatory	No	Yes, by special counsel
ABSCAM (House)	H.Res. 67, 97th Cong., (1981).	Member	Letters Rogatory	No	Yes, by special counsel
ABSCAM (Senate)	S.Res. 350, 97th Cong., (1982).	Member/ Staff	No	No	No
Iran-Contra House and Senate	H.Res. 12, 100th Cong., (1987). S.Res. 23, 100th Cong., (1987).	Member/ Staff	Letters Rogatory, Commissions, Depositions	Yes	Yes
Judge Hastings Impeachment	H.Res. 320, 100th Cong., (1987).	Staff	No	No	No
Judge Nixon Impeachment	H.Res. 562, 100th Cong., (1988).	Staff	No	No	No
October Surprise	H.Res. 258, 102nd Cong., (1991).	Member/ Staff	Letters Rogatory, Commissions, Depositions	No	Yes
Senate Whitewater(I)	S.Res. 229, 103rd Cong., (1994).	Staff	No	No	No
Senate Whitewater (II)	S.Res. 120, 104th Cong., (1995).	Staff	Letters Rogatory, Commissions	Yes	No
White House Travel Office	H.Res. 369, 104th Cong., (1996).	Member/ Staff	No	No	No

Investigation	Authority Citation	Deposition Authority	International Information Gathering Authority	Tax Information Access Authority	Authority to Participate In Judicial Proceedings
House Campaign Finance	H.Res. 167, 105th Cong., (1997).	Member/ Staff	Letters Rogatory, Commissions	No	No
Senate Campaign Finance	S.Res. 54, 105th Cong., (1997).	Staff	No	No	No
Select Committee on National Security Commercial Concerns	H.Res. 463, 105th Cong., (1998).	Member/ Staff	Letters Rogatory, Depositions	Yes	Yes, by House General Counsel
Teamsters Election Investigation	H.Res. 507, 105th Cong., (1998).	Member/ Staff	No	No	No
Benghazi	H.Res. 567, 113th Cong. (2013).	Member/ Staff	No	No	No

Note: More comprehensive compilations of authorities and rules of Senate and House special investigatory committees may be found in Senate Committee on Rules and Administration, "Authority and Rules of Senate Special Investigatory Committees and Other Senate Entities, 1973-97," S.Doc. 105-16, 105th Cong., 1st sess. (1998), and CRS Report 95-949, *Staff Depositions in Congressional Investigations*, by Jay R. Shampansky.

Selected Oversight Techniques

Many oversight techniques are self-explanatory. There are several techniques, however, for which explanation or elaboration may prove helpful for a better understanding of their utility.

Identifying the Committee's Jurisdiction

A basic step in oversight preparation is to determine the laws, programs, activities, functions, advisory committees, agencies, and departments within a committee's jurisdiction. This is essential if a committee is to know the full range of its oversight responsibilities. To accomplish this general goal, House and Senate committees might:

1. Prepare a document, as needed, which outlines for each subcommittee of a standing committee the agencies, laws, programs activities, functions, advisory committees, and required agency reports that fall within its jurisdictional purview.

2. Publish, as needed, a compilation of all the basic statutes in force within the jurisdiction of each subcommittee or for the committee itself if it has no subcommittees.

3. Request the assistance of the various legislative support agencies (the Congressional Budget Office, the Congressional Research Service, or the Government Accountability Office) in identifying the full range of federal programs and activities under a committee's jurisdiction.

Orientation and Periodic Review Hearings with Agencies

Oversight hearings (or even "pre-hearings") may be held for the purposes of briefing members and staff on the organization, operations, and programs of an agency, and determining how an agency intends to implement any new legislation. The hearings can also be used as a way to obtain information on the administration, effectiveness, and economy of agency operations and programs.

Agency officials can be noticeably influenced by the knowledge and expectation that they will be called before a congressional committee regularly to account for the activities of their agencies. Such hearings benefit the committee by, for example:

- helping committee members keep up-to-date on important administrative developments;

- serving as a forum for exchanging and communicating views on pertinent problems and other relevant matters;

- providing background information which could assist members in making sound legislative and fiscal judgments;

- identifying program areas within each committee's jurisdiction that may be vulnerable to waste, fraud, abuse, or mismanagement; and

- determining whether new laws are needed or whether changes in the administration of existing laws will be sufficient to resolve problems.

The ability of committee members during oversight hearings to focus on meaningful issues and to ask penetrating questions will be enhanced if staff have accumulated, organized, and evaluated relevant data, information, and analyses about administrative performance.

Ideally, each standing committee should regularly monitor the application of laws and implementation of programs within its jurisdiction. A prime objective of the "continuous watchfulness" mandate (Section 136) of the Legislative Reorganization Act of 1946 is to encourage committees to take an active and ongoing role in administrative review and not wait for public revelations of agency and program inadequacies before conducting oversight. As Section 136 states in part: "each standing committee of the Senate and House of Representatives shall exercise continuous watchfulness of the execution by the administrative agencies concerned of any laws, the subject matter of which is within the jurisdiction of such committee."

Committee personnel could be assigned to maintain active liaison with appropriate agencies and to record their pertinent findings routinely. Information compiled in this fashion will be useful not only for regular oversight hearings, but also for oversight hearings called unexpectedly with little opportunity to conduct an extensive background study.

It is important that specific letters be directed by the committee to the agency witnesses so that they will be on notice about what they will have to answer. In this way witnesses will be responsive in providing worthwhile testimony at hearings; testify "to the point" and avoid rambling and/or evasive statements; and restrict their use of this kind of answer to questions: "I didn't know you wanted that information...."

Casework

An important check against bureaucratic indifference or inefficiency is casework. Typically, Members of Congress hear from individual constituents and communities about problems they are having with various federal agencies and departments. As a House member once said:

> Last year, one of my constituents, a 63-year old man who requires kidney dialysis, discovered that he would no longer be receiving Medicare because the Social Security Administration thought he was dead. Like many residents who have problems dealing with the federal bureaucracy, this man contacted my district office and asked for help. Without difficulty, he convinced my staff that he was indeed alive, and we in turn convinced the Social Security Administration to resume sending him benefits.[342]

Casework is important not only in resolving problems that constituents are having with bureaucrats but also in identifying limitations in the law. As a scholar of constituency service explained: "Casework allows ad hoc correction of bureaucratic error, impropriety, and laxity, and can lead a senator or representative to consider changes in laws because of particularly flagrant or persistent problems that casework staff discovered."[343]

Audits

Periodic auditing of executive departments is among the strongest techniques of legislative oversight. Properly utilized, the audit enables Congress to hold executive officers to a strict accounting for their use of public funds and the conduct of their administration.

Government auditing encompasses more than checking and verifying accounts, transactions, and financial statements. Many federal, state, and some foreign audit agencies are moving in the direction pioneered by Government Accountability Office (GAO), which may evaluate whether claimed achievements are supported by adequate and reliable evidence and data and are in compliance with legislatively established objectives, and whether resources are being used efficiently, effectively, and economically.

In reviewing agencies' own evaluations, or in undertaking an initial evaluation, auditors are advised by GAO to ask questions such as the following:

- How successful is the program in accomplishing the intended results? Could program objectives be achieved at less cost?

- Has agency management clearly defined and promulgated the objectives and goals of the program or activity?

- Have performance standards been developed?

---

[342] Lee H. Hamilton, "Constituent Service and Representation," *The Public Manager*, summer 1992, p. 12.

[343] John R. Johannes, "Constituency Service," in Donald Bacon, et al., eds., *The Encyclopedia of the United States Congress* (New York: Simon and Schuster, 1995), p. 544.

- Are program objectives sufficiently clear to permit agency management to accomplish effectively the desired program results? Are the objectives of the component parts of the program consistent with overall program objectives?

- Are program costs reasonably commensurate with the benefits achieved?

- Have alternative programs or approaches been examined, or should they be examined to determine whether objectives can be achieved more economically?

- Were all studies, such as cost-benefit studies, appropriate for analyzing costs and benefits of alternative approaches?

- Is the program producing benefits or detriments that were not contemplated by Congress when it authorized the program?

- Is the information furnished to Congress by the agency adequate and sufficiently accurate to permit Congress to monitor program achievements effectively?

- Does top management have the essential and reliable information necessary for exercising supervision and control and for ascertaining directions or trends?

- Does management have internal review or audit facilities adequate for monitoring program operations, identifying program and management problems and weaknesses, and insuring fiscal integrity?

In addition to GAO and other governmental audits, Congress may have access to the internal audit reports of agency audit teams.

- Internal audit reports are designed to meet the needs of executive officials.

- This information is useful in conducting oversight; however, executive agencies are sometimes reluctant to provide internal audit reports to Congress.

- A large number of governmental and private organizations conduct audits of expenditures. Every major federal agency, for example, has its own statutory Inspector General and each of the 50 states plus hundreds of local governments have their own audit offices. Many government agencies also contract with public accounting firms to perform financial audits. For assistance in finding audit reports or in learning how to commission audit reports, congressional staff might consult with officials at the GAO, which is the auditing arm of Congress.

Monitoring the *Federal Register*

The Federal Register, available at https://www.federalregister.gov/, is published daily, Monday through Friday, except official holidays, by the Office of the Federal Register, National Archives and Records Administration (NARA). It provides a uniform system for making available to the public regulations and legal notices issued by Federal agencies. These include presidential proclamations and executive orders, federal agency documents having general applicability and legal effect, documents required to be published by act of Congress, and other Federal agency documents of public interest. Final regulations are codified by subject in the *Code of Federal Regulations* (CFR).

Federal Register subscription options include receiving the table of contents of each day's issue via an email message or an RSS notification. To learn how to subscribe to the daily table of contents and how to create customized subscriptions, visit the "User Information" page, at https://www.federalregister.gov/learn/user-information. The website also includes social media tools that enable a user to share documents through, for example, Twitter, Facebook, and RSS feeds.

Documents are on file for public inspection in the Office of the Federal Register the day before they are published, unless the issuing agency requests earlier filing. The list of documents on file for public inspection can be accessed at https://www.federalregister.gov/public-inspection. Regular scrutiny of the *Federal Register* by committees and staff may help them to identify proposed rules and regulations in their subject areas that merit congressional review as to need and likely effect.

Another website, http://www.reginfo.gov/public/, also includes information about proposed and completed regulatory actions of federal agencies. OMB's Office of Information and Regulatory Affairs (OIRA) and the Regulatory Information Service Center (RISC) of the General Services Administration are responsible for this website.

Special Studies and Investigations by Staff, Support Agencies, Outside Contractors, and Others

Staff Investigations. The staffs of committees and individual members play a vital role in the legislative process. Committee staffs, through field investigations or on-site visits, for example, can help a committee develop its own independent evaluation of the effectiveness of laws.

Support Agencies. The legislative support agencies, directly or indirectly, can assist committees and members in conducting investigations and reviewing agency performance.[344] The Government Accountability Office is the agency most involved in investigations, audits, and program evaluations. It has a large, professional investigative staff and produces numerous reports useful in oversight.

Outside Contractors. The 1974 Budget Act, as amended, and the Legislative Reorganization Act of 1970 authorize House and Senate committees to enlist the services of individual consultants or organizations to assist them in their work.

- A committee might contract with an independent research organization or employ professional investigators for short-term studies.

- Committees may also utilize, subject to appropriate approvals, federal and support agency employees to aid them in their oversight activities.

- Committees might also establish a voluntary advisory panel to assist them in their work.

---

[344] "Oversight Information Sources and Consultant Services" for information on the capabilities of the Congressional Research Service (CRS), Government Accountability Office (GAO), and Congressional Budget Office (CBO).

Communicating with the Media

Public exposure of a problem is an effective oversight technique, and will often help bring about a solution to that problem. Public officials often seem much more responsive to correcting deficiencies after the issue has been described in widely circulated news stories. Effective communication with the media is based on knowledge and understanding of each of the media forms and the *advantages* and *disadvantages* of each.

Wire Services

- Timeliness, brevity, and accuracy are the main criteria for dealing with the wire services.

- Personal contact with wire service reporters gets the best results.

Daily Newspapers

- Obtain information on the operational procedures and deadlines of daily newspapers, and how they are affected by time.

- Since regular news for Monday is usually low, it may be useful to issue statements and releases for "Monday a.m." use.

- Saturday usually has the lowest circulation and Sunday has the widest.

- Stories for weekend publication should be given to reporters during the middle of the week or earlier.

Magazines

- Magazines and other periodicals are generally wider ranging and focus on why something happens, not what happened.

- Weeklies do not ordinarily respond to member press conferences and releases in the same manner as the other media; personal meetings and telephone conversations are usually more effective.

- Deadlines Vary

  - Obtain information on operational procedures.

  - Weekends are generally production periods for most magazines.

Trade Periodicals

Many of these topically oriented magazines and newsletters are produced by publishing firms which utilize the services of the periodical press galleries in the Capitol.

Television

- House and Senate rules identify procedures for radio and television broadcasting of committee hearings. (See House Rule XI and Senate Rule XXVI.)

- News of a committee's oversight activities may appear in diverse forms on television. For example, it could appear on the networks as a brief report on the morning or evening news, air on a cable news channel, or arise in the course of live House or Senate floor debate telecast over C-SPAN (the Cable Satellite Public Affairs Network).

- Washington-based news organizations may also provide daily television coverage of Congress to independent television stations. Public television and cable news organizations occasionally broadcast live coverage of committee oversight hearings.

- To encourage television coverage of a committee's oversight activities, the following checklist might be helpful to staff.

  - Alert correspondents and Washington bureau chiefs of upcoming hearings several days in advance via press releases; follow up with personal or telephone notification of certain "must-contact" correspondents.

  - Notify the Associated Press, Reuters, and other news services of a scheduled hearing or meeting at least a day in advance. Allow enough lead time to permit inclusion of the committee activity in the wire services' calendars of daily events for the next day.

  - If widespread media interest is anticipated, reserve at least a week in advance a hearing room large enough to accommodate television cameras.

  - Alert interested correspondents or assignment editors when House or Senate floor action is likely on a matter related to the committee's oversight function.

  - Provide or have available for the media background information on oversight issues awaiting committee action or consideration by the House or Senate.

  - Consider making committee members readily available for television cameras either before or after any executive sessions (e.g., allowing television crews in briefly at the start to take video footage of the committee, or arranging for a press conference after the committee session).

  - Video, where appropriate, committee members discussing topical oversight issues for distribution to interested television stations.

  - Keep the contact person of each of the network news interview programs ("Meet the Press," etc.) apprised of a committee's oversight activities, and their relevance to topical national issues. Suggest the appearance of committee members on interview programs when a committee oversight issue becomes especially newsworthy.

  - Be alert to live television interview possibilities for committee members that can be arranged on relatively short notice (e.g., newsmaker interviews on cable news channels).

Radio

- Time is of the essence. Radio news reporters want congressional reaction *immediately*, not hours later when the story breaks in the newspaper or on television.

- Members who are readily available for quick interviews are frequently broadcast within minutes or the next morning coast-to-coast on hundreds of radio stations. In most cases an interview will be aired repeatedly over a period of several hours.

- Congressional offices should contact radio reporters directly through the House and Senate press galleries.

Press Conferences

- Time

    - The periods between 10 a.m. and 2 p.m. are often preferable.

    - Early morning press conferences usually have low attendance because reporters on daily papers do not start work until mid-morning.

    - Late afternoon press conferences are often unattended because these occur too close to the evening news program and reporters do not have adequate time to prepare and deliver coverage of these for that particular day.

    - Check with the press galleries. They keep a running log of most scheduled news events and can provide information on possible competition at any time on any day.

- Place

    - Committee rooms are good, but they are frequently in use at the best time for a conference.

    - A member's office or the press galleries can be adequate, but keep in mind that the reporters and cameramen need room to operate.

    - It might be wise to go to the radio-TV galleries after the conference and do a repeat to get electronic coverage.

- Notification

    - Notify the press galleries in writing as far in advance as possible.

    - Also notify the wire services and television networks directly at their downtown offices.

- Form

    - A press conference should be viewed as an open house with everybody invited and everybody welcome.

    - A brief opening statement should be read or summarized. After copies of it have been distributed, the questioning should begin.

        - Leave plenty of time for questions.

        - Do not restrict the areas of questioning.

- Anticipate the questions and have answers prepared.

- The normal time for a routine press conference is about one-half hour.

News Releases

- A good news release answers in one page or less the questions where, when, who, what, how, why, and, for some topics, how much (e.g., cost) or how many (e.g., beneficiaries). It should:

    - contain the name, telephone number, and e-mail of your press contact;

    - be for immediate release (better than embargo);

    - quote the member directly;

    - avoid excessive use of the member's name;

    - avoid needless big words, long sentences, and long paragraphs; and

    - make the point quickly, clearly, directly, and then end.

The Internet and Social Media

Members and committees can use the Internet to communicate with media representatives and constituents to explain their views and positions with respect to oversight activities. The Internet permits lawmakers and committees to rely less on traditional journalistic sources for coverage and more on direct communication with the citizenry.

The Internet can be employed in a variety of ways to mobilize public interest in congressional oversight. For example, lawmakers can conduct on-line discussions with interested citizens, or use Twitter or Facebook to share information with constituents. Committees can establish their own websites to solicit input from individuals and organizations about executive branch departments and programs.

There are various bloggers who monitor federal spending. With numerous government websites that enable attentive individuals to monitor the expenditure of federal funds, Congress gets additional oversight assistance from the "public as watchdog."

Reporting Requirements, Consultation, and Other Sources of Information

Congressional oversight of the executive branch is dependent to a large degree upon information supplied by the agencies being overseen. In the contemporary era, reporting and prior consultation provisions have increased in an attempt to ensure congressional access to information, statistics, and other data on the workings of the executive. The result is that approximately 4,000 reports arrive annually on Capitol Hill. Concerns about unnecessary, duplicative, and wasteful reports, however, have prompted efforts to eliminate these. One such initiative, in part stimulated by earlier recommendations from the Vice President's National Performance Review and from the GAO, resulted in the Federal Reports Elimination and Sunset Acts of 1995 and 1998. Nonetheless, reductions in the number of required reports have not kept pace with new or continuing requirements, such as those identified in the 2001 act to Prevent the Elimination of Certain Reports (P.L. 107-74).

Reporting Requirements

Reporting requirements affect executive and administrative agencies and officers, including the President; independent boards and commissions; and federally chartered corporations (as well as the judiciary). These statutory provisions vary in terms of the specificity, detail, and type of information that Congress demands. Reports may be required at periodic intervals, such as semiannually or at the end of a fiscal year, or submitted only if and when a specific event, activity, or set of conditions exists. The reports may also call upon an agency, commission, or officer to:

- study, and provide recommendations, about a particular problem or concern;

- alert Congress or particular committees and subcommittees in advance about a proposed or planned activity or operation;

- provide information about specific on-going or just-completed operations, projects, or programs; or

- summarize an agency's activities for the year or the prior six months.

Examples of Reporting Requirements in Law

Initial Requirement in the 1789 Treasury Department Act:

"That it shall be the duty of the Secretary of the Treasury ... to make report, and give information to either branch of the legislature, in person or in writing (as he may be required), respecting all matters referred to him by the Senate or House of Representatives, or which shall appertain to his office...." 1 Stat. 65-66 (1789)

Reporting on Covert Action in the 1991 Intelligence Oversight Act:

"The President shall ensure that the intelligence committees are kept fully and currently informed of the intelligence activities of the United States, including any significant anticipated intelligence activity ...

(1) The President shall ensure that any finding [authorizing a covert action] shall be reported to the intelligence committees as soon as possible after such approval and before the initiation of the covert action, except as otherwise provided in paragraph (2) and paragraph (3).

(2) If the President determines that it is essential to limit access to the finding to meet extraordinary circumstances affecting the vital interests of the United States, the finding may be reported to the chairmen and ranking minority members of the intelligence committees, the Speaker and minority leader of the House of Representatives, the majority and minority leaders of the Senate, and such other members of the congressional leadership as may be included by the President.

(3) Whenever a finding is not reported [in advance to the committees], the President shall fully inform the intelligence committees in a timely fashion and shall provide a statement of the reasons for not giving prior notice." 105 Stat. 441-443 (1991)

Prior Consultation

In the past, explicit prior consultation provisions were rarely incorporated into law. However, there appears to be an increase in statutory provisions as well as in committee reports that accompany legislation specifying conditions for such discussion.

A Sample Prior Consultation Provision

A provision in the Conference Committee report on the 1978 Ethics in Government Act illustrates this development: "The conferees expect the Attorney General to *consult* with the Judiciary Committees of both Houses of Congress *before* substantially expanding the scope of authority or mandate of the Public Integrity Section of the Criminal Division."

Other Significant Sources of Information

A number of general management laws provide for additional sources of information, data, and material that can aid congressional oversight endeavors.

Chief Financial Officers Act of 1990, as Amended (104 Stat. 2838, 108 Stat. 3410, 110 Stat. 3009-389, and 116 Stat. 2049)

The CFO act is designed to improve financial management throughout the federal government, through various procedures and mechanisms.

- The 1990 act created two new posts within OMB, along with a new position of chief financial officer in each of 23 major federal agencies, including all Cabinet departments. Subsequently, two other agencies have been added (the Department of Homeland Security and the Social Security Administration) and one subtracted (when the Federal Emergency Management Agency was merged into DHS). Of these 24 posts, 17 are filled by presidential appointees subject to Senate confirmation; these are in the 15 Cabinet departments plus the Environmental Protection Agency and the National Aeronautics and Space Administration. The remaining seven positions directly under the CFO act are in the Agency for International Development, General Services Administration, National Science Foundation, Nuclear Regulatory Commission, Office of Personnel Management, Small Business Administration, and the Social Security Administration.

- The CFO act also provides for improvements in agency systems of accounting, financial management, and internal controls to assure the issuance of reliable financial information and to deter fraud, as well as waste and abuse of government resources.

- The enactment, furthermore, calls for the production of complete, reliable, timely, and consistent financial information for use by both the executive and the legislature in the financing, management, and evaluation of federal programs.

- The act, as amended, requires most executive branch entities to submit audited financial statements annually.

Government Performance and Results Act, as Amended (107 Stat. 285 and 124 Stat. 3866)

This act—commonly known as "GPRA" or the "Results Act," and amended substantially by the GPRA Modernization Act—requires federal agencies to submit long-range strategic plans, annual performance plans based on these, follow-up yearly assessments, and government-wide performance plans.

- *Strategic Plans*. The strategic plans specify five-year goals and objectives for agencies, based on their basic missions and underlying statutory or other

---

authority of the agency. These plans, initially required in 1997, were to be developed in consultation with relevant congressional offices and with information from "stakeholders" and then submitted to Congress.

- *Annual Performance Plans and Goals.* Based on these long-term plans, which may be modified if conditions and agency responsibilities change, the agencies are directed to set annual performance goals and to measure the results of their programs in achieving these goals. The objective of GPRA is to focus on outcomes (i.e., the results and accomplishments of a program, such as a decline in the use of illegal drugs for an anti-drug abuse program) rather than outputs (i.e., other measures of agency activity and operations, such as the number of anti-drug agents in the field). The annual plans, which are also *available to Congress*, began with FY1999.

- *Annual Assessments.* Each agency is to issue yearly follow-up reports assessing the implementation of its annual plan. Beginning in 2000, these are required six months after the end of the fiscal year.

- *Government-wide Plans and Goals.* GPRA, as amended in 2010, calls for a federal government performance plan and priority goals, under the direction of the Office of Management and Budget. These are to include "outcome-oriented goals covering a limited number of crosscutting policy areas; and goals for management improvements needed across the Federal Government."

Congressional Review Act (110 Stat. 868)

This Act (5 U.S.C. §§ 801, *et seq.*) established, for the first time, a mechanism by which Congress can review and disapprove virtually any federal rule or regulation.[345] It requires that:

1. All agencies promulgating a covered rule must submit a report to each house of Congress and the Comptroller General, containing specific information about the rule before it can go into effect.

2. Rules designated by the Office of Management and Budget as "major" may normally not go into effect until 60 days after submission, while non-major rules may become effective "as otherwise allowed in law," usually 30 days after publication in the *Federal Register*.

3. All covered rules are subject to fast-track disapproval by passage of a joint resolution, even if they have already gone into effect, for a period of at least 60 days. Upon enactment of such a joint resolution, no new rule that is "substantially the same" as the disapproved rule may be issued until it is specifically authorized by a law enacted subsequent to the disapproval of the original rule.

4. There can be no judicial review of actions taken (or not taken) by Congress, the Comptroller General, or OMB; but the failure of an agency to submit a covered rule for congressional review may be subject to sanction by a federal court.

---

[345] For a detailed discussion, *see* CRS Report IF10023, *The Congressional Review Act (CRA)*, by Alissa M. Dolan, Maeve P. Carey, and Christopher M. Davis.

Paperwork Reduction Act of 1995 (109 Stat. 163)

This most recent version of paperwork reduction legislation builds on a heritage of statutory controls over government paperwork that dates to 1940.

1. Among other things, the current act and its 1980 predecessor more clearly defined the oversight responsibilities of OMB's Office of Information and Regulatory Affairs (OIRA); it is authorized to develop and administer uniform information policies in order to ensure the availability and accuracy of agency data collection.

2. Congressional oversight has been strengthened through its subsequent reauthorizations and the requirement for Senate confirmation of OIRA's administrator.

Federal Managers' Financial Integrity Act (FMFIA) of 1982 (96 Stat. 814)

FMFIA is designed to improve the government's ability to manage its programs by strengthening internal management and financial controls, accounting systems, and financial reports.

1. The internal accounting systems are to be consistent with standards that the Comptroller General prescribes, including a requirement that all assets be safeguarded against waste, fraud, loss, unauthorized use, and misappropriation.

2. FMFIA also provides for ongoing evaluations of the internal control and accounting systems that protect federal programs against waste, fraud, abuse, and mismanagement.

3. The enactment further mandates that the head of each agency report annually to the President and Congress on the condition of these systems and on agency actions to correct any material weakness which the reports identify.

4. FMFIA is also connected to the Chief Financial Officers Act of 1990, which calls upon the director of OMB to submit a financial management status report to appropriate congressional committees; part of this report is to be a summary of reports on internal accounting and administrative control systems as required by FMFIA.

Cash Management Improvement Act of 1990 (104 Stat. 1058)

This enactment is intended to improve efficiency, effectiveness, and equity in the exchange of funds between the federal government and state governments. Its fundamental objective is to prevent either level of government from engaging in cash management practices that allow it to earn interest on cash reserves at the expense of the other.

Clinger-Cohen Act of 1996 (110 Stat. 679)

This act requires that agencies buy the best and most cost-effective information technology available. To do so, the act gave more responsibility to individual agencies, revoking the primary role that the General Services Administration had played previously, and established the position of chief information officer (CIO) in federal agencies to provide relevant advice to agency heads.

Federal Advisory Committee Act (FACA)

Congress formally acknowledged the merits of using advisory committees to obtain expert views drawn from business, academic, government, and other interests when it enacted the Federal Advisory Committee Act (FACA) in 1972 (5 U.S.C. Appendix; 86 Stat. 700). Congressional enactment of FACA established the first requirements for the management and oversight of federal advisory committees to ensure impartial and relevant expertise. As required by FACA, the General Services Administration (GSA) administers and provides management guidelines for advisory committees. From 1972 until 1997, GSA submitted a hard copy of its annual comprehensive review of agency federal advisory committees to the President and Congress. Since 1998, however, GSA has maintained a specialized, federal government, interagency, information-sharing database that collects data on federal advisory committee activities government-wide and is publicly available on the web. The database is available at http://www.facadatabase.gov.

Federal Information Security Management Act of 2002

The Federal Information Security Management Act of 2002 (FISMA) replaced what has been commonly referred to as the Government Information Security Reform Act (GISRA), which expired at the end of the 107th Congress. Both GISRA and FISMA represent an effort by Congress to improve federal agency compliance with information security standards and guidelines. Congress put into statute certain requirements, including a directive that federal agencies submit their information security programs to an annual independent review, along with a requirement that the Director of the Office of Management and Budget report the results of these reviews to Congress.

Accountability of Tax Dollars Act of 2002

The Accountability of Tax Dollars Act (ATDA) of 2002 (P.L. 107-289; 116 Stat. 2049) was intended "to expand the types of Federal agencies that are required to prepare audited financial statements to all executive branch agencies in the federal government." In fact, ATDA brings almost all executive branch agencies under the requirement for preparation of annual audited financial statements that previously applied only to the 24 major departments and agencies covered by the Chief Financial Officers (CFO) Act. Specifically, Section 2(a) changes the list of agencies covered by the audited annual financial statements requirement in 31 U.S.C. § 3515 by deleting the cross-reference to CFO Act agencies and inserting "each covered executive agency."

Federal Financial Management Improvement Act of 1996

The Federal Financial Management Improvement Act of 1996 (FFMIA) (110 Stat. 3009-389; 31 U.S.C. §3512 note) incorporates in statute certain financial management system requirements already established as executive branch policy. The law also requires auditors to report on agency compliance with these requirements, and agency heads and management to correct deficiencies within certain time periods. FFMIA reflects an ongoing effort to reform financial management in the federal government. The 1996 law builds upon prior legislation, including the Chief Financial Officers Act of 1990, the Government Performance and Results Act of 1993, and the Government Management Reform Act of 1994.

Unfunded Mandates Reform Act of 1995

After considerable debate, the Unfunded Mandates Reform Act (P.L. 104-4; 109 Stat. 48-71; 2 U.S.C. §§1501-1571) was enacted early in the 104th Congress. Generally, unfunded intergovernmental mandates include responsibilities or duties that federal programs, standards, or requirements impose on governments at other levels without providing for the payment of the costs of carrying out these responsibilities or duties. The intent of the mandate legislation was to limit the ability of the federal government to impose costs on state and local governments through unfunded mandates. The enactment has three components: revised congressional procedures regarding future mandates; new requirements for federal agency regulatory actions; and authorization for a study of existing mandates to evaluate their current usefulness. The primary objective was to create procedures that would retard and spotlight, if not stop, congressional authorization of new unfunded mandates on state and local governments.

Federal Funding Accountability and Transparency Act

On September 26, 2006, President George W. Bush signed into law the Federal Funding Accountability and Transparency Act (FFATA) (P.L. 109-282; 31 U.S.C. §6101). As required by this Act, OMB established a searchable, free, and public website that enables anyone to go online to find information that names the recipients and dollar amounts of most federal grants, loans, and contracts.[346] A key concept of FFATA is to provide citizens with greater transparency as to how Federal funds are spent and thus be better able to hold public officials accountable for funding decisions.

Resolutions of Inquiry

The House of Representatives can call upon the executive for factual information through resolutions of inquiry (House Rule XIII, clause 7). This is a *simple resolution*, approved by only the House. Resolutions of inquiry are addressed to either the President or heads of departments and agencies to supply specific factual information to the chamber. The resolutions usually "*request*" the President or "*direct*" administrative heads to supply such information. In calling upon the President for information, especially about foreign affairs, the qualifying phrase—"if not incompatible with the public interest"—is often added.

Such resolutions are to ask for facts, documents, or specific information; these devices are *not* to request an opinion or require an investigation (see box below). Resolutions of inquiry can be instrumental in triggering other congressional methods of obtaining information, such as through supplemental hearings or the regular legislative process.

Resolutions of Inquiry in Practice

The first resolution of inquiry was approved on March 24, 1796, when the House sought documents in connection with the Jay Treaty negotiations:

---

[346] Two federal government websites resulted from the enactment of FFATA. USAspending.gov, at http://www.usaspending.gov/, includes spending data for contracts, grants, direct payments, insurance, and loans/guarantees. The FFATA Search Portal, at http://www.ffata.org/ffata/, contains information about contracts and grants.

> *Resolved*, That the President of the United States be requested to lay before this House a copy of the instructions to the minister of the United States, who negotiated the treaty with the King of Great Britain ... together with the correspondence and other documents relative to the said treaty; excepting such of the said papers as any existing negotiation may render improper to be delivered. (*Journal of the House of Representatives*, 4th Cong., 1st sess., March 24, 1796. p. 480.)

A contemporary illustration occurred on March 1, 1995, when the House adopted H.Res. 80, as amended (104th Cong., 1st sess., 407-21). The resolution sought information about the Mexican peso crisis at the time and an Administration plan to use up to $20 billion in resources from the Exchange Stabilization Fund to help stabilize the Mexican currency and financial system. The resolution read:

> "*Resolved*, That the President, is hereby requested to provide the House of Representatives (consistent with the rules of the House), not later than 14 days after the adoption of this resolution, the following documents in the possession of the executive branch, if not inconsistent with the public interest...." The House request then specified the matters that the documents were to cover: The condition of the Mexican economy; consultations between the Government of Mexico, on the one hand, and the U.S. Secretary of the Treasury and/or the International Monetary fund, on the other; market policies and tax policies of the Mexican Government; and repayment agreements between Mexico and the United States; among other things.

A resolution of inquiry is privileged and may be considered in the House after it is reported. If the resolution is not reported within 14 legislative days after its introduction, any member can move to discharge the committee of jurisdiction and bring the resolution to the floor. However, action by a committee within the 14 days to reject the resolution effectively sidetracks House action on the resolution.

Limitations and Riders on Appropriations

Congress uses a two-step legislative procedure: authorization of programs in bills reported by legislative committees followed by the financing of those programs in bills reported by the Committees on Appropriations. Congressional rules generally encourage these two stages to be distinct and sequential. Authorizations should not be in general appropriation bills, nor appropriations in authorization measures. However, there are various exceptions to the general principle that Congress should not make policy through the appropriations process. One exception is the practice of permitting "limitations" in an appropriations bill. "Riders" (language extraneous to the subject of the bill) are also added to control agency actions.

Limitations

Although House rules forbid in any general appropriations bill a provision "changing existing law," certain "limitations" may be admitted. "Just as the House under its rules may decline to appropriate for a purpose authorized by law, so it may by limitation prohibit the use of the money for part of the purpose while appropriating for the remainder of it." *Constitution, Jefferson's Manual, and Rules of the House of Representatives*, H. Doc. No. 111-157, 111th Cong., 2d Sess. §1053 (2011). Limitations can be an effective device in oversight by strengthening Congress's ability to exercise control over federal spending and to reduce unnecessary or undesired expenditures. Under House Rule XXI, no provision changing existing law can be reported in any general appropriation bill "except germane provisions that retrench expenditures by the reduction of amounts of money covered by the bill" (the Holman rule, rarely used in modern practice).

A Sample Appropriations Limitation

The Hyde Amendment, Labor-HHS Appropriations Act for fiscal 1998, 111 Stat. 1516, sec. 509 & 510 (1997): "None of the funds appropriated under this Act shall be expended for any abortion ... [except] (1) if the pregnancy is the result of an act of rape or incest; or (2) in the case where a woman suffers from a physical disorder, physical injury, or physical illness, including a life-endangering physical condition caused by or arising from the pregnancy itself, that would, as certified by a physician, place the woman in danger of death unless an abortion is performed."

Rule XXI was amended in 1983 in an effort to restrict the number of limitations on appropriations bills. The rule was changed again in 1995 by granting the majority leader a central role in determining consideration of limitation amendments. The procedures for limitation in the House are set forth in the House rulebook, sections 1044(b), 1053-62.

Riders

Unlike limitations, legislative riders are extraneous to the subject matter of the bill to which they are added. Riders appear in both authorization bills and appropriations bills. In the latter, they may be subject to a point of order in the House on the ground that they are attempts to place legislation in an appropriations bill. In the Senate, Rule XVI prohibits on a point of order the addition to general appropriations bills of amendments that are legislative or non-germane. Both chambers have procedures to waive these prohibitions.

A Sample Appropriations Rider

Department of Homeland Security Appropriations Act, 2007, P.L. 109-295 §550, 120 Stat. 1355 (2006): "(a) No later than six months after the date of enactment of this Act, the Secretary of Homeland Security shall issue interim final regulations establishing risk-based performance standards for security of chemical facilities and requiring vulnerability assessments and the development and implementation of site security plans for chemical facilities: Provided, That such regulations shall apply to chemical facilities that, in the discretion of the Secretary, present high levels of security risk: Provided further, That such regulations shall permit each such facility, in developing and implementing site security plans, to select layered security measures that, in combination, appropriately address the vulnerability assessment and the risk-based performance standards for security for the facility: Provided further, That the Secretary may not disapprove a site security plan submitted under this section based on the presence or absence of a particular security measure, but the Secretary may disapprove a site security plan if the plan fails to satisfy the risk-based performance standards established by this section: Provided further, That the Secretary may approve alternative security programs established by private sector entities, Federal, State, or local authorities, or other applicable laws if the Secretary determines that the requirements of such programs meet the requirements of this section and the interim regulations: Provided further, That the Secretary shall review and approve each vulnerability assessment and site security plan required under this section: Provided further, That the Secretary shall not apply regulations issued pursuant to this section to facilities regulated pursuant to the Maritime Transportation Security Act of 2002, P.L. 107-295, as amended; Public Water Systems, as defined by section 1401 of the Safe Drinking Water Act, P.L. 93-523, as amended; Treatment Works as defined in section 212 of the Federal Water Pollution Control Act, Public Law 92-500, as amended; any facility owned or operated by the Department of Defense or the Department of Energy, or any facility subject to regulation by the Nuclear Regulatory Commission..."

Legislative Veto and Advance Notice

Many acts of Congress have delegated authority to the executive branch on the condition that proposed executive actions be submitted to Congress for review and possible disapproval before they can be put into effect. This way of ensuring continuing oversight of policy areas follows two paths: the legislative veto and advance notification.

Legislative Veto

Beginning in 1932, Congress delegated authority to the executive branch with the condition that proposed executive actions would be first submitted to Congress and subjected to disapproval by a committee, a single house, or both houses. Over the years, other types of legislative veto were added, allowing Congress to control executive branch actions without having to enact a law. In 1983, the Supreme Court ruled that the legislative veto was unconstitutional on the ground that all exercises of legislative power that affect the rights, duties, and relations of persons outside the legislative branch must satisfy the constitutional requirements of bicameralism and presentment of a bill or resolution to the President for his signature or veto. INS v. Chadha, 462 U.S. 919 (1983). Despite this ruling, Congress has continued to enact proscribed legislative vetoes and it has also relied on informal arrangements to provide comparable controls.

Statutory Legislative Vetoes

Congress responded to *Chadha* by converting some of the one-house and two-house legislative vetoes to joint resolutions of approval or disapproval, thus satisfying the requirements of bicameralism and presentment. However, Congress continues to rely on legislative vetoes. Since the *Chadha* decision, hundreds of legislative vetoes have been enacted into public law, usually in appropriations acts. These legislative vetoes are exercised by the Appropriations Committees. Typically, funds may not be used or an executive action may not begin until the Appropriations Committees have approved or, at least, not disapproved the planned action, often within a specified time limit.

A Sample Statutory Legislative Veto Provision

Department of Transportation and Related Agencies Appropriations Act 2001, 114 Stat. 1356A-2 (2000): For the appropriation account "Transportation Administrative Service Center," no assessments may be levied against any program, budget activity, subactivity or project funded by this statute "unless notice of such assessments and the basis therefore are presented to the House and Senate Committees on Appropriations and are approved by such Committees."

Informal Legislative Vetoes

Unlike a formal legislative veto, where the arrangement is spelled out in the law, the informal legislative veto occurs where an executive official pledges not to proceed with an activity until Congress or certain committees agree to it. An example of this appeared during the 101st Congress. In the "bipartisan accord" on funding the contras in Nicaragua, the Administration pledged that no funds would be obligated beyond November 30, 1989, unless affirmed by letter from the relevant authorization and appropriations committees and the bipartisan leadership of Congress.

Advance Notification or Report-and-Wait

Statutory provisions may stipulate that before a particular activity can be undertaken by the executive branch or funds obligated, Congress must first be advised or informed, ordinarily through a full written statement, of what is being proposed. These statutory provisions usually provide for a period of time during which action by the executive must be deferred, giving Congress an opportunity to pass legislation prohibiting the pending action or using political pressure to cause executive officials to retract or modify the proposed action. This type of "report and wait" provision has been upheld by the Supreme Court. The Court noted: "The value of the reservation of the power to examine proposed rules, laws and regulations before they become effective is well understood by Congress. It is frequently, as here, employed to make sure that the action under the delegation squares with the Congressional purpose." *Sibbach* v. *Wilson*, 312 U.S. 1 (1941).

A Sample Report-and-Wait Provision

Comprehensive Anti-Apartheid Act of 1986, P.L. 99-440, § 311: "The President may suspend or modify any of the measures required by this title or section 501(c) or section 504(b) thirty days after he determines, and so reports to the Speaker of the House of Representatives and the chairman of the Committee on Foreign Relations of the Senate, that the Government of South Africa has [taken certain actions] unless the Congress enacts within such 30-day period, in accordance with section 602 of this Act, a joint resolution disapproving the determination of the President under this subsection."

Independent Counsel

The statutory provisions for the appointment of an independent counsel (formerly called "special prosecutor") were originally enacted as Title VI of the Ethics in Government Act of 1978, and codified at 28 U.S.C. §§ 591-599. The independent counsel was reauthorized in 1983, 1987, and 1994. It expired on June 30, 1999. The mechanisms of the independent counsel law were triggered by the receipt of information by the Attorney General that alleged a violation of any federal criminal law (other than certain misdemeanors or "infractions") by a person covered by the act. Certain high-level federal officials, including the President, Vice President, and heads of departments, were automatically covered by the law. In addition, the Attorney General had discretion to seek an independent counsel for any person for whom there may exist a personal, financial or political conflict of interest for Justice Department personnel to investigate; and the Attorney General could seek an independent counsel for any member of Congress when the Attorney General deemed it to be in the "public interest."

After conducting a limited review of the matter (a 30-day threshold review of the credibility and specificity of the charges, and a subsequent 90-day preliminary investigation, with a possible 60-day extension), the Attorney General, if he or she believed that "further investigation is warranted", would apply to a special "division of the court," a federal three-judge panel appointed by the Chief Justice of the Supreme Court, requesting that the division appoint an independent counsel. The Attorney General of the United States was the *only* officer in the government authorized to apply for the appointment of an independent counsel. The special division of the court selected and appointed the independent counsel, and designated his or her prosecutorial jurisdiction, based on the information provided the court by the Attorney General. The independent counsel had the full range of investigatory and prosecutorial powers and functions of the Attorney General or other Department of Justice employees.

Collisions between Congress and Independent Counsels

"The Congress' role here is terribly important. It is for them to present to the public as soon as possible a picture of the actual facts as to the Iran/Contra matter. This is so because there has been so much exposed without sufficient clarity to clear up the questions. There is a general apprehension that this is damaging. Congress properly wants to bring this to an end soon and that gives them a real feeling of urgency for their investigation.

"[The House and Senate Iran-Contra Committees] are trying to provide a factual predicate which will enable Congress to decide intelligently whether there is a need for a statutory amendment or for a closer oversight over covert activities and other matters.... As they quite properly point out, they cannot wait for Independent Counsel to satisfy himself as to whether a crime may or may not have been committed. They have a problem of their own.

"... We are proceeding with much greater detail than Congress would think necessary for their purposes. We come into collision when the question of immunity arises.

"... There is a greater pressure on Congress to grant immunity to central figures than there is for Independent Counsel. Over the last three months, we have had long negotiations over this question of immunity....

"If the Congress decides to grant immunity, there is no way that it can be avoided. They have the last word and that is a proper distribution of power....

"... The reason why Congress must have this power to confer immunity is because of the importance of their role. The legislative branch has the power to decide whether it is more important perhaps even to destroy a prosecution than to hold back testimony they need."

Lawrence E. Walsh, "The Independent Counsel and the Separation of Powers," Houston Law Review, v. 25 (1988):1.

There was no specific term of appointment for independent counsels. They could serve for as long as it took to complete their duties concerning that specific matter within their defined and limited jurisdiction. Once a matter was completed, the independent counsel filed a final report. The special division of the court could also find that the independent counsel's work was completed and terminate the office. A periodic review of an independent counsel for such determination was to be made by the special division of the court. An independent counsel, *prior* to the completion of his or her duties, could be removed from office (other than by impeachment and conviction) only by the Attorney General of the United States for good cause, physical or mental disability, or other impairing condition, and such removal could be appealed to the court. The procedures for appointing and removing the independent counsel were upheld by the Supreme Court in *Morrison* v. *Olson*, 487 U.S. 654 (1988).

Investigation by the independent counsel could compete with parallel efforts by congressional committees to examine the same issue. Congress could decide to accommodate the needs of the independent counsel, such as delaying a legislative investigation until the independent counsel completed certain phases of an inquiry (see box above).

Although Congress could call on the Attorney General to apply for an independent counsel by a written request from the House or Senate Judiciary Committee, or a majority of members of either party of those committees, the Attorney General is not required to begin a preliminary investigation or to apply for an independent counsel in response to such a request. However, in such cases the Justice Department was required to provide certain information to the requesting committee.

The independent counsel was directed by statutory language to submit to Congress an annual report on the activities of such independent counsel, including the progress of investigations and any prosecutions. Although it was recognized that certain information would have to be kept confidential, the statute stated that "information adequate to justify the expenditures that the office of the independent counsel has made" should be provided. 28 U.S.C. § 595(a)(2).

The conduct of an independent counsel was subject to congressional oversight and an independent counsel was required to cooperate with that oversight. 28 U.S.C. § 595(a)(1). In addition, the independent counsel was required to report to the House of Representatives any "substantial and credible" information that may constitute grounds for any impeachment. 28 U.S.C. § 595(c). On September 11, 1998, Independent Counsel Kenneth W. Starr forwarded to the House a report concluding that President Clinton may have committed impeachable offenses. The House passed two articles of impeachment (perjury and obstruction of justice), but the Senate voted only 45 to 55 on the perjury charge and 50 to 50 on the obstruction of justice charge, both votes short of the two-thirds majority required under the Constitution.

The independent counsel statute expired in 1992, partly because of criticism directed at Lawrence Walsh's investigation of Iran-Contra. The statute was reauthorized in 1994, but objections to the investigations conducted by Kenneth Starr into Whitewater, Monica Lewinsky, and other matters, put Congress under pressure to let the statute lapse on June 30, 1999.

Unless Congress in the future reauthorizes the independent counsel, the only available option for an independent counsel is to have the Attorney General invoke existing authority to appoint a special prosecutor to investigate a particular matter. For example, when the independent counsel statute expired in 1992 and was not reauthorized until 1994, Attorney General Janet Reno appointed Robert Fiske in 1993 to investigate the Clintons' involvement in Whitewater and the death of White House aide Vincent Foster. On July 9, 1999 Attorney General Reno promulgated regulations concerning the appointment of outside, temporary counsels, to be called "Special Counsels," in certain circumstances to conduct investigations and possible prosecutions of certain sensitive matters, or matters which may raise a conflict for the Justice Department (28 C.F.R. Part 600). Such special counsels will have substantially less independence than the statutory independent counsel, including removal for "misconduct, dereliction of duty, incapacity, conflict of interest, or for other good cause, including violation of Department policies."

Statutory Offices of Inspector General: Establishment and Evolution

Inspectors general (IGs), whose origins date back to the mid-1970s, have been granted substantial independence and powers to combat waste, fraud, and abuse within designated federal departments and agencies. To execute their missions, offices of inspector general (OIGs) conduct and publish audits and investigations—among other duties. Established by public law as permanent, nonpartisan, and independent offices, OIGs exist in more than 70 federal agencies, including all departments and larger agencies, along with numerous boards and commissions and other entities.[347]

The overwhelming majority of IGs are governed by the Inspector General Act of 1978, as amended (hereinafter referred to as the IG Act).[348] The IG Act provided the blueprint for IG appointments and removals, powers and authorities, and responsibilities and duties—and

---

[347] Three other inspector general posts (in the armed forces departments) are recognized in public law: Air Force (10 U.S.C. §8020), Army (10 U.S.C. §3020), and Navy (10 U.S.C. §5020). These offices, however, are not examined here, because they have a significantly different heritage; set of authorities; operational structure and organization; and degree of independence.

[348] 5 U.S.C. (IG Act) Appendix.

explicitly created OIGs in 12 "federal establishments."[349] Since its enactment in 1978, the IG Act has been substantially amended twice:

- The Inspector General Act Amendments of 1988 created a new set of IGs in "designated federal entities" (DFEs), which are usually smaller federal agencies.[350] The IG Act of 1988 also added to the reporting obligations of all IGs and agency heads, among other things.

- The Inspector General Reform Act of 2008 established a new Council of the Inspectors General for Integrity and Efficiency (CIGIE); amended reporting obligations, salary, bonus, and award provisions; amended IG removal requirements; and added budget protections—including requiring that Congress see IGs' unaltered original budget submissions.[351]

Typically, the jurisdiction of an inspector general includes only the programs and operations of a single affiliated agency and its components. Some IGs, however, have authority to conduct audits and investigations in more than a single agency, organization, program, or activity. Examples include the IG of the IC, the IG for the Department of State and the Broadcasting Board of Governors, and the IG for the Federal Reserve System and the Bureau of Consumer Financial Protection.[352]

Other pieces of legislation have established or amended IGs in specified agencies or programs—either directly under the IG Act or as separate units. Still other enactments have enhanced IG independence or have added new responsibilities and powers on a selective basis.[353] As a result, statutory IGs are not all created equal. In certain cases, differences among IGs are significant.

---

[349] P.L. 95-452. Two IGs whose origins pre-dated the IG Act served as models; in 1976, in the Department of Health, Education, and Welfare, now Health and Human Services (P.L. 94-505); and in 1977, in the then-new Department of Energy (P.L. 95-91). The IG Act of 1978, as amended, establishes offices of inspectors general in many federal agencies as well as defines the IG as the head of each of these offices. The act assigns to the IG specific duties and authorities, including the authority "to select, appoint, and employ such officers and employees as may be necessary for carrying out the functions, powers, and duties of the Office." (5 U.S.C. (IG Act) Appendix §6(a)(7)).

[350] P.L. 100-504.

[351] P.L. 110-409.

[352] 5 U.S.C. (IG Act) Appendix §§2-4 and 8G(g)(1). The Inspector General of the Intelligence Community (IC), created by the Intelligence Authorization Act for Fiscal Year 2010 (P.L. 111-259, §405), has express cross-agency jurisdiction; this enactment recognizes the continued authority of the existing statutory inspectors general over IC components. The same law (P.L. 111-259, §431) created inspector general posts in four Defense Department agencies, identified as "designated federal entities" under the IG Act: the Defense Intelligence Agency, National Geospatial-Intelligence Agency, National Reconnaissance Office, and National Security Agency. The Inspector General of the Department of State and Broadcasting Board of Governors has jurisdiction over the Department of State and the Broadcasting Board of Governors (recognizing the Broadcasting Board of Governors as a separate organization outside the State Department; P.L. 105-277, Division G, Title XIII, Chapter 3, §1322(a)(3); 112 Stat. 2681-777 and 2681-778). In 2010, the Inspector General of the Board of Governors for the Federal Reserve System was given jurisdiction over a new organization—the Bureau of Consumer Financial Protection, which was established as an "independent bureau" in the Federal Reserve System by the Dodd-Frank Wall Street Reform and Consumer Protection Act (P.L. 111-203, §1011). To reflect this expanded coverage, the IG was retitled the Inspector General of the Board of Governors of the Federal Reserve System and the Bureau of Consumer Financial Protection (P.L. 111-203, §1081(1)-(2)). Most recently, P.L. 113-6, enacted on March 26, 2013, requires, among other things, the Government Accountability Office (GAO) IG to concurrently serve as the IG for the Commission on Civil Rights (P.L. 113-6; 127 Stat. 266).

[353] For instance, the inspectors general of federal banking agencies and of the Federal Reserve System had been given review and reporting mandates in separate legislation (12 U.S.C. §1831o(k) and 12 U.S.C. §1790d(j), respectively), which were modified in 2010 by the Dodd-Frank Wall Street Reform and Consumer Protection Act (P.L. 111-203, §§987(a) and 988(a)).

Nonetheless, in general, statutory IGs follow the standards, guidelines, and directives in the IG Act.[354]

Types and Categories

As noted above, statutory offices of inspector general are currently authorized in more than 70 federal establishments, designated federal entities, and other agencies or programs.[355] Authority for most of the IGs is provided by the IG Act.[356]

The statutory IGs may be grouped by these criteria: the method of appointment, the authorizing statute, and the branch of government in which it is located.

- **Appointment by the President with the Advice and Consent of the Senate, Under the IG Act.** *"Federal establishments,"* as identified in the IG Act, include the 15 Cabinet departments and larger federal agencies. Each IG is appointed by the President with the advice and consent of the Senate and can be removed by the President, but *not* by the affiliated agency head.[357]

- **Appointment by the Head of the Parent Agency, Under the IG Act.** *"Designated federal entities"* *(DFEs),* also as identified in the IG Act, include the usually smaller boards, commissions, foundations, and government enterprises. Each IG is appointed by and removable by the head of the affiliated agency.[358]

- **Appointment by the President with the Advice and Consent of the Senate, Enacted Under Separate Statutory Authority.** *Two other permanent executive agencies* operate under their own statutory authorities. These are the Inspector General in the Central Intelligence Agency (P.L. 101-193) and the Inspector General of the Intelligence Community within the Office of the Director of

---

[354] OIGs may follow additional regulations, policies, or standards in addition to the IG Act. For example, the Council of the Inspectors General on Integrity and Efficiency maintains "Quality Standards for Inspection and Evaluation," which all OIG employees are required to follow when conducting inspections or evaluations. Available at http://www.ignet.gov/pande/standards/iestds12r.pdf.

[355] Some now-defunct statutory IGs have been abolished or transferred either when their parent agency met the same fate or when superseded by another inspector general office. For example, the Office of Inspector General in the Office of the Director of National Intelligence (DNI)—which operated under the full discretionary authority of the DNI (P.L. 108-458)—was supplanted by the Inspector General of the IC; the new IC IG post was established by the Intelligence Authorization Act of 2010 (P.L. 111-259, §405) with substantially broader authority, jurisdiction, and independence than the previous IG.

[356] Nine other operational IGs have been established by and are governed by statutes other than the IG Act: the Inspector General in the Central Intelligence Agency (CIA), the Inspector General of the Intelligence Community within the Office of the Director of National Intelligence (ODNI) with cross-agency jurisdiction, the Inspector General of the Architect of the Capitol, the Inspector General for the Government Accountability Office, the Inspector General of the Government Printing Office, the Inspector General of the Library of Congress, the Special Inspector General for Afghanistan Reconstruction, the Special Inspector General for the Troubled Asset Relief Program, and the Inspector General for the U.S. Capitol Police...

[357] 5 U.S.C. (IG Act) Appendix §2. For a listing of IGs in federal establishments, see U.S. Government Accountability Office, *Inspectors General: Reporting on Independence, Effectiveness, and Expertise*, GAO-11-770, September 2011, p. 21, at http://www.gao.gov/assets/330/323642.pdf.

[358] For a listing of IGs in DFEs, see U.S. Government Accountability Office, *Inspectors General: Reporting on Independence, Effectiveness, and Expertise*, p. 22.

National Intelligence, whose jurisdiction extends across all Intelligence Community (IC) elements or components (P.L. 111-259). Each IG is appointed by the President with the advice and consent of the Senate and is removable by the President.

- **Varied Appointment Structure, Enacted Under Separate Statutory Authority, and Temporary.** *Two temporary programs* operate under their own authorities and reflect different appointment structures.[359] These IGs are:

  - the Special Inspector General for Afghanistan Reconstruction (SIGAR), a direct presidential appointee, unique among IGs (P.L. 110-181); and

  - the Special Inspector General for the Troubled Asset Relief Program (SIGTARP), who is appointed by the President with the advice and consent of the Senate (P.L. 110-343).[360]

- **Varied Appointment Structure, Enacted Under Separate Statutory Authority, and Located in the Legislative Branch.** *Five legislative branch IGs* operate under statutory authorities other than the IG Act. Each IG is appointed and removable by the head of their affiliated agency. These are:

  - the Architect of the Capitol (P.L. 110-161);

  - Government Accountability Office (P.L. 110-323);

  - Government Printing Office (P.L. 100-504);

  - Library of Congress (P.L. 109-55); and

  - U.S. Capitol Police (P.L. 109-55).

Purposes

Under Section 2 of the IG Act, the three principal purposes of inspectors general who are governed by the IG Act are:

- conducting and supervising audits and investigations related to agency programs and operations;

- providing leadership and coordination and recommending policies for activities designed to promote the economy, efficiency, and effectiveness and the

---

[359] A third, temporary special IG, the Special Inspector General for Iraq Reconstruction (SIGIR), was established by the Emergency Supplemental Appropriations Act for Defense and for the Reconstruction of Iraq and Afghanistan, as amended (P.L. 108-106). SIGIR was abolished in October 2013. SIGIR's final report is available from the IG's archived website here: http://cybercemetery.unt.edu/archive/sigir/20131001092420/http://www.sigir.mil/files/quarterlyreports/September2013/Report_-_September_2013.pdf#view=fit.

[360] The Troubled Asset Relief Program investment authority expired on October 3, 2010. The termination of that authority did not affect the Treasury Department's ability to administer existing troubled asset purchases and guarantees and its ability to expend TARP funds for obligations entered into before the closing date. Consequently, SIGTARP's oversight mandate did not end. Rather, the special inspector general is authorized to carry out the office's duties until the Government has sold or transferred all assets and terminated all insurance contracts acquired under TARP. See SIGTARP, *Quarterly Report to Congress*, July 25, 2012, p. 15.

---

prevention and detection of fraud and abuse in such programs and operations; and

- keeping the agency head and Congress fully and currently informed about problems and deficiencies relating to such programs and the necessity for and progress of corrective action.[361]

- Over time and as conditions dictated, IGs have acquired additional related responsibilities, on a selective basis. For instance, the Dodd-Frank Wall Street Reform and Consumer Protection Act contains a number of provisions that add to the duties of IGs over certain federally insured funds and aid in coordination among relevant IGs via a Council of Inspectors General on Financial Oversight.[362]

Authorities

To carry out their purposes, IGs covered by the IG Act have been granted broad authority to:

- conduct audits and investigations;

- access directly the records and information related to agency programs and operations;

- request assistance from other federal, state, and local government agencies;

- subpoena information and documents; administer oaths when conducting interviews;

- hire staff and manage their own resources;

- receive and respond to complaints from agency employees, whose identity is to be protected; and

- implement the cash incentive award program in their agency for employee disclosures of waste, fraud, and abuse.[363]

Notwithstanding these broad powers, IGs are *not* authorized to take corrective action themselves. Moreover, the IG Act prohibits the transfer of "program operating responsibilities" to an IG.[364]

---

[361] IGs not covered by the IG Act generally have similar or identical purposes to those that are governed by it, although some IG missions may vary.

[362] P.L. 111-203, §§989E(a)-989E(b).

[363] 5 U.S.C. (IG Act) Appendix §§6(a), 6(e), and 7; 5 U.S.C. §4512. IGs not explicitly covered by the IG Act may have similar or identical authorities, although some IGs may have additional authorities or be prohibited from exercising the authorities listed here.

[364] 5 U.S.C. (IG Act) Appendix §8G(b) and §9(a)(2). One rationale for this proscription is that it would be difficult, if not impossible, for IGs to audit or investigate programs and operations impartially and objectively if they were directly involved in carrying them out.

Reporting Requirements (to the Attorney General, Agency Head, Congress, and the Public)

IGs have various reporting obligations to Congress, the Attorney General, agency head(s), and the public. One such obligation is to report suspected violations of federal criminal law directly and expeditiously to the Attorney General.[365] IGs are also required to report semiannually (twice per year) about their activities, findings, and recommendations to the agency head, who must submit the IG's report to Congress within 30 days.[366] The agency head's submission must provide the IG's report unaltered, but it may include any additional comments from the agency head. These semiannual reports are to be made available to the public within 60 days of their submission to Congress.[367] IGs are also to report "particularly serious or flagrant problems" immediately to the agency head, who must submit the IG report (unaltered but with his or her comments) to Congress within seven days.[368]

Independence

IGs have broad powers and protections that support their independence, including the authority to hire their own staff. Their independent status is reinforced in other ways, including, for example, by law enforcement powers.[369] Moreover, inspectors general determine the priorities and projects for their offices without outside direction, in most cases. IGs may decide to conduct a review requested by the agency head, President, legislators, employees, or anyone for that matter; but they are not obligated to do so, unless it is called for in law.[370] Congress, however, has mandated in legislation that OIGs conduct certain reviews.

IGs serve under the "general supervision" of the agency head, reporting exclusively to the head or to the officer next in rank if such authority is delegated.[371]

---

[365] 5 U.S.C. (IG Act) Appendix §4(d).

[366] 5 U.S.C. (IG Act) Appendix §5(a), (b).

[367] 5 U.S.C. (IG Act) Appendix §5(c).

[368] 5 U.S.C. (IG Act) Appendix §5(d). IGs are to keep the agency head and Congress "fully and currently informed" by means of the required reports and "otherwise." (5 U.S.C. (IG Act) Appendix. §4(a)(5)).

[369] 5 U.S.C. (IG Act) Appendix §§6(a)(4) and 6(e). Twenty-five federal IG offices are explicitly provided law enforcement authority by the IG Act. The act also provides the Attorney General the authority to vest IG offices with law enforcement authority. Additionally, five IG offices are provided law enforcement authority by statutes other than the IG Act. For more information on IGs and law enforcement authority, see CRS Report R43722, *Offices of Inspectors General and Law Enforcement Authority: In Brief*, by Wendy Ginsberg.

[370] Pursuant to the IG Act, the heads of only six agencies—the Departments of Defense, Homeland Security, Justice, and Treasury, plus the U.S. Postal Service and Federal Reserve Board—may prevent or halt the IG from initiating, carrying out, or completing an audit or investigation, or issuing a subpoena, and then only for certain reasons: to preserve national security interests or to protect ongoing criminal investigations, among a few others. (U.S.C. App. §§8, 8D(a), 8E(a), 8G(f), 8G(g)(3), and 8I(a)). When exercising this power, the IG Act generally provides for congressional notification of the exercise of such authority, either via the agency head or the inspector general, who must transmit an explanatory statement for such action to specified congressional committees within 30 days. (5 U.S.C. (IG Act) Appendix. §§8(b)(3)-8(b)(4), which states that the Secretary of Defense must "submit a statement concerning" the exercise of such power to various congressional committees within 30 days and must also submit a "statement of the reasons for the exercise of power" to the congressional committees within an additional 30 days after the submission of the first statement. See also 5 U.S.C. (IG Act) Appendix. §8E(a)(2), which requires the Attorney General to notify the IG in writing of the exercise of such power and mandating that the IG transmit a copy of such notice to certain congressional committees).

[371] 5 U.S.C. (IG Act) Appendix §§3(a), 8G(d).

Budgets and Appropriations

Pursuant to the IG Act, presidentially-appointed IGs in establishments are provided a separate appropriations account for their offices.[372] This requirement prevents agency administrators from limiting, transferring, or otherwise reducing IG funding once it has been specified in law. In contrast, each DFE IG's budget is part of the affiliated entity's budget and may be susceptible to some reallocation of funds.

The Inspector General Reform Act of 2008, moreover, amended the budget process for establishment and DFE OIGs. Pursuant to the reform act amendments, OIG budget estimates (i.e., budget proposals, which are to include operations, IG training, and other costs to support the federal IG council[373]) are to be provided to the affiliated agency. The affiliated agency's aggregated budget request to the President is required to include the OIG's original budget estimate and any response from the IG to the agency head's suggested changes. The President, in turn, must then include in his budget submission to Congress: the IG's original budget estimate; the President's requested amounts for the IG; and comments of the affected IG, if he or she determines that the President's budget would "substantially inhibit" the IG from performing his or her duties.[374] Similar provisions apply to the inspectors general for the CIA and of the Intelligence Community.[375]

Appointment, Removal, and Term Limits

Some variations occur with regard to the appointment and removal of inspectors general, reflecting—to a degree—the status, location, and permanency of the affiliated agency. All IGs, however, follow certain laws and practices to help ensure impartiality and political nonpartisanship.

Pursuant to the Inspector General Act and other statutes, IGs are to be selected without regard to political affiliation and solely on the basis of integrity and demonstrated ability in accounting, auditing, financial and management analysis, law, public administration, or investigations.[376] IGs who are presidential appointees with the advice and consent of the Senate can be removed only by the President (or through the impeachment process in Congress).[377]

---

[372] 31 U.S.C. §1105(a)(25). The IGs in the CIA and of the Intelligence Community have similar safeguards for their budget accounts (50 U.S.C. §403(q)(17)(f) and 50 U.S.C. §. 403-3H(m), respectively).

[373] The federal IG council, known as the Council on Inspectors General of the Inspectors General for Integrity and Efficiency (CIGIE), will be discussed below in greater detail.

[374] 5 U.S.C. (IG Act) Appendix §6(f)(1)-(3).

[375] 50 U.S.C. §403q(17)(f) and 50 U.S.C. §403-3(n), respectively.

[376] 5 U.S.C. (IG Act) Appendix §§3(a) and 8G(c). The CIA IG and the IC IG, who operate under different statutes, are to be selected under these criteria as well as prior experience in the field of foreign intelligence or national security and in compliance with the relevant security standards (50 U.S.C. §403(q)(b) and §403-3H(c), respectively, for the CIA IG and the IC IG).

[377] 5 U.S.C. (IG Act) Appendix §3. When exercising removal authority, the President must communicate the reasons to Congress in writing 30 days prior to the scheduled removal date. This advance notice allows the inspector general, Congress, or other interested parties to examine and possibly object to the planned removal (5 U.S.C. (IG Act) Appendix. §3(b) for PAS IGs under the IG Act; 50 U.S.C. §403(q)(b) for the IG in the CIA; and 50 U.S.C. §403-3(H)(c)(4)) for the IG of the Intelligence Community).

IGs in designated federal entities and legislative branch agencies vary in appointment structure, removal procedure, and term limits. The DFE IGs are appointed by and can be removed by the agency head, who must notify Congress in writing 30 days in advance when exercising the removal authority.[378] Furthermore, the U.S. Postal Service (USPS) IG is the only inspector general with the restriction that he or she can be removed only "for cause" and then only by the written concurrence of at least seven of the nine presidentially-appointed governors of USPS. In other cases, the Dodd-Frank Wall Street Reform and Consumer Protection Act amended the IG Act to require the written concurrence of a two-thirds majority of board or commission members for removal of an IG in any designated federal entity in which the board or commission is considered the DFE head.[379]

Coordination and Controls

Coordination among the IGs and controls over their actions, which might include investigating charges of wrongdoing by the IGs themselves, exists through several channels—including interagency councils created by public law or administrative directive.

Council of the Inspectors General for Integrity and Efficiency. Perhaps the most important coordinating body for IGs is the Council of the Inspectors General for Integrity and Efficiency (CIGIE), created by the IG Reform Act of 2008.[380] CIGIE is designed to aid coordination among IGs and maintain one or more academies for the professional training of auditors, investigators, inspectors, and evaluators, and other personnel in IG offices.[381] CIGIE includes all statutory IGs along with other relevant officers, such as a representative of the Federal Bureau of Investigation (FBI) and the Special Counsel of the Office of Special Counsel.[382] The council chairperson is an inspector general chosen from within its ranks, while the executive chairperson is the OMB deputy director of management.[383]

Other Coordinative Bodies. Other interagency mechanisms have been created by law or administrative directive to assist coordination among IGs. For example, a separate Council of Inspectors General on Financial Oversight—chaired by the Treasury IG, and composed of IGs from nine financial agencies—was established by statute to facilitate information sharing among them and develop ways to improve financial oversight.[384] In 2010, Congress enacted a bill requiring the establishment of the Intelligence Community Inspectors General Forum. The forum consists of all statutory or administratively-established inspectors with oversight responsibility of

---

[378] 5 U.S.C. (IG Act) Appendix §8G(c) and (e). Differences, however, arise over who might be considered to be the "head of the agency" in a DFE. The agency head may be: an individual serving as the administrator or director or as spelled out in law (e.g., the Archivist of the United States in the National Archives and Records Administration), the chairperson of a board or commission, a full board or council as specified in law (e.g., the National Council on the Arts in the National Endowment of the Arts), or a certain super-majority of a governing board. (5 U.S.C. (IG Act) Appendix. §§8G(f)(1)-(2) and (4)). In the United States Postal Service (USPS), for instance, the governors appoint the inspector general.

[379] 5 U.S.C. (IG Act) Appendix §8G(e)(1).

[380] 5 U.S.C. (IG Act) Appendix §11.

[381] 5 U.S.C. (IG Act) Appendix §11(c)(E).

[382] 5 U.S.C. (IG Act) Appendix §11(b)(1).

[383] 5 U.S.C. (IG Act) Appendix §11(b)(2).

[384] P.L. 111-203, §989E.

an element of the IC and is chaired by the IC Inspector General.[385] At least two administrative organizations have also been created to help coordinate IG activities and capabilities in selected areas: the Homeland Security Roundtable; and the Defense Council on Integrity and Efficiency, composed primarily of DOD audit and investigative units and chaired by the DOD inspector general.[386]

Investigation of Alleged OIG Wrongdoing. Investigation of alleged misconduct by OIG officials—including inspectors general themselves—is the province of a special Integrity Committee in CIGIE.[387] The special committee receives, reviews, and refers for investigation allegations of wrongdoing by these officials, with the relevant processes and procedures spelled out in the IG Act. The committee is composed of four IGs on the Council, along with the Special Counsel, the Director of the Office of Government Ethics, and the FBI representative on the council, who chairs the committee.[388]

Oversight Information Sources and Consultant Services

Congress calls upon a variety of sources for information and analysis to support its oversight activities. Most of this assistance is provided by legislative support agencies: The Congressional Research Service, the Congressional Budget Office, and the Government Accountability Office. In addition, the Offices of Senate Legal Counsel and House General Counsel are valuable oversight resources. A range of outside interest groups and research organizations also provide rich sources of information.

Congressional Research Service (CRS)

CRS Mission Statement

"The Congressional Research Service serves the Congress throughout the legislative process by providing comprehensive and reliable legislative research and analysis that are timely, objective, authoritative, and confidential, thereby contributing to an informed national legislature."

Organization

CRS is organized into five interdisciplinary research divisions: American Law; Domestic Social Policy; Foreign Affairs, Defense and Trade; Government and Finance; and Resources, Science and Industry. The Knowledge Services Group provides research support services to CRS analysts and attorneys in their preparation of authoritative and reliable information research and policy analysis to Congress.

---

[385] P.L. 111-259, §405; 50 U.S.C. §403-3h(h).

[386] Office of Inspector General, Department of Defense, *Defense Council on Integrity and Efficiency: Charter*, at http://www.dodig.mil/dcie.html.

[387] 5 U.S.C. (IG Act) Appendix §11(d)(1).

[388] 5 U.S.C. (IG Act) Appendix §11(d)(2).

Staff of CRS

CRS has about 600 employees on its permanent staff. The professional staff are diverse, including, among others, attorneys, economists, engineers, social science analysts, information scientists, librarians, defense and foreign affairs analysts, political scientists, public administrators, and physical and biological scientists.

Analytical and Research Services

Policy analysis and research. CRS staff anticipates and responds to congressional needs for policy analysis, research and information in an interdisciplinary, integrated manner. CRS provides timely and objective responses to congressional inquiries for policy analysis, research and information at every stage of the legislative process. Legislative attorneys and paralegal staff respond to congressional needs for legal information and analysis to support the legislative, oversight, and representational functions of Congress.

Information research. Information research specialists and resource specialists are available to provide information research and reference assistance. The staff also provides copies of articles in newspapers, journals, legal and legislative documents and offers assistance with a wide variety of electronic files.

Briefings, seminars, and workshops

CRS conducts briefings, seminars, and workshops for members of Congress and their staffs. On these occasions CRS analysts and other experts discuss public policy issues, international concerns, and the legislative process.

Briefings. CRS analysts and specialists are available to give one-on-one briefings to members and staff on public policy issues, the legislative process, congressional office operations, committee matters, or a general orientation to CRS.

Issue seminars and workshops. In anticipation of congressional interest or at the request of a member or committee, CRS organizes and conducts seminars and workshops on issues of current interest to members and staff of Congress. CRS and outside experts participate in these events with members and staff.

Federal Law Update. This series, offered twice yearly by the American Law Division, focuses on developments on important issues of law directly related to the legislative business of Congress. The series can meet continuing legal education (CLE) requirements in some states.

CRS Legislative Institutes. This two-part series provides training in the work of Congress and the legislative process. Topics include the federal budget process, committee system and procedures, floor procedures, amendments, and resolutions.

District and Staff Institutes. These institutes provide orientation for staff of district offices that includes discussions of CRS services, the legislative and budget processes, casework, member allowances, ethics, and franking. The program is supported by the House and Senate.

New Member Seminar. Every two years CRS offers new members an orientation seminar on public policy issues. These sessions are held in January at the beginning of each new Congress.

For additional information about CRS seminars and events, call 7-7904.

CRS Products

Customized Memoranda. Confidential memoranda prepared for a specific office are a major form of CRS written communication. These memoranda are solely for the use of the requesting office and are not distributed further unless permission has been given by that office. Memoranda are often used by CRS attorneys and analysts to respond to inquiries focused on legislative and policy matters of individual member interest.

CRS Reports. Reports for Congress on specific issues take many forms: policy analyses, statistical reviews, economic studies, legal analyses, historical studies, and chronological reviews. Reports are available on the CRS website at http://www.crs.gov.

Congressional Distribution Memoranda. Matters that are not suitable for treatment in a CRS Report, but that may be of interest to more than one congressional office, can be the subject of general distribution memoranda provided to a congressional office upon request. General distribution memoranda differ from Reports because they are tailored; are directed to a specific question or concern; or are more technical or focused in nature.

Reading Rooms and Research Centers

Staff in the congressional reading rooms and research centers provide telephone reference assistance and in-person consultation on resources and research for congressional staff. A selected research collection, newspapers and journals, and assistance with online searching are available.

- La Follette Congressional Reading Room

  - Monday-Thurs: 10:00 a.m. – 8:00 p.m.; Friday: 10:00 a.m. – 6:00 p.m.; Saturday: 10:00 a.m. – 5:00 p.m. except during recess or district/state work periods.

  - When Congress is in session on a Sunday or holiday, the hours are posted to the website.

- Rayburn Research Center: Monday-Friday 10:00 a.m. – 4:00 p.m.

- CRS Senate Center: Monday-Friday 10:00 a.m. – 4:00 p.m. Hours may change when Congress is not in session.

- Jefferson Congressional Reading Room: a Members-only facility staffed by CRS information professionals providing in-person service.

  - Monday-Friday 8:30 a.m. – 5:00 p.m. except during recess or district/state work periods.

Events

- Russell Senate Center, B07
  - Monday-Friday 10:00 a.m. – 4:00 p.m. Doors may open earlier for events.

Electronically Accessible Products and Services

CRS Website. http://www.crs.gov. The CRS website provides 24-hour access to an array of CRS services including full text of reports, a weekly "Floor Agenda," updates and analyses of the annual appropriations legislation, an interactive guide to the legislative process, online registration for CRS seminars, and complete information on other CRS services. In operation since the 104th Congress, the CRS website is accessible only to House and Senate offices and other legislative branch agencies. A linked format allows the user to move easily within a CRS online document and link to the text and summary of relevant legislation and other CRS products on the topic.

Legislative Information System. http://www.congress.gov. The Legislative Information System (LIS) was available for the first time on Capnet at the beginning of the 105th Congress. The system provides Members of Congress and their staff with access to the most current and comprehensive legislative information available. It can be accessed only by the House and Senate and the legislative support agencies. The LIS has been developed under the policy direction of the Senate Committee on Rules and Administration and the House Committee on House Administration. It has been a collaborative project of the offices and agencies of the legislative branch, including the Secretary of the Senate and the Clerk of the House; House Information Resources and the Senate Sergeant at Arms; the Government Printing Office; the Government Accountability Office; the Congressional Budget Office; the Congressional Research Service; and the Library of Congress. CRS has responsibility for the overall coordination of the retrieval system; the Library of Congress is responsible for its technical development and operation.

Floor Agenda. The "Floor Agenda: CRS Products" page, a weekly compendium of CRS products relevant to scheduled or expected floor action in the House and Senate, is available on the CRS website and through e-mail subscription to all Members, committees, subcommittees, and congressional staff. All CRS products listed on the Floor Agenda are linked for electronic delivery to subscriber desktops.

CRS Programs Listserv. Launched in fiscal 2001, this e-mail notification system provides subscribers with descriptions of current CRS programs and links to online registration forms.

Issues Before Congress. The Issues Before Congress (IBC) system, accessible to Congress from the CRS Home Page, reflects policy areas identified by CRS research staff as active and of current importance to Congress. All products presented as IBCs are maintained to address significant policy developments. On occasion the system is used to facilitate the contribution of CRS expertise in situations requiring immediate attention of Congress on an unanticipated basis. CRS typically develops and maintains about 150 IBCs a year.

Appropriations. The CRS Appropriations web page continues to provide comprehensive legislative tracking and access to legislative analysis of each of the 12 annual appropriations bills.

Audiovisual Products and Services

CRS provides a variety of audiovisual products and technical assistance in support of its service to Congress. These include producing video or audio copies of CRS institutes and seminars that congressional staff can request for viewing in DVD format. In addition, CRS provides two hours of television programming each weekday for the Senate closed-circuit system.

CRS Divisional Responsibilities

CRS has adopted an interdisciplinary and integrative approach as it responds to requests from Congress. The Service seeks to define complex issues in clear and understandable ways, identify basic causes of the problems under consideration, and highlight available policy choices and potential effects of action. CRS is organized into the following divisions and offices to support the analysis, research, and information needs of Congress.

Divisions

American Law Division. The American Law Division provides Congress with legal analysis and information on the range of legal questions that emerge from the congressional agenda. Division lawyers and paralegals work with federal, state, and international legal resources in support of the legislative, oversight, and representational needs of Members and committees of Congress. The division's work involves the constitutional framework of separation of powers, congressional-executive relations and federalism; the legal aspects of congressional practices and procedures; and the myriad questions of administrative law, constitutional law, criminal law, civil rights, environmental law, business and tax law, and international law that are implicated by the legislative process. In addition, the division prepares *The Constitution of the United States of America—Analysis and Interpretation* (popularly known as the Constitution Annotated).

Domestic Social Policy Division. The Domestic Social Policy Division offers Congress research and analysis in the broad area of domestic social policies and programs. Analysts use multiple disciplines in their research, including program and legislative expertise, quantitative methodologies, and economic analysis. Issue and legislative areas include education and training, health care and financing, Social Security, public and private pensions, welfare, nutrition assistance, housing, immigration, drug control, crime and criminal justice, labor and occupational safety, unemployment and workers compensation, and issues related to children and families, persons with disabilities, the aged, the poor, and veterans.

Foreign Affairs, Defense, and Trade. The Foreign Affairs, Defense, and Trade Division is organized into seven regional and functional sections. Analysts follow worldwide political and economic and security developments for Congress, including U.S. relations with individual countries and transnational issues such as terrorism, refugees, global economic problems, and global institutions such as the International Monetary Fund and the United Nations. They also address U.S. foreign aid programs, strategies, and resource allocations; State Department budget and functions; international debt; public diplomacy; and legislation on foreign relations. Research responsibilities also include national security policy, military strategy, U.S. and foreign weapons systems, military operations, defense acquisition, military compensation, military health, the defense budget, and U.S. military bases. Trade-related legislation, policies, programs, and U.S. trade performance and investment flows are examined, as are trade negotiations and agreements, export promotion, import regulations, and tariffs.

Government and Finance Division. The Government and Finance Division responds to congressional requests for assistance on all aspects of Congress. These include the congressional budget and appropriations process, the legislative process, congressional administration and staffing, and the organization and operations of Congress and legislative branch agencies. Among the financial issues covered by the division are banking, financial institutions, insurance, mortgages, and securities; taxation, public finance, fiscal and monetary policy, and the public debt; the interaction between taxes and interest rates; and macroeconomic policy. In addition, the division responds to requests on the organization and management of the federal executive and judicial branches; judicial and executive branch nominations; government personnel and the civil service; the presidency and vice presidency; government information policy and privacy issues; intergovernmental relations and forms of federal aid; federalism; statehood and U.S. territories; the District of Columbia; economic developments; federal planning for and response to emergencies, disasters, and acts of terrorism in the United States; survey research and public opinion polls; the census; reapportionment and redistricting; elections, campaign finance, lobbying, and political parties; constitutional amendments; and constitutional history.

Resources, Science, and Industry Division. The Resources, Science, and Industry Division covers an array of legislative issues for Congress involving natural resources and environmental management, science and technology, and industry and infrastructure. Resources work includes policy analysis on public lands and other natural resources issues; environment; agriculture, food, and fisheries; and energy and minerals. Science coverage includes policy analysis on civilian and military research and development issues, information and telecommunications, space, earth sciences, and general science and technology. Support on transportation and industry issues includes policy analysis on transportation and transportation infrastructure issues, industrial market structure and regulation, and sector-specific industry analysis.

Knowledge Services Group. The Knowledge Services Group includes information professionals who respond to congressional requests and partner with CRS analysts and attorneys in providing authoritative and reliable information research and policy analysis to Congress. They write descriptive products and contribute to analytical products in policy research areas, advise analysts and Congress in finding solutions for their information needs, make recommendations for incorporating new research materials in print and digital formats and provide or coordinate specialized training on these resources. They also evaluate, acquire, and maintain research data and geospatial information to address various public policy issue areas. They work closely with the research divisions to provide seminars, institutes, and other in-person briefings to Members and their staff, and also provide direct support to Congress in congressional reading rooms and research centers.

Offices

Office of Communications. The Office of Communications is responsible for coordinating and overseeing CRS communications with internal and external audiences. The office assists CRS staff in understanding how Service policies, procedures, decisions, and activities relate to the CRS mission of serving Congress and how staff efforts fulfill that mission. To achieve that goal, the office advises on communications-related aspects of CRS initiatives; ensures that internal and external communications are clear, consistent, and aligned with the CRS mission; coordinates efforts to improve the use of existing communications channels; and plans, develops, and implements new uses of communications channels.

Office of Finance and Administration. The Office of Finance and Administration oversees the financial, procurement, and administrative programs of the Service. This includes coordinating the strategic planning; preparing the budget request; formulating and executing the financial operating plan; performing contracting and procurement actions; supervising the Service's status, role, activities, and interaction with the Library in performing these functions.

Office of the Counselor to the Director. The Office of the Counselor to the Director examines and defines policy and legal questions and issues affecting all aspects of the Service, and serves as the principal legal and policy advisor to the CRS Director, Deputy Director, and other senior management officials. The office develops and coordinates matters relating to internal CRS policies, particularly as they affect the Service's relationship with congressional clients and other legislative support agencies, and ensures that the Service complies with applicable guidelines and directives contained in the Reorganization Act, in statements by appropriations and oversight committees, and in Library regulations and CRS policy statements. The Office of the Counselor to the Director also addresses policy and legal questions with respect to such matters as congressional requests, potential conflicts of interest and activities on the part of staff, and personnel policy and labor-management issues.

Office of Congressional Information and Publishing. The Office of Congressional Information and Publishing facilitates and enhances congressional access to CRS expertise and legislative information. The office manages congressional research requests for CRS services and collects and organizes data about the use of CRS by Congress; edits, provides graphics support for, and publishes, CRS reports exclusively for Congress; organizes, analyzes, and publishes legislative information (including summaries of pending legislation); and coordinates Congress's Legislative Information System (LIS) in partnership with the Clerk of the House, Secretary of the Senate, and a number of other legislative branch offices and agencies.

Office of Information Management and Technology. The Office of Information Management and Technology provides the information management capabilities and support required for CRS legislation-related activities, communications, and service to Congress. This includes planning, procurement, development, operations, security, and maintenance of the information technology infrastructure and systems required to support the CRS mission. The office is also responsible for the overall information architecture and maintains information resources by identifying, assessing, acquiring, organizing, preserving, and tracking materials.

The Office of Workforce Management and Development. The Office of Workforce Management and Development manages the Service's ability to attract, develop, and retain quality talent needed to respond to the dynamic research, analysis, and information needs of Congress. The office provides a comprehensive package of services and programs to support and strengthen human capital capabilities. These services and programs extend to the areas of staffing and workforce planning; performance management, training and development, and staff recognition; data management and analysis; workforce flexibilities; and personnel security. The office also serves as liaison and collaborates with other Library offices on human resource management issues and initiatives.

Interdisciplinary Teams

As part of Service-wide planning efforts, CRS managers attempt to anticipate major congressional issues. The program identifies and defines major issues, structures them for more effective scrutiny by Congress, and provides effective, timely, and comprehensive products and services to Congress, which usually require multi-disciplinary and interdivisional contributions. The issues chosen are national in scope, receive widespread public attention, have significant effects on the federal budget, economy, or social fabric of the Nation, and are virtually certain to be the subject of congressional hearings and legislative action.

Limitations

The Legislative Reorganization Act of 1970 and specific provisions in various other Acts direct and authorize CRS to provide a great range of products and services to Congress. However, pursuant to these statutory authorities and understandings reached over time in consultation with the relevant oversight committees, the Service has developed the following policies limiting or barring certain types of assistance. When it appears that a congressional request should be declined on these policy grounds, that decision and notification to the requestor is to be made only after consultation with the appropriate Section Research Manager or Assistant Director.

- CRS cannot prepare reports, seminars or undisclaimed products that are of a partisan nature or advocate bills or policies. But CRS will respond to requests for "directed writing"—statement drafts, casemaking or other disclaimed products clearly identified as prepared at the direction of the client and not for attribution as CRS analysis or opinion. In no case is excessive partisanship, incorrect factual data, moral denigration of opponents, or personal research damaging to Members permissible.

- CRS cannot provide researched information focusing on individual Members or living former Members of Congress (other than holders of, or nominees to, federal appointive office), except at the specific request or with permission of the member concerned.

- Members of the CRS staff shall not appear as witnesses before committees of Congress in their capacity as CRS employees or on matters relating to their official duties without the express consent of the Director.

- CRS does not draft bills (a function of the office of the legislative counsels), but will assist with the preparation of legislative proposals.

- CRS cannot meet deadlines or demands that could only be met by dropping or jeopardizing the quality of responses to urgent legislative requests related to the public policy work of Congress, but the Service will respond to all requests as rapidly as is feasible under prevailing workload conditions.

- CRS cannot accept "rush" or priority deadlines on constituent inquiries but will respond as expeditiously as is possible without compromising the quality of responses relating to current legislative business.

- CRS cannot undertake casework or provide translating services or briefings for constituents, but can lend assistance in responding to constituent matters, including identification of the appropriate agency or private entity to contact for further pursuit of the matter.

- CRS cannot give personal legal or medical advice, but will assist in the provision of background information, the identification of relevant issues for further scrutiny, and advice on sources of additional assistance.

- CRS cannot undertake scholastic or personal research for office staff, but can, on a nonpriority basis, help with bibliographic and reference services.

- CRS assistance for former Members of Congress should be limited to use of the La Follette Reading Room and reference centers, the hotline service, the provision of readily available information and previously prepared CRS congressional distribution products. CRS cannot undertake original research for former Members, but on a nonpriority basis responds to requests for reference services and research guidance.

- CRS is not authorized to provide congressional offices with clerical assistance (e.g., typing, duplication, maintenance of mailing lists, continuing clipping services, etc.).

- CRS must not use its staff to index hearings or congressional documents other than those prepared by the Service itself.

- The Library of Congress is not authorized to subscribe to or lend on a regular basis current issues of periodicals and newspapers for the purpose of furnishing them regularly to individual congressional offices.

- CRS must not use its staff to support executive or other commissions that are not funded through the Legislative Branch Appropriations Act. In those instances where Members of Congress are official members of a commission not served by CRS, the Service may supply customary assistance to the Members, but queries should be placed through the members' offices by their official staffs, and the replies should be sent to the Members' offices, not to the office of the commission.

- CRS does not conduct audits or field investigations.

- CRS is not authorized to provide its services in support of political campaign organizations.

- While CRS reference and research specialists serve all Members and committees of Congress, the Director has the authority to assign staff to work temporarily for particular committees on request. In current circumstances, however, no full-time assignments may be approved, and staff assigned to close support of a committee must be available to serve other clients. When staff is adequate to permit the loan of subject specialists for short periods, the Director may approve formal requests without reimbursement; staff loans for periods of over 60 days must be reimbursed. No full-time assignment of staff is approved if the assignment leaves the Service unable to serve Congress adequately.

- As a general rule, the services of CRS are provided exclusively to Congress and, to the extent provided by law, to other congressional support agencies. Because of the benefits derived from the exchange of information with other governmental bodies (including elected and appointed officials of foreign governments), the Service may also at the discretion of the Director exchange courtesies and services of a limited nature with such organizations, so long as such assistance benefits CRS services to Congress.

- CRS does not provide its services to congressional Member organizations and informal caucuses not funded by legislative branch appropriations but will provide its normal services to the offices of Members who belong to such entities and to formal congressional party organizations. Current lists of organizations that may place requests directly are available from the Congressional Services Section.

Contact Information

Fast Access to all CRS services

- Phone 7-5700 (Press 1-5 to speak to an information specialist)
- Website http://www.crs.gov
- Fax 7-6745
- Website navigation assistance 7-7100

CRS Experts

- Phone 7-5700 (press 1-5 to request an expert)
- Dial by name 7-5700 (press 1-4 and spell last name then first name)

CRS Products

- Website (retrieve full text) http://www.crs.gov

In-Person Services and CRS Products
(Note: Hours may change when Congress is not in session.)

- Hotline (quick facts, statistics and web assistance) 7-7100
- La Follette Congressional Reading Room, Madison, LM 202, 707-7100 (7-7100)
  - Monday-Thurs: 10:00 a.m. – 8:00 p.m.; Friday: 10:00 a.m. – 6:00 p.m.; Saturday: 10:00 a.m. – 5:00 p.m. except during recess or district/state work periods.
  - When Congress is in session on a Sunday or holiday, the hours are posted on the website.
- Rayburn Research Center B355; 5-6958, Monday - Friday 10:00 a.m. – 4:00 p.m.
- Jefferson Congressional Reading Room, Jefferson 159
  - *Members of Congress Only*
  - Monday - Friday 9:00 a.m. – 5:00 p.m.

Events

- CRS Senate Center, Russell B07, 4-3550
  - Monday-Friday, 10:00 a.m. – 4:00 p.m. Doors may open earlier for events.

Programs and Training

- For information, call 7-7904 or visit http://www.crs.gov and select the Programs and Events tab.

To set up a borrowing account with the Library of Congress Collection

- Email: loanref@loc.gov

- Phone: 7-5441

- Fax: 7-5986

- To request book pick-up: 7-5717

Mailing Address

Mary B. Mazanec, Director
Congressional Research Service
The Library of Congress, LM 203
Washington, DC 20540-7210
(Note: Hill offices may use Inside Mail)

For questions, comments, or problems about CRS services, please call 7-3915.

Congressional Budget Office (CBO)

Since its founding in 1974, the Congressional Budget Office (CBO) has produced independent analyses of budgetary and economic issues to support the congressional budget process. The agency is strictly nonpartisan and conducts objective, impartial analysis, which is evident in each of the dozens of reports and hundreds of cost estimates that its economists and policy analysts produce each year. All CBO employees are appointed solely on the basis of professional competence, without regard to political affiliation. CBO does not make policy recommendations, and each report and cost estimate discloses the agency's assumptions and methodologies. All of CBO's products apart from informal cost estimates for legislation being developed privately by Members of Congress or their staffs are available to the Congress and the public on CBO's website.

CBO's Products

CBO provides budgetary and economic information in a variety of ways and at various points in the legislative process.

Baseline Budget Projections and Economic Forecasts

- CBO's reports on the budget and economic outlook cover the 10-year period used in the Congressional budget process. Those reports present and explain CBO's baseline budget projections and economic forecast, which are generally based on current law regarding federal spending and revenues. The reports also describe the differences between the current projections and previous ones, compare the economic forecast with those of other forecasters, and show the budgetary impact of some alternative policy assumptions.

- Produced: Several times annually. The budget projections and economic forecast are generally issued each January and updated in August. In addition, the budget projections are updated in March.

Analysis of the President's Budget

- CBO estimates the budgetary impact of the proposals in the President's budget using the agency's own economic forecast and estimating assumptions. CBO's independent "reestimate" of the President's budget allows the Congress to compare the Administration's spending and revenue proposals with CBO's baseline spending and revenue projections and with other proposals using a consistent set of economic and technical assumptions.

- Produced: Annually. The budgetary analysis is generally issued in March, followed in April by an analysis of the impact of the President's budgetary proposals on the economy and, in turn, indirectly on the federal budget.

Budget Options

- Periodically, CBO produces a reference volume examining options for reducing budget deficits. The volume includes a wide range of options, derived from many sources, for reducing spending and increasing revenues. For each option, the volume presents an estimate of its effects on the budget and a discussion of its pros and cons but makes no recommendations. In addition, CBO produces numerous reports (discussed below) that examine policy options for specific federal programs and aspects of the tax code.

- Produced: Generally in odd-numbered years, to correspond to the beginning of each new Congress.

Long-Term Budget Projections

- CBO provides the Congress with budget projections that go beyond the standard 10-year budget window. Those projections typically span 25 years but can extend as far as 75 years into the future. The projections show the impact of long-term demographic trends and rising health care costs on federal spending, revenues, and deficits. CBO also projects the economic impact of alternative long- term budget policies.

- Produced: Annually, usually in June.

Cost Estimates

- CBO provides formal, written estimates of the cost of virtually every bill "reported" (approved) by Congressional committees to show how the bill would affect spending or revenues over the next 5 or 10 years, depending on the type of spending involved. Each cost estimate includes a section describing the basis for the estimate. For most tax legislation, CBO uses estimates provided by the staff of the Joint Committee on Taxation, a separate group that works closely with the congressional tax-writing committees. In addition to formal, written estimates, CBO provides a far greater number of preliminary, informal estimates as committees are considering what legislation to advance, as amendments to legislation are being debated, and at other stages in the legislative process.

- Produced: Throughout the year, with formal estimates typically numbering between 500 and 700 annually.

Analyses of Federal Mandates

- CBO analyzes the costs that proposed legislation would impose on state, local, and tribal governments and on the private sector. If the estimated five-year cost of such a mandate exceeds specified thresholds, the agency reports the cost and provides the basis of the estimate. CBO produces mandate statements with its cost estimates for each committee-approved bill.

- Produced: Throughout the year. In addition, CBO produces a report each spring listing all of its work analyzing mandates in the previous year.

Monthly Budget Review

- CBO issues a monthly analysis of federal spending and revenue totals for the previous month, the current month, and the fiscal year to date. Those analyses help to inform the Congress and the public about the monthly status of the budget.

- Produced: The fifth working day of each month.

Scorekeeping for Enacted Legislation

- CBO provides the budget and appropriations committees with frequent tabulations of Congressional action affecting spending and revenues. Those scorekeeping reports provide information about whether legislative actions are consistent with the spending and revenue levels set by the budget resolution.

- Produced: Periodically during the year.

Compilations of Unauthorized Appropriations and Expiring Authorizations

- CBO prepares a report listing all programs and activities funded for the current fiscal year for which authorizations of appropriations have expired or will expire during the current fiscal year.

- Produced: Annually, in January.

Reports on the Troubled Asset Relief Program

- The Congress established the Troubled Asset Relief Program (TARP) in 2008 to stabilize financial markets. CBO regularly provides its estimate of the costs of the program and a comparison of that estimate to the preceding estimate from the Administration's Office of Management and Budget (OMB).

- Produced: Within 45 days of the TARP report produced by OMB; annually starting in 2013 and twice per year in previous years.

Reports on the American Recovery and Reinvestment Act

- The American Recovery and Reinvestment Act of 2009 (ARRA) requires CBO to comment on reports filed by recipients of ARRA funding about the number of jobs funded by ARRA. CBO's reports provide the agency's own estimates of the effects of ARRA on total output and jobs.

- Produced: Annually starting in 2013 and quarterly in previous years.

Sequestration Reports

- Under the Balanced Budget and Emergency Deficit Control Act of 1985, as amended by the Budget Control Act of 2011, CBO is required to issue reports that provide estimates of certain limits on discretionary budget authority (that is, the authority provided by appropriation acts for the government to incur financial obligations). Separately, on the basis of its own estimates, OMB will determine whether a sequestration (cancellation of budgetary resources) is required under those laws and, if so, the allocation of the cancellation of resources.

- Produced: Twice a year.

Analytic Reports

- In addition to the reports discussed above, CBO prepares analytic reports that examine specific federal programs, aspects of the tax code, and budgetary and economic challenges. The reports cover a wide range of subjects, including health care, economic growth, income security, education, taxes, energy, the environment, national security, financial issues, infrastructure, and more. Most CBO reports present a set of options for changes in the federal programs or tax rules being examined. Such reports generally include estimates of each option's budgetary effects, economic effects, or both, as well as a discussion of each option's pros and cons. As with the agency's other products, these reports make no recommendations. Some CBO reports provide background information about CBO's other analyses to enhance the transparency of the agency's work.

- Most CBO reports are written at the request of the chairman or ranking minority member of a committee or subcommittee or of the leadership of either party in the House or Senate. The agency may also present its analyses as testimony before Congressional committees rather than in report format. In addition, CBO managers and analysts sometimes make presentations to professional groups, and slides from those presentations are generally posted on CBO's website. The agency also sometimes summarizes its analyses in less traditional formats (such as infographics), and those summaries are also available on CBO's website.

- Produced: Throughout the year.

Working Papers

- CBO's working papers include papers that provide technical descriptions of official CBO analyses and papers that represent independent research by CBO analysts. Through those papers, CBO aims to enhance the transparency of its work and to encourage external review of that work. Working papers are not subject to CBO's regular review and editing process.

- Produced: Throughout the year.

Data and Technical Information

- To provide more detail about CBO's budgetary and economic projections and to add to the transparency of CBO's other analyses, the agency posts a considerable amount of data and other technical information on its website.

- Produced: Throughout the year.

CBO's Organization

The Speaker of the House of Representatives and the President pro tempore of the Senate jointly appoint the CBO Director, after considering recommendations from the two budget committees. Directors are appointed for four-year terms, and they may be reappointed to the position; in addition, a director serving at the expiration of a term may continue to serve until his or her successor is appointed. The Congressional Budget and Impoundment Control Act of 1974 specifies that CBO's director is to be chosen without regard to political affiliation.

The rest of CBO's staff, including the Deputy Director, are appointed by the Director. CBO directors have established a firm tradition of retaining staff from their predecessors. Directors appoint all CBO employees solely on the basis of professional competence, without regard to political affiliation.

Doug Elmendorf is CBO's current Director. He was initially appointed on January 22, 2009, to complete the previous four-year term of office. He was later reappointed to serve through January 3, 2015.

Offices of Senate Legal Counsel and House General Counsel

For over three decades the offices of Senate Legal Counsel and House General Counsel have developed parallel yet distinctly unique and independent roles as institutional legal "voices" of the two bodies they represent. Familiarity with the structure and operation of these offices and the nature of the support they may provide committees in the context of an investigative oversight proceeding is essential.

Senate Legal Counsel

The Office of Senate Legal Counsel[389] was created by Title VII of the Ethics in Government Act of 1978[390] "to serve the institution of Congress rather than the partisan interests of one party or another."[391] The counsel and deputy counsel are appointed by the president pro tempore of the Senate upon the recommendation of the majority and minority leaders. The appointment of each is made effective by a resolution of the Senate, and each may be removed from office by a resolution of the Senate. The term of appointment of the counsel and deputy counsel is two Congresses. The appointment of the counsel and deputy counsel and the counsel's appointment of assistant Senate Legal Counsel are required to be made without regard to political affiliation. The office is responsible to a bipartisan Joint Leadership Group, which is comprised of the majority and minority leaders, the president pro tempore, and the chairman and ranking minority member of the Committees on the Judiciary and on Rules and Administration.[392]

---

[389] A full description of the Office of Senate Legal Counsel and its work may be found in Floyd M. Riddick and Alan S. Frumin, Riddick's Senate Procedure, S.Doc. 28, 101st Cong., 2nd sess. 1236 (1992). *See* Charles Tiefer, The Senate and House Counsel Offices: Dilemmas of Representing in Court the Institutional Congressional Client, Law and Contemporary Problems, vol. 61: no. 2, spring 1998:48-63 (providing a more recent discussion of the history, development and work of both the Senate and House counsels' offices).

[390] P.L. 95-520, §§701 *et seq.*, 92 Stat. 1824, 1875 (1978), *codified principally in* 2 U.S.C. §§288, *et seq.*

[391] S.Rept. 95-170, 95th Cong., 2nd sess. 84 (1978).

[392] 2 U.S.C. §288(a) and (b), 288a.

The act specifies the activities of the office, two of which are of immediate interest to committee oversight concerns: representing committees of the Senate in proceedings to aid them in investigations, and advising committees and officers of the Senate.[393]

Proceedings to Aid Investigations by Senate Committees

The Senate Legal Counsel may represent committees in proceedings to obtain evidence for Senate investigations. Two specific proceedings are authorized.

The first proceeding is under the law providing committees the authority to grant witness immunity (18 U.S.C. §6005). It provides that a committee or subcommittee of either house of Congress may request an immunity order from a U.S. district court when the request has been approved by the affirmative vote of two-thirds of the members of the full committee. By the same vote, a committee may direct the Senate Legal Counsel to represent it or any of its subcommittees in an application for an immunity order.[394]

The second proceeding involves authority under the Ethics in Government Act of 1978 which permits the Senate Legal Counsel to represent a committee or subcommittee of the Senate in a civil action to enforce a subpoena. Prior to the Ethics Act, subpoenas of the Senate could be enforced only through the cumbersome method of a contempt proceeding before the bar of the Senate or by a certification to the U.S. attorney and a prosecution for criminal contempt of Congress under 2 U.S.C. §§ 192, 194. The Ethics Act authorizes the Senate to enforce its subpoenas through a civil action in the U.S. District Court for the District of Columbia.[395] The House chose not to avail itself of this procedure and this enforcement method applies only to Senate subpoenas. Senate subpoenas have been enforced in several civil actions. See, for example, proceedings to hold in contempt a recalcitrant witness in the impeachment proceedings against Judge Alcee L. Hastings[396] and proceedings to enforce a subpoena *duces tecum* for the production of diaries of Senator Bob Packwood.[397]

The statute details the procedure for directing the Senate Legal Counsel to bring a civil action to enforce a subpoena. In contrast to an application for an immunity order, which may be authorized by a committee, only the full Senate by resolution may authorize an action to enforce a subpoena.[398] The Senate may not consider a resolution to direct the counsel to bring an action unless the investigating committee reports the resolution by a majority vote. The statute specifies the required contents of the committee report; among other matters, the committee must report on the extent to which the subpoenaed party has complied with the subpoena, the objections or privileges asserted by the witness, and the comparative effectiveness of a criminal and civil

---

[393] In addition, the office is called upon to defend the Senate, its committees, officers and employees in civil litigation relating to their official responsibilities or when they have been subpoenaed to testify or to produce Senate records; and to appear for the Senate when it intervenes or appears as amicus curiae in a lawsuit to protect the powers or responsibilities of Congress.

[394] 2 U.S.C. §288b(d)(2), 288f.

[395] 28 U.S.C. §1365.

[396] *See* S.Rept. 98, 101st Cong., 1st sess. (1989).

[397] *See* Senate Select Committee on Ethics v. Packwood, 845 F. Supp. 17 (D.D.C. 1994), *petition for stay pending appeal denied*, 510 U.S. 1319 (1994).

[398] 2 U.S.C. §288d and 28 U.S.C. §1365.

proceeding.[399] A significant limitation on the civil enforcement remedy is that it excludes from its coverage actions against officers or employees of the federal government acting within their official capacities, except where the refusal to comply is based on the assertion of a personal privilege or objection and not on a governmental privilege or objection that has been authorized by the executive branch.[400] Its reach is limited to natural persons and to entities acting or purporting to act under the color of state law.[401]

Advice to Committees and Officers of the Senate and Other Duties

The Ethics act details a number of advisory functions of the Office of Senate Legal Counsel. Principal among these are the responsibility of advising members, committees, and officers of the Senate with respect to subpoenas or requests for the withdrawal of Senate documents, and the responsibility of advising committees about their promulgation and implementation of rules and procedures for congressional investigations. The office also provides advice about legal questions that arise during the course of investigations.[402]

The act also provides that the counsel shall perform such other duties consistent with the nonpartisan purposes and limitations of Title VII as the Senate may direct.[403] Thus, in 1980, the office was used in the investigation relating to President Carter's brother, Billy, and his connection to Libya. The office worked under the direction of the chairman and vice-chairman of the subcommittee charged with the conduct of that investigation.[404] Members of the office have also undertaken special assignments such as the Senate's investigation of "Abscam" and other undercover activities,[405] the impeachment proceedings of Judge Harry Claiborne,[406] Judge Walter L. Nixon, Jr.,[407] Judge Alcee L. Hastings Jr.,[408] Judge G. Thomas Porteous, Jr.[409] and the confirmation hearings of Justice Clarence E. Thomas. The office was called upon to assist in the Senate's conduct of the impeachment trial of President Clinton.

In addition, the counsel's office provides information and advice to members, officers, and employees on a wide range of legal and administrative matters relating to Senate business. Unlike the House practice, the Senate Legal Counsel plays no formal role in the review and issuance of subpoenas. However, since it may become involved in civil enforcement proceedings, it has welcomed the opportunity to review proposed subpoenas for form and substance prior to their issuance by committees. The Office of Senate Legal Counsel can be reached at 224-4435.

---

[399] 2 U.S.C. §288 d(c).

[400] *See* 28 U.S.C. §1365 (a).

[401] Id.

[402] 2 U.S.C. §288g(a)(5) and (6).

[403] 2 U.S. 288g(c).

[404] *See* S.Rept. 1015, 96th Cong., 2nd sess. (1980).

[405] *See* S.Rept. 682, 97th Cong., 2nd sess. (1982).

[406] *See* S.Rept. 812, 99th Cong., 2nd sess. (1986).

[407] *See* S.Rept. 164, 101st Cong., 1st sess. (1989).

[408] *See* S.Rept. 156, 101st Cong., 1st sess. (1989).

[409] *See* S. Rept. 347, 111th Cong., 2nd sess. (2010).

House General Counsel

The House Office of General Counsel has evolved since the mid-1970s, from its original role as a legal advisor to the Clerk of the House on a range of matters that fell within the jurisdiction of the Clerk's office, to that of counsel for the institution. At the beginning of the 103rd Congress, it was made a separate House office, reporting directly to the Speaker, charged with the responsibility "of providing legal assistance and representation to the House."[410] While the function and role of the House Office of General Counsel and Senate Legal Counsel with respect to oversight assistance to committees and protection of institutional prerogatives are similar, there are some differences that will be noted below.

The General Counsel, Deputy General Counsel, and other attorneys of the office are appointed by the Speaker and serve at his pleasure.[411] The office "function[s] pursuant to the direction of the Speaker, who shall consult with a Bipartisan Legal Advisory Group," which consists of the Speaker himself, the Majority Leader, Majority Whip, Minority Leader, and Minority Whip.[412] The office has statutory authority to appear before state or federal courts in the course of performing its functions. 2 U.S.C. § 130f. The office may appear as amicus curiae on behalf of the Speaker and the Bipartisan Legal Advisory Group in litigation involving the institutional interests of the House.[413] Where authorized by statute or resolution, the office may represent the House itself in judicial proceedings.[414] The office also represents House officers in litigation affecting the institutional interests and prerogatives of the House.[415] Finally, the office defends the House, its committees, officers, and employees in civil litigation relating to their official responsibilities, or when they have been subpoenaed to testify or to produce House records (see House Rule VIII).

Unlike Senate committees, House committees may only issue subpoenas under the seal of the Clerk of the House. In practice, committees often work closely with the Office of General Counsel in drafting subpoenas and every subpoena issued by a committee is reviewed by the office for substance and form. Committees frequently seek the advice and assistance of the Office of General Counsel in dealing with various asserted constitutional, statutory, and common-law privileges,[416] in responding to executive agencies and officials that resist congressional oversight,[417] and in navigating the statutory process for obtaining a contempt citation with respect to a recalcitrant witness.[418]

---

[410] *See* H. Res. 5, §11, 139 Cong. Rec. H5 (daily ed. Jan. 5, 1993).

[411] House Rule II(8) of the Rules of the 108th Congress.

[412] Id.

[413] *See, e.g.,* Elk Grove Unified School District v. Newdow, 124 S. Ct. 2301 (2004); Raines v. Byrd, 521 U.S. 811 (1997); Beverly Enterprises, Inc. v. Trump, 182 F.3d 183 (3d Cir. 1999); United States v. McDade, 28 F.3d 283 (3d Cir. 1994); Cano v. Davis, No. 01-8477 (C.D. Cal. March 28, 2002) (unpublished order granting motions to quash subpoenas to Members).

[414] *See, e.g.,* Department of Commerce v. U.S. House of Representatives, 525 U.S. 316 (1999) (litigation in which the General Counsel was authorized by statute, P.L. 105-119, §209(b) (1997), to represent the House in a challenge to the legality of the Department of Commerce's plan to use statistical sampling in the 2000 census).

[415] *See, e.g.,* Adams v. Clinton, 90 F. Supp. 2d 35, *aff'd sub nom.* Alexander v. Mineta, 531 U.S. 940, 941 (2000); Schaffer v. Clinton, 240 F.3d 878 (10th Cir. 2001); Skaggs v. Carle, 110 F.3d 831 (D.C. Cir. 1997); Newdow v. Eagen, No. 02-01704 (D.D.C. filed March 24, 2004).

[416] *See, e.g.,* H.Rept. 105-797, *In the Matter of Representative Jay Kim,* Committee on Standards of Official Conduct, 105th Cong., 2nd sess. 84-85 (Oct. 8, 1998).

[417] *See, e.g.,* Hearing, "The Attorney General's Refusal to Provide Congressional Access to 'Privileged' Inslaw (continued...)

The Office of General Counsel represents the interests of House committees in judicial proceedings in a variety of circumstances. The office represents committees in federal court on applications for immunity orders pursuant to 18 U.S.C. § 6005; appears as amicus curiae in cases affecting House committee investigations;[419] defends against attempts to obtain direct or indirect judicial interference with congressional subpoenas or other investigatory authority;[420] represents committees seeking to prevent compelled disclosure of non-public information relating to their investigatory or other legislative activities;[421] and appears in court on behalf of committees seeking judicial assistance in obtaining access to documents or information such as documents that are under seal or materials which may be protected by Rule 6(e) of the Federal Rules of Criminal Procedure.[422]

Like the Senate Legal Counsel's office, the House General Counsel's office also devotes a large portion of its time to rendering informal advice to individual members and committees. The office can be reached at (202) 225-9700. Its website address is http://generalcounsel.house.gov/, which is available only to House offices.

Government Accountability Office (GAO)

The Government Accountability Office, formerly called the General Accounting Office, was established by the Budget and Accounting Act of 1921 (31 U.S.C. § 702) as an independent auditor of government agencies. Over the years, Congress has expanded GAO's audit authority, added new responsibilities and duties, including performance, management and accountability evaluations, and strengthened GAO's ability to perform independently of the executive branch. GAO's mission is to support the Congress in meeting its constitutional responsibilities and to help improve the performance and ensure the accountability of the federal government.

GAO is led by the Comptroller General of the United States, who is appointed by the President, with the advice and consent of the Senate, from a list of candidates selected by a bipartisan, bicameral congressional commission. The Comptroller General serves a term of 15 years. GAO

(...continued)

Documents," before the Subcommittee on Economic and Commercial Law, Committee on the Judiciary, 101st Cong., 2nd sess. 77-104 (Dec. 5, 1990).

[418] *See. e.g.,* 132 Cong Rec. 3036-38 (1986) (floor consideration of contempt citation against two witnesses who refused to testify concerning alleged assistance provided to former Philippines President Ferdinand E. Marcos and his wife).

[419] *See, e.g., Dornan v. Sanchez,* 978 F. Supp. 1315, 1317 n.1 (C.D. Cal. 1997).

[420] *See, e.g., Harris v. Board of Governors,* 938 F.2d 720 (7th Cir. 1991); United States v. United States House of Representatives, 556 F. Supp. 150 (D.D.C. 1983).

[421] *See, e.g.,* Pentagon Technologies Int'l, Ltd. v. Committee on Appropriations of the United States House of Representatives, 20 F. Supp. 2d 41 (D.D.C. 1998), *aff'd* 194 F.3d 174 (D.C. Cir. 1998); United States v. McDade, No. 96-1508 (3d Cir. July 12, 1996) (unpublished order quashing subpoena to the Committee on Standards of Official Conduct); Brown & Williamson Tobacco Corp. v. Williams, 62 F.3d 408 (D.C. Cir. 1995); United States v. Arthur Andersen, LLP, No. 02-121 (S.D. Tex. filed May 15, 2002) (unpublished order quashing subpoena to the Committee on Energy and Commerce).

[422] *See, e.g.,* In re Harrisburg Grand Jury, 638 F. Supp. 43 (M.D. Pa. 1986). *Cf.* United States v. Moussaoui, No. 01-455-A, 2002 WL 1990900 (E.D. Va. Aug. 29, 2002) (order denying the "Expedited Motion of the United States for Clarification Regarding the Applicability of the Protective Order for Unclassified But Sensitive Material and Local Rule 57 to Information That May Be Made Public in Congressional Proceedings").

---

issues hundreds of reports, testimony statements, and legal opinions each year. GAO's staff are located in Washington, D.C. and in field offices throughout the country.

Working with Congress

Most GAO reports are prepared in response to requests from Members of Congress, or requirements in statute or committee or conference reports. GAO is required to do work requested by committee chairs and, as a matter of policy, assigns equal status to requests from ranking minority members, and subcommittee leaders. A small percentage of reviews are undertaken under the Comptroller General's authority. GAO's policies for accepting and prioritizing mandates and requests are laid out in its *Congressional Protocols*. GAO's Watchdog website, available on House and Senate intranet, provides information on the *Congressional Protocols*, how to request GAO reports, and information about ongoing reviews, among other things. GAO encourages Members and staff to consult with its staff when considering a request or mandate for a report.

Upon receiving a request, GAO will contact the requester to confirm acceptance, or to discuss issues needing to be resolved. Such issues are outlined in the *Protocols*, and may include:

- Existence of similar or duplicate requests. In these cases GAO may suggest consolidating requests.

- An issue in litigation. GAO will typically not undertake reviews in these circumstances

- GAO's authority to do the work and obtain data. For example, GAO does not have authority to obtain information from the private sector or state and local governments without a connection to federal spending or programs.

- Whether GAO is the most appropriate organization to undertake the work. GAO will refer to requester to other organizations in these cases.

- GAO's available resources. GAO may not have resources to undertake the scope of work requested, or may not have staff with expertise available to begin the work right away. GAO will work with the requesters on scope and priorities in these cases.

Upon beginning work, GAO will consult with requesters and conduct research to design methodologies that can answer the agreed-upon questions in an objective, fact-based, nonpartisan, nonideological, fair, and balanced way. GAO will confirm in writing the questions to be addressed, and the methodological approach.GAO will keep requesters informed throughout its work.

Approach to Work

GAO's reports typically support Congressional oversight through focusing on:

- auditing agency operations to determine whether federal funds are being spent efficiently and effectively;

- identifying opportunities to address duplication, overlap, waste or inefficiencies in the use of public funds;

- reporting on how well government programs and policies are meeting their objectives; performing policy analyses and outlining options for congressional consideration; or

- investigating allegations of illegal and improper activities.

GAO's objective is to produce high-quality reports, testimonies, briefings, and other products and services that are objective, fact-based, nonpartisan, nonideological, fair, and balanced. The agency operates under strict professional standards, including Government Auditing Standards and a quality assurance framework. GAO obtains information through surveys, interviews, database analysis, and document reviews, among other techniques. All numbers and statements of fact presented in GAO work are thoroughly checked and referenced. GAO obtains comments on its findings and recommendations from the agencies it reviews, and includes these comments in its reports.

GAO's products include oral briefings, testimony and written reports. All non-classified reports are made available to the public through posting on GAO's website. GAO can also provide technical assistance to Members and staff, based on its past work, through, for example, briefings by its subject-matter experts.

Additional Services

In addition to its audits and evaluations, GAO offers a number of other services.

Forensic Audits and Investigative Service. The Forensic Audits and Investigative Services (FAIS) team conducts forensic audits and investigations of fraud, waste, and abuse. Its primary mission is to support Congress by improving the performance and accountability of government through auditing and investigating allegations of illegal or improper conduct related to federal funds, programs, or activities. FAIS also conducts evaluations of security vulnerabilities and supports other GAO reviews where an investigative component is needed. FAIS conducts its work in accordance with the Government Auditing Standards and the standards for investigations established by the Council of Inspectors General on Integrity and Efficiency

Legal Services. GAO provides various legal services. For example, upon request, GAO may render a legal decision or opinion on questions involving the use of, and accountability for, public funds or on other legal issues of interest to congressional committees. GAO publishes the Principles of Federal Appropriations Law (known as the Red Book) and teaches a class that provides an orientation to federal fiscal laws. GAO attorneys are available for informal technical assistance. In addition, under the Competition in Contracting Act, GAO provides an objective, independent, and impartial forum for the resolution of bid protests of awards of federal contracts in 100 days. Under other authorities, GAO reviews all major rules proposed by federal agencies and provides reports to Congress; and received agency reports about vacancies in Presidentially appointed, Senate confirmed positions and issues legal opinions under the Federal Vacancies Reform Act of 1998.

Accounting and Financial Management Policy. GAO prescribes accounting principles and standards for the executive branch. The Comptroller General appoints the Advisory Council on Government Auditing Standards, which advises GAO's preparation of the *Generally Accepted Government Audit Standards*, which is used by auditors of government entities, and entities that receive government awards, among others.

Audit/Evaluation Community Support. GAO also provides other services to help the audit and evaluation community improve and keep abreast of current developments. For example, it publishes and distributes papers on current audit and evaluation methodologies and approaches; assists in various training programs sponsored by these organizations, and sponsors an international auditor fellowship program to help other nations improve their audit functions.

Committee Support. Occasionally, on request of committee leadership, GAO details staff to work for congressional committees for up to one year. In these cases, the staff assigned represent a committee and not GAO.

Contacting GAO

GAO encourages Members and staff to consult with its staff when considering a request or mandate for a report. GAO's Office of Congressional Relations (512-4400) will help identify an appropriate GAO point of contact. Additional information is available on http://www.gao.gov or the "Watchdog" site which is available only to Members and staff via the House and Senate intranets. Request letters should be addressed to:

The Honorable Gene L. Dodaro
Comptroller General of the United States
441 G Street NW
Washington DC 20548

GAO will accept letters attached to email sent to congrel@gao.gov or in hard copy. They may also be sent to staff of the Congressional Relations Office, whose contact information is listed on the Watchdog site.

Office of Management and Budget (OMB)

The Office of Management and Budget, http://www.whitehouse.gov/omb, came into existence in 1970; its predecessor agency, the Bureau of the Budget, was established in 1921. Initially created as a unit in the Treasury Department, since 1939 the agency has been a part of the Executive Office of the President (EOP).

Capabilities

OMB, though created by Congress, is the President's agent for the management and implementation of policy, including the federal budget. OMB's major responsibilities include:

- Assisting the President in the preparation of budget proposals and development of a fiscal program.

- Supervising and controlling the administration of the budget in the executive branch, including transmittal to Congress of proposals for deferrals and rescissions.

- Keeping the President informed about agencies' activities (proposed, initiated, and completed), in order to coordinate efforts, expend appropriations economically, and minimize overlap and duplication.

- Administering the process of review of draft proposed and final agency rules established by Executive Order 12866.

- Administering the process of review and approval of collections of information by federal agencies and reducing the burden of agency information collection on the public under the Paperwork Reduction Act of 1995.

- Overseeing the manner in which agencies disseminate information to the public (including electronic dissemination); how agencies collect, maintain, and use statistics; how agencies' archives are maintained; how agencies develop systems for insuring privacy, confidentiality, security, and the sharing of information collected by the government; and how the government acquires and uses information technology, pursuant to the Paperwork Reduction Act of 1995, the Clinger-Cohen Act of 1996, and other legislation.

- Studying and promoting better governmental management, including making recommendations to agencies regarding their administrative organization and operations.

- Clearing and coordinating agencies' draft testimony and legislative proposals and making recommendations about presidential action on legislation.

- Assisting in the preparation, consideration, and clearance of executive orders and proclamations.

- Planning and developing information systems that provide the President with agency and program performance data.

- Establishing and overseeing implementation of financial management policies and requirements for the federal government as required by the Chief Financial Officers Act of 1990.

- Assisting in development of regulatory reform proposals and programs for paperwork reduction, and then the implementation of these initiatives.

- Improving the economy and efficiency of the federal procurement process by providing overall direction for procurement policies, regulations, procedures, and forms.

- Establishing policies and methods that reduce fraud, waste, and abuse, and coordinating the work of the inspectors general through the Council of the Inspectors General on Integrity and Efficiency (P.L. 110-409).

Limitations

OMB is inevitably drawn into institutional and partisan struggles between the President and Congress. Difficulties for Congress notwithstanding, OMB is the central clearinghouse for executive agencies and is, therefore, a rich source of information for investigative and oversight committees.

Budget Information

Since enactment of the 1974 Budget Act, as amended, Congress has more budgetary information than ever before. Extensive budgetary materials are also available from the executive branch.

Some of the major sources of budgetary information are available on and off Capitol Hill. They include (1) the President and executive agencies (recall that under the Budget and Accounting Act of 1921, the President presents annually a national budget to Congress); (2) the Congressional Budget Office; (3) the House and Senate Budget Committees; (4) the House and Senate Appropriations Committees; and (5) the House and Senate legislative committees. In addition, CRS and GAO prepare reports that address the budget and related issues.

Worth mention is that discretionary spending, the component of the budget that the Appropriations Committees oversee through the appropriations process, accounts for about one-third of federal spending. Other House and Senate committees, particularly Ways and Means and Finance, oversee more than $1 trillion in spending through reauthorizations, direct spending measures, and reconciliation legislation. In addition, Ways and Means and Finance oversee a diverse set of programs, including tax collection, tax expenditures, and some user fees, through the revenue process. The oversight activities of all of these committees is enhanced through the use of the diverse range of budgetary information that is available to them.

Executive Branch Budget Products

Budget of the United States Government, Fiscal Year 2012 contains the Budget Message of the President and information on the President's budget proposals by budget function.

Analytical Perspectives, Budget of the United States Government, Fiscal Year 2012 contains analyses that are designed to highlight specified subject areas or provide other significant presentations of budget data that place the budget in perspective. This volume includes economic and accounting analyses; information on Federal receipts and collections; analyses of Federal spending; information on Federal borrowing and debt; baseline or current services estimates; and other technical presentations. The Analytical Perspectives volume also contains supplemental material with several detailed tables, including tables showing the budget by agency and account and by function, subfunction, and program, that is available on the Internet and as a CD-ROM in the printed document.

Historical Tables provides data on budget receipts, outlays, surpluses or deficits, Federal debt, and Federal employment over an extended time period, generally from 1940 or earlier to 2012 or 2015. To the extent feasible, the data have been adjusted to provide consistency with the 2012 Budget and to provide comparability over time.

The Appendix, Budget of the United States Government, Fiscal Year 2012 contains detailed information on the various appropriations and funds that constitute the budget. The Appendix contains financial information on individual programs and appropriation accounts. It includes for each agency: the proposed text of appropriations language; budget schedules for each account; legislative proposals; explanations of the work to be performed and the funds needed; and proposed general provisions applicable to the appropriations of entire agencies or group of agencies. Information is also provided on certain activities whose transactions are not part of the budget totals.

Several other points about the President's budget and executive agency budget products are worth noting. First, the President's budgetary communications to Congress continue after the January/February submission and usually include a series of budget amendments and supplementals, the Mid-Session Review, Statements of Administration Policy (SAPs) on legislation, and even revised budgets on occasion. Second, most of these additional communications are issued as House documents and are available on the web from GPO Access or the OMB Home Page (in the case of SAPs). Third, the initial budget products often do not provide sufficient information on the President's budgetary recommendations to enable committees to begin developing legislation, and that further budgetary information is provided in the "justification" materials (see below) and the later submission of legislative proposals. Finally, the internal executive papers (such as agency budget submissions to OMB) often are not made available to Congress.

Some Other Sources of Useful Budgetary Information

Committees on Appropriations. The subcommittees of the House and Senate Appropriations Committees hold extensive hearings on the fiscal year appropriations requests of federal departments and agencies. Each federal department or agency submits *justification material* to the Committees on Appropriations. Their submissions can run from several hundreds of pages to over two thousand pages. The Appropriations Subcommittees typically print this material with the hearing record of the federal officials concerning these requests.

Budget Committees. House and Senate Budget Committees, in preparing to report the annual concurrent budget resolution, conduct hearings on overall federal budget policy. These hearings and other fiscal analyses made by these panels address various aspects of federal programs and funding levels which can be useful sources of information.

Other Committees. To assist the Budget Committees in developing the concurrent budget resolution, other committees are required to prepare "views and estimates" of programs in their jurisdiction. Committee views and estimates, usually packaged together and issued as a committee print, also may be a useful source of detailed budget data.

Internal Agency Studies and Budget Reviews. These agency studies and reviews are often conducted in support of budget formulation and can yield useful information about individual programs. The budgeting documents, evaluations, and priority rankings of individual agency programs can provide insights into executive branch views of the importance of individual programs.

Beneficiaries, Private Organizations, and Interest Groups

Committees and members can acquire useful information about executive branch programs and performance from the beneficiaries of those programs, private organizations, and interest groups. An effective oversight device, for example, is to ask beneficiaries how well federal programs and services are working. A variety of methods might be employed to solicit the views of those on the receiving end of federal programs and services, including investigations and hearings, field and on-site meetings, surveys and opinion polls, and websites. The results of such efforts can assist committees in obtaining policy-relevant information about program performance and in evaluating the problems people might be having with federal administrators and agencies.

There are numerous think tanks, universities, or associations, for instance, that periodically conduct studies of public policy issues and advise members and others on how well federal agencies and programs are working. Similarly, numerous interest groups are active in monitoring areas such as civil rights, education, or health and they are not reluctant to point out alleged bureaucratic failings to committees and members. Some of these groups may also assist committees and members in bringing about improvements in agencies and programs. For example, the Project on Government Oversight (POGO), an independent, nonprofit organization, that seeks a more effective, accountable, open, and ethical federal government. The group's web site is: http://www.pogo.org.

There are also scores of social, political, scientific, environmental, and humanitarian nongovernmental organizations (NGOs) located around the world. Working with governments, corporations, foundations, and other entities are such NGOs as Greenpeace, Amnesty International, the World Resources Institute, the Red Cross, and the Save the Children Fund. Many NGOs might provide valuable assistance to congressional overseers because they "do legal, scientific, technical, and policy analysis; provide services; shape, implement, monitor, and enforce national and international commitments; and change institutions and norms."[423]

---

[423] Jim Bencivenga, "Critical Mass," *Christian Science Monitor*, February 3, 2000, p. 15. Also see "NGOs," *The Economist*, January 29, 2000, pp. 25-27.

Appendix A. Illustrative Subpoena

Subpena Duces Tecum

𝔅𝔶 𝔄𝔲𝔱𝔥𝔬𝔯𝔦𝔱𝔶 𝔬𝔣 𝔱𝔥𝔢 𝔥𝔬𝔲𝔰𝔢 𝔬𝔣 𝔚𝔢𝔭𝔯𝔢𝔰𝔢𝔫𝔱𝔞𝔱𝔦𝔟𝔢𝔰 𝔬𝔣 𝔱𝔥𝔢 ℭ𝔬𝔫𝔤𝔯𝔢𝔰𝔰 𝔬𝔣 𝔱𝔥𝔢 𝔘𝔫𝔦𝔱𝔢𝔡 𝔖𝔱𝔞𝔱𝔢𝔰 𝔬𝔣 𝔄𝔪𝔢𝔯𝔦𝔠𝔞

———

To ..Custodian.of.Documents.International.Brotherhood.of.Teamsters..............

You are hereby commanded to produce the things identified on the attached schedule before the Subcommittee on Oversight
and..Investigations. Committee on ...Education.and.the.Workforce...............................

of the House of Representatives of the United States, of which the Hon. Pete.Hoekstra..........

.... is chairman, by producing such things in Room ...B-346A... of the

..........Rayburn.............. Building ...., in the city of Washington, on

..........March..17,..1998......, at the hour of ....5:00..p.m................

To .Any..staff.member.or.agent.of.the.Committee.on.Education.and.the.Workfor
of the age of 18 years or older or to any United States Marshal
to serve and make return.

Witness my hand and the seal of the House of Representatives

of the United States, .at the city of Washington, this

.....10th..... day of ......March................., 19..98...

Peter Hoekstra

The Honorable Pete Hoekstra   *Chairman.*

Attest:

....
    Clerk.

Subpena for..Custodian.of.Documents....

International.Brotherhood.of.Teamsters

25.Louisiana.Avenue,.N.W....................

Washington,.D.C..20001......................

before the Committee on the.Education....

and.the.Workforce,.Subcommittee.on.

Oversight.and.Investigations...........

Served........ ....

....

....

....

....

....

....

...........................House of Representatives

GENERAL INSTRUCTIONS

1. In complying with this Subpoena, you are required to produce all responsive documents that are in your possession, custody, or control, whether held by you or your past or present agents, employees, and representatives acting on your behalf. You are also required to produce documents that you have a legal right to obtain, documents that you have a right to copy or have access to, and documents that you have placed in the temporary possession, custody, or control of any third party. No records, documents, data or information called for by this request shall be destroyed, modified, removed or otherwise made inaccessible to the Committee.

2. In the event that any entity, organization or individual denoted in this subpoena has been, or is also known by any other name than that herein denoted, the subpoena shall be read to also include them under that alternative identification.

3. Each document produced shall be produced in a form that renders the document susceptible of copying.

4. Documents produced in response to this subpoena shall be produced together with copies of file labels, dividers or identifying markers with which they were associated when this subpoena

was served. Also identify to which paragraph from the subpoena that such documents are responsive.

5. It shall not be a basis for refusal to produce documents that any other person or entity also possesses non-identical or identical copies of the same document.

6. If any of the subpoenaed information is available in machine-readable form (such as punch cards, paper or magnetic tapes, drums, disks, or core storage), state the form in which it is available and provide sufficient detail to allow the information to be copied to a readable format. If the information requested is stored in a computer, indicate whether you have an existing program that will print the records in a readable form.

7. If the subpoena cannot be complied with in full, it shall be complied with to the extent possible, which shall include an explanation of why full compliance is not possible.

8. In the event that a document is withheld on the basis of privilege, provide the following information concerning any such document: (a) the privilege asserted; (b) the type of document; (c) the general subject matter; (d) the date, author and addressee; and (e) the relationship of the author and addressee to each other.

9. If any document responsive to this subpoena was, but no longer is, in your possession, custody, or control, identify the document (stating its date, author, subject and recipients) and explain the circumstances by which the document ceased to be in your possession, or control.

10. If a date set forth in this subpoena referring to a communication, meeting, or other event is inaccurate, but the actual date is known to you or is otherwise apparent from the context of the request, you should produce all documents which would be responsive as if the date were correct.

11. Other than subpoena questions directed at the activities of specified entities or persons, to the extent that information contained in documents sought by this subpoena may require production of donor lists, or information otherwise enabling the re-creation of donor lists, such identifying information may be redacted.

12. The time period covered by this subpoena is included in the attached Schedule A.

13. This request is continuing in nature. Any record, document, compilation of data or information, not produced because it has not been located or discovered by the return date, shall be produced immediately upon location or discovery subsequent thereto.

14. All documents shall be Bates stamped sequentially and produced sequentially.

15. Two sets of documents shall be delivered, one set for the Majority Staff and one set for the Minority Staff. When documents are produced to the Subcommittee, production sets shall be delivered to the Majority Staff in Room B346 Rayburn House Office Building and the Minority Staff in Room 2101 Rayburn House Office Building.

GENERAL DEFINITIONS

1. The term "document" means any written, recorded, or graphic matter of any nature whatsoever, regardless of how recorded, and whether original or copy, including, but not limited to, the

following: memoranda, reports, expense reports, books, manuals, instructions, financial reports, working papers, records notes, letters, notices, confirmations, telegrams, receipts, appraisals, pamphlets, magazines, newspapers, prospectuses, interoffice and intra office communications, electronic mail (E-mail), contracts, cables, notations of any type of conversation, telephone call, meeting or other communication, bulletins, printed matter, computer printouts, teletypes, invoices, transcripts, diaries, analyses, returns, summaries, minutes, bills, accounts, estimates, projections, comparisons, messages, correspondence, press releases, circulars, financial statements, reviews, opinions, offers, studies and investigations, questionnaires and surveys, and work sheets (and all drafts, preliminary versions, alterations, modifications, revisions, changes, and amendments of any of the foregoing, as well as any attachments or appendices thereto), and graphic or oral records or representations of any kind (including without limitation, photographs, charts, graphs, microfiche, microfilm, videotape, recordings and motion pictures), and electronic, mechanical, and electric records or representations of any kind (including, without limitation, tapes, cassettes, discs, and recordings) and other written, printed, typed, or other graphic or recorded matter of any kind or nature, however produced or reproduced, and whether preserved in writing, film, tape, disc, or videotape. A documents bearing any notation not a part of the original text is to be considered a separate document. A draft or non-identical copy is a separate document within the meaning of this term.

2. The term "communication" means each manner or means of disclosure or exchange of information, regardless of means utilized, whether oral, electronic, by document or otherwise, and whether face to face, in a meeting, by telephone, mail, telexes, discussions, releases, personal delivery, or otherwise.

3. The terms "and" and "or" shall be construed broadly and either conjunctively or disjunctively to bring within the scope of this subpoena any information which might otherwise be construed to be outside its scope. The singular includes plural number, and vice versa. The masculine includes the feminine and neuter genders.

4. The term "White House" refers to the Executive Office of the President and all of its units including, without limitation, the Office of Administration, the White House Office, the Office of the Vice President, the Office of Science and Technology Policy, the Office of Management and Budget, the United States Trade Representative, the Office of Public Liaison, the Office of Correspondence, the Office of the Deputy Chief of Staff for Policy and Political Affairs, the Office of the Deputy Chief of Staff for White House Operations, the Domestic Policy Council, the Office of Federal Procurement Policy, the Office of Intergovernmental Affairs, the Office of Legislative Affairs, Media Affairs, the National Economic Council, the Office of Policy Development, the Office of Political Affairs, the Office of Presidential Personnel, the Office of the Press Secretary, the Office of Scheduling and Advance, the Council of Economic Advisors, the Council on Environmental Quality, the Executive Residence, the President's Foreign Intelligence Advisory Board, the National Security Council, the Office of National Drug Control, and the Office of Policy Development.

March 10, 1998

Custodian of Documents
International Brotherhood of Teamsters
25 Louisiana Avenue, N.W.
Washington, D.C. 20001

SCHEDULE A

1. All organizational charts and personnel rosters for the International Brotherhood of Teamsters ("Teamsters" or "IBT"), including the DRIVE PAC, in effect during calendar years 1991 through 1997.

2. All IBT operating, finance, and administrative *manuals* in effect during calendar years 1991 through 1997, including, but not limited to those that set forth (1) operating policies, practices, and procedures; (2) internal financial practices and reporting requirements; and (3) authorization, approval, and review responsibilities.

3. All annual audit reports of the IBT for the years 1991 through 1996 performed by the auditing firm of Grant Thornton.

4. All IBT annual reports to its membership and the public for years 1991 through 1997, including copies of IBT annual audited financial statements certified to by independent public accountants.

5. All books and records showing receipts and expenditures, assets and liabilities, profits and losses, and all other records used for recording the financial affairs of the IBT including, journals (or other books of original entry) and ledgers including cash receipts journals, cash disbursements journals, revenue journals, general journals, subledgers, and workpapers reflecting accounting entries.

6. All Federal Income Tax returns filed by the IBT for years 1991 through 1997.

7. All minutes of the General Board, Executive Board, Executive Council, and all Standing Committees, including any internal ethics committees formed to investigate misconduct and corruption, and all handouts and reports prepared and produced at each Committee meeting.

8. All documents referring or relating to, or containing information about, any contribution, donation, expenditure, outlay, in-kind assistance, transfer, loan, or grant (from DRIVE, DRIVE E&L fund, or IBT general treasury) to any of the following entities/organizations:

   a. Citizen Action

   b. Campaign for a Responsible Congress

   c. Project Vote

   d. National Council of Senior Citizens

   e. Vote Now '96

   f. AFL-CIO

   g. AFSCME

   h. Democratic National Committee

   i. Democratic Senatorial Campaign Committee ("DSCC")

j. Democratic Congressional Campaign Committee ("DCCC")

k. State Democratic Parties

1. Clinton-Gore '96

m. SEIU

9. All documents referring or relating to, or containing information about any of the following individuals/entities:

a. Teamsters for a Corruption Free Union

b. Teamsters for a Democratic Union

c. Concerned Teamsters 2000

d. Martin Davis

e. Michael Ansara

f. Jere Nash

g. Share Group

h. November Group

i. Terrence McAuliffe

j. Charles Blitz

k. New Party

1. James P. Hoffa Campaign

m. Delancy Printing

n. Axis Enterprises

o. Barbara Arnold

p. Peter McGourty

q. Charles McDonald

r. Theodore Kheel

10. All documents referring or relating to, or containing information on about, communications between the Teamsters and the White House regarding any of the following issues:

a. United Parcel Service Strike

b. Diamond Walnut Company Strike

c. Pony Express Company organizing efforts

d. Davis Bacon Act

e. NAFTA Border Crossings

f. Ron Carey reelection campaign

g. IBT support to 1996 federal election campaigns.

i. All documents referring or relating to, or containing information about, communications between the Teamsters and the Federal Election Commission.

12. All documents referring or relating to, or containing information about, communications between the Teamsters and the Democratic National Committee, DSCC, or DCCC.

13. All documents referring or relating to, or containing information about, communications between the Teamsters and the Clinton-Gore '96 Campaign Committee.

14. All documents referring or relating to, or containing information about, policies and procedures in effect during 1996 regarding the approval of expenditures from the IBT general treasury, DRIVE E&L fund, and DRIVE PAC.

15. All documents referring or relating to, or containing information about the retention by the IBT of the law firm Covington & Burling and/or Charles Ruff.

16. All documents referring or relating to, or containing information about work for the IBT performed by the firm Palladino & Sutherland and/or Jack Palladino.

17. All documents referring or relating to, or containing information about work for the IBT performed by Ace Investigations and/or Guerrieri, Edmund, and James.

18. All documents referring or relating to, or containing information about IBT involvement in the 1995-1996 Oregon Senate race (Ron Wyden vs. Gordon Smith).

19. All documents referring or relating to, or containing information about, Ron Carey's campaign for reelection as general president of the Teamsters.

20. All documents referring or relating to, or containing information about organization, planning, and operation of the 1996 IBT Convention.

21. All documents referring or relating to, or containing information about the following:

a. Trish Hoppey

b. John Latz

c. any individual with the last name of "Golovner".

d. Convention Management Group.

22. All documents referring or relating to, or containing information about the Household Finance Corporation.

23. All documents referring or relating to, or containing information about, any "affinity credit card" program or other credit card program sponsored by or participated in by the IBT.

24. A list of all bank accounts held by the International Brotherhood of Teamsters including the name of the bank, account number, and bank address.

25. All documents referring or relating to, or containing information about, payments made by the IBT to any official or employee of the Independent Review Board.

26. Unless otherwise indicated, the time period covered by this subpoena is between January 1991 and December 1997.

Appendix B. Examples of White House Response to Congressional Requests

THE WHITE HOUSE

November 4, 1982

MEMORANDUM FOR THE HEADS OF EXECUTIVE DEPARTMENTS AND AGENCIES

SUBJECT: Procedures Governing Responses to Congressional Request for Information

The policy of this administration is to comply with Congressional Requests for information to the fullest extent consistent with the constitutional and statutory obligations of the Executive Branch. While this Administration, like its predecessors, has an obligation to protect the confidentiality of some communications, executive privilege will be asserted only in the most compelling circumstances, and only after careful review demonstrates that assertion of the privilege is necessary. Historically, good faith negotiations between Congress and the executive branch has minimized the need for invoking executive privilege, and this tradition of accommodation should continue as the primary means of resolving conflicts between the Branches. To ensure that every reasonable accommodation is made to the needs of Congress, executive privilege shall not be invoked without specific Presidential authorization.

The Supreme Court has held that the Executive Branch may occasionally find it necessary and proper to preserve the confidentiality of national security secrets, deliberative communications that form a part of the decision-making process, or other information important to the discharge of the Executive Branch's constitutional responsibilities. Legitimate and appropriate claims of privilege should not thoughtlessly be waived. However, to ensure that this Administration acts responsibly and consistently in the exercise of its duties, with due regard for the responsibilities and prerogatives of Congress, the following procedures shall be followed whenever Congressional requests for information raise concerns regarding the confidentiality of the information sought:

1. Congressional requests for information shall be complied with as promptly and as fully as possible, unless it is determined that compliance raises a substantial question of executive privilege. A "substantial question of executive privilege" exists if disclosure of the information requested might significantly impair the national security (including the conduct of foreign relations), the deliberative processes of the Executive Branch or other aspects of the performance of the Executive Branch's constitutional duties.

2. If the head of an executive department or agency ("Department Head") believes, after consultation with department counsel, that compliance with a Congressional request for information raises a substantial question of executive privilege, he shall promptly notify and consult with the Attorney General through the Assistant Attorney General for the Office of Legal Counsel, and shall also promptly notify and consult with the Counsel to the President. If the information requested of a department or agency derives in whole or in part or from information received from another department or agency, the latter entity shall also be consulted as to whether disclosure of the information raises a substantial question of executive privilege.

3. Every effort shall be made to comply with the Congressional request in a manner consistent with the legitimate needs of the Executive Branch. The Department Head, the Attorney "General and the Counsel to the President may, in the exercise of their discretion in the circumstances, determine that executive privilege shall not be invoked and release the requested information.

4. If the Department Head, the Attorney General or the Counsel to the President believes, after consultation, that the circumstances justify invocation of executive privilege, the issue shall be presented to the President by the Counsel to the President, who will advise the Department Head and the Attorney General of the President's decision.

5. Pending a final Presidential decision on the matter, the Department Head shall request the Congressional body to hold its request for the information in abeyance. The Department Head shall expressly indicate that the purpose of this request is to protect the privilege pending a Presidential decision, claim of privilege.

6. If the President decides to invoke executive privilege, the Department Head shall advise the requesting Congressional body that the claim of executive privilege is being made with the specific approval of the President.

Any questions concerning these procedures or related matters should be addressed to the Attorney General, through the Assistant Attorney General for the Office of Legal Counsel, and to the Counsel to the President.

Ronald Reagan

THE WHITE HOUSE

September 28, 1994

MEMORANDUM FOR ALL EXECUTIVE DEPARTMENT AND AGENCY GENERAL COUNSELS

FROM: LLOYD N. CUTLER, SPECIAL COUNSEL TO THE PRESIDENT

SUBJECT: Congressional Requests to Departments and Agencies for Documents Protected by Executive Privilege

The policy of this Administration is to comply with congressional requests for information to the fullest extent consistent with the constitutional and statutory obligations of the Executive Branch. While this Administration, like its predecessors, has an obligation to protect the confidentiality of core communications, executive privilege will be asserted only after careful review demonstrates that assertion of the privilege is necessary to protect Executive Branch prerogatives.

The doctrine of executive privilege protects the confidentiality of deliberations within the White House, including its policy councils, as well as communications between the White House and executive departments and agencies. Executive privilege applies to written and oral communications between and among the White House, its policy councils and Executive Branch agencies, as well as to documents that describe or prepares for such communications (e.g.

"talking points"). This has been the view expressed by all recent White House Counsels. In circumstances involving communications relating to investigations of personal wrongdoing by government officials, it is our practice not to assert executive privilege, either, in judicial proceedings or in congressional investigations and hearings. Executive privilege must always be weighed against other competing governmental interests, including the judicial need to obtain relevant evidence, especially in criminal proceedings, and the congressional need to make factual findings for legislative and oversight purposes.

In the last resort, this balancing is usually conducted by the courts. However, when executive privilege is asserted against a congressional request for documents, the courts usually decline to intervene until after the other two branches have exhausted the possibility of working out a satisfactory accommodation. It is our policy to work out such an accommodation whenever we can, without unduly interfering with the President's need to conduct frank exchange of views with his principal advisors.

Historically, good faith negotiations between Congress and the Executive Branch have minimized the need for invoking executive privilege.

Executive privilege belongs to the President, not individual departments or agencies. It is essential that all requests to departments and agencies for information of the type described above be referred to the White House Counsel before any information is furnished. Departments and agencies receiving such request should therefore follow the procedures set forth below, designed to ensure that this Administration acts responsibly and consistently with respect to executive privilege issues, with due regard for the responsibilities and prerogatives of Congress:

First, any document created in the White House, including a White House policy council, or in a department or agency, that contains the deliberations of, or advice to or from, the White House, should be presumptively treated as protected by executive privilege. This is so regardless of the document's location at the time of the request or whether it originated in the White House or in a department or agency.

Second, a department or agency receiving a request for any such document should promptly notify the White House Counsel's Office, and direct any inquiries regarding such a document to the White House Counsel's Office.

Third, the White House Counsel's Office, working together with the department or agency (and, where appropriate, the Department of Justice), will discuss the request with appropriate congressional representatives to determine whether a mutually satisfactory recommendation is available.

Fourth, if efforts to reach a mutually satisfactory accommodation are unsuccessful, and if release of the document would pass a substantial question of executive privilege, the Counsel to the President will consult with the Department of Justice and other affected agencies to determine whether to recommend that the President invoke the privilege.

We believe this policy will facilitate the resolution of issues relating to disclosures to Congress and maximize the opportunity for reaching mutually satisfactory accommodations with Congress. We will of course try to cooperate with reasonable congressional requests for information in ways that preserve the President's ability to exchange frank advice with his immediate staff and the heads of the executive departments and agencies.

Appendix C. Selected Readings

Aberbach, Joel D. Keeping a Watchful Eye: The Politics of Congressional Oversight. Washington: Brookings Institution, 1990. JK585.A63

Congressional Oversight: Methods and Techniques. Committee Print, Prepared for the Subcommittee on Oversight Procedures of the Senate Committee on Government Operations by the Congressional Research Service and the General Accounting Office, 94th Congress, 2nd session. Washington: GPO, 1976.

Fisher, Louis. Constitutional Conflicts between Congress and the President. Lawrence, Kansas: University Press of Kansas, 2007, 5th Revised Edition. KF4565.F57 1997.

Foreman, Christopher H. Signals from the Hill: Congressional Oversight and the Challenge of Social Regulation. New Haven: Yale University Press, 1988. JK585.F68

Hamilton, James. The Power to Probe: A Study of Congressional Investigations. New York: Vintage Books, 1976.

Harris, Joseph P. Congressional Control of Administration. Washington: Brookings Institution, 1964. JK1061.H3

History of the United States House of Representatives, 1789-1994. H.Doc. 103-324, 103rd Congress, 2nd session. Washington: GPO, 1994. Chapter XI, "Oversight," pp. 233-266.

CRS Report 97-936, *Congressional Oversight*, by Elaine Halchin and Frederick M. Kaiser.

_____. Congressional Oversight of the Presidency. Annals, vol. 499, September 1988, pp. 75-89.

CRS Report RL32113, *Congressional Intervention in the Administrative Process: Legal and Ethical Considerations*, by Jack Maskell.

CRS Report RL32617, *A Perspective on Congress's Oversight Function*, by Walter J. Oleszek.

Mayhew, David R. Divided We Govern: Party Control, Lawmaking, and Investigations, 1946-1990. New Haven: Yale University Press, 1991. JK2261.M36

McCubbins, Mathew D. and Thomas Schwartz. Congressional Oversight Overlooked: Police Patrol Versus Fire Alarms. American Journal of Political Science, vol. 2, February 1984, pp. 165-79.

National Academy of Public Administration. Panel on Congress and the Executive. Beyond Distrust: Building Bridges Between Congress and the Executive. Washington: NAPA, 1992.

Ogul, Morris S. Congress Oversees the Bureaucracy: Studies in Legislative Supervision. Pittsburgh: University of Pittsburgh Press, 1976. JK585.O48

Oleszek, Walter J. Congressional Procedures and the Policy Process, 6th ed. Washington: Congressional Quarterly Press, 2004. Chapter 10, Legislative Oversight. KF4937.O44

Ornstein, Norman F. and Thomas E. Mann. When Congress Checks Out. Foreign Affairs, vol. 85, 2006, pp. 67-80.

Rosenberg, Morton. Congress's Prerogative Over Agencies and Agency Decisionmakers: The Rise and Demise of the Reagan Administration's Theory of the Unitary Executive. George Washington Law Review, vol. 57, January 1989, pp. 627-703.

Rosenbloom, David H. Building a Legislative-Centered Public Administration: Congress and the Administrative State, 1946-1999. Tuscaloosa, Ala.: The University of Alabama Press, 2000. KF1601.R58

Schlesinger, Arthur M. and Roger Bruns, eds. Congress Investigates: A Documented History, 1792-1974 (5 vols.) New York: Chelsea House Publishers, 1975. JK1123.A2S34

Study on Federal Regulation: Congressional Oversight of Regulatory Agencies. Senate Doc. 95-26, 95th Congress, 1st session. Washington: GPO, 1977.

U.S. General Accounting Office. Investigators' Guide to Sources of Information. GAO Report OSI-97-2. Washington: GAO, 1997.

West, William F. Controlling the Bureaucracy: Institutional Constraints in Theory and Practice. Armonk, New York and London, England: M.E. Sharpe: 1995. JK421.W44

The Budget Process

Fisher, Louis. Presidential Spending Power. Princeton, N.J.: Princeton University Press, 1975. 345 p. HJ257.2.F57

CRS Report 98-720, *Manual on the Federal Budget Process*, by Robert Keith and Allen Schick.

Schick, Allen. Congress and Money. Washington: Urban Institute, 1980. 604 p. HJ2051.S34

Wilmerding, Lucius, Jr. The Spending Power: A History of the Efforts of Congress to Control Expenditures. New Haven, Conn.: Yale University Press, 1943. 317 p. HJ2013.U5W5

Authorization and Appropriation Processes

Devins, Neal E. Regulation of Government Agencies Through Limitation Riders, Duke Law Journal, v. 1987, 1987:456.

Fisher, Louis. Annual Authorizations: Durable Roadblocks to Biennial Budgeting, Public Budgeting & Finance, v. 3, Spring 1983: 24.

_____. The Authorization-Appropriation Process in Congress: Formal Rules and Informal Practices, Catholic University Law Review, v. 29, 1979: 51.

Fenno, Richard F., Jr. The Power of the Purse. Boston, Mass.: Little, Brown, 1966. 704 p. JK1074.F4

LeBoeuf, Jacques B. Limitations on the Use of Appropriations Riders by Congress to Effectuate Substantive Policy Changes, Hastings Constitutional Law Quarterly, v. 19, Winter 1992: 457.

LeLoup, Lance T. Appropriations Politics in Congress: The House Appropriations Committee and the Executive Agencies, Public Budgeting & Finance, v. 4, Winter 1984: 78.

U.S. General Accounting Office, Office of the General Counsel. Principles of Federal Appropriations Law. Vols. I, II, and III. 2004.

The Confirmation Process

Carter, Stephen L. The Confirmation Mess: Cleaning Up the Federal Appointments Process. New York: Basic Books, 1994. 252 p. JK736.C37

Gerhardt, Michael J. The Federal Appointments Process. Durham and London: Duke University Press, 2000. 400 p. JK731.G47

_____. Toward a Comprehensive Understanding of the Federal Appointments Process, Harvard Journal of Law and Public Policy, v. 21, no. 4, 1998: 468.

Harris, Joseph P. The Advice and Consent of the Senate: A Study of the Confirmation of Appointments by the United States Senate. Berkeley, Cal.: University of California Press, 1953. 457 p. JK1274.H3

Hogue, Henry. The Law: Recess Appointments to Article III Courts, Presidential Studies Quarterly, v. 34, 2004: 656.

Haynes, George H. The Senate of the United States: Its History and Practice. Boston, Mass.: Houghton Mifflin Co., 1938. 2 vols. 1118 p. JK1161.H28

Kim, Haeryon. Congressional Influence on the FCC: An Analysis of Confirmation Hearings for Commission Chairmen, 1969-1989, Communications and the Law, v. 15, 1993: 37.

Mackenzie, G. Calvin. The Politics of Presidential Appointments. New York: The Free Press, 1981. 298 p. JK736.M33

CRS Report RL32551, *9/11 Commission Recommendations: The Senate Confirmation Process for Presidential Nominees*, by Betsy Palmer.

Ross, William G. The Senate's Constitutional Role in Confirming Cabinet Nominees and Other Executive Officials, Syracuse Law Review, vol. 48, 1998: 1123.

The Impeachment Process

Bazan, Elizabeth B. *Impeachment: An Overview of Constitutional Provisions, Procedure, and Practice.* CRS Report 99-186 (out of print; available from the authors).

Black, Charles L., Jr. Impeachment: A Handbook. New Haven, Conn.: Yale University Press, 1974. 80 p. LC 73-92315

Bushnell, Eleanor. Crimes, Follies, and Misfortunes: The Federal Impeachment Trials. Urbana, Ill.: University of Chicago Press, 1992. 380 p. KF8781.B87

Gerhardt, Michael J. The Federal Impeachment Process: A Constitutional and Historical Analysis. Princeton, N.J.: Princeton University Press, 1996. 233 p. KF4958.G47

Labowitz, John R. Presidential Impeachment. New Haven: Yale University Press, 1978. 257 p. KF5075.L33

Maskell, Jack. *Censure of the President by the Congress.* CRS Report 98-343 (out of print; available from the authors).

Posner, Richard A. An Affair of State: The Investigation, Impeachment, and Trial of President Clinton. Cambridge, Mass.: Harvard University Press, 1999. 276 p. KF5076.C57P67

Rae, Nicol C. and Colton C. Campbell. Impeaching Clinton: Partisan Strife on Capitol Hill. Lawrence: University Press of Kansas, 2004. 234 p. E886.2.R435

Rehnquist, William H. Grand Inquests: The Historic Impeachments of Justice Samuel Chase and President Andrew Johnson. New York: William Morrow and Co., 1992. 303 p. E302.6C4R44

U.S. Congress. Impeachment: Selected Materials, Committee on the Judiciary, House of Representatives, 93rd Congress, 1st session, October 1973. 718 p.

_____. Impeachment: Selected Materials on Procedure, Committee on the Judiciary, House of Representatives, 93rd Congress, 2nd session, January 1974. 900 p.

_____. Constitutional Grounds for Impeachment: Modern Precedents, Committee on the Judiciary, House of Representatives, 105th Congress, 2nd session, Ser. No. 9, November 1998. 94 p.

_____. Impeachment: Selected Materials, Committee on the Judiciary, House of Representatives, 105th Congress, 2nd session, Ser. No. 10, November 1998. 1854 p.

The Investigative Process

Beard, Glenn A. Congress v. The Attorney-Client Privilege: A "Full and Frank" Discussion, American Criminal Law Review, v. 35, 1997: 119.

Berger, Raoul. Congressional Subpoenas to Executive Officials. Columbia Law Review, v. 75, 1975: 865.

Berger, Raoul. Executive Privilege: A Constitutional Myth. Cambridge, Mass.: Harvard University Press, 1974.

Brand, Stanley M. Battle Among the Branches: The Two Hundred Year War. North Carolina Law Review, v. 65, 1987: 901.

Brand, Stanley M. and Connelly, Sean. Constitutional Confrontations: Preserving a Prompt and Orderly Means By Which Congress May Enforce Investigative Demands Against Executive Branch Officials. Catholic University Law Review, v. 36, 1986: 71.

Bush, Joel D. Congressional Executive Access Disputes: Legal Standards and Political Settlements. Journal of Law and Politics, v. 9, Summer 1993: 719.

Clavelaux, Ronald L. The Conflict Between Executive Privilege and Congressional Oversight: The Gorsuch Controversy. Duke Law Journal, v. 1983, No. 6: 1333.

Cole, Lance. The Fifth Amendment and Compelled Production of Personal Documents after United States v. Hubbell—New Protection for Private Papers? American Journal of Criminal Law, v. 29, Spring 2002: 123.

Devins, Neal. Congressional-Executive Information Disputes: A Modest Proposal—Do Nothing. Administrative Law Review, vol. 48, Winter 1996: 109.

Dimock, Marshall E. Congressional Investigating Committees. Baltimore: Johns Hopkins University Press, 1929. JK1123.A2E2

CRS Report R42811, *Congressional Investigations of the Department of Justice, 1920-2012: History, Law, and Practice*, by Alissa M. Dolan and Todd Garvey.

Fisher, Louis. The Politics of Executive Privilege. Durham, N.C.: Carolina Academic Press, 2004. 272 p. JK468.S4F57

CRS Report RL34097, *Congress's Contempt Power and the Enforcement of Congressional Subpoenas: Law, History, Practice, and Procedure*, by Todd Garvey and Alissa M. Dolan.

CRS Report RL34114, *Congress's Contempt Power and the Enforcement of Congressional Subpoenas: A Sketch*, by Todd Garvey and Alissa M. Dolan.

CRS Report R42670, *Presidential Claims of Executive Privilege: History, Law, Practice, and Recent Developments*, by Todd Garvey and Alissa M. Dolan.

CRS Report RL31351, *Presidential Advisers' Testimony Before Congressional Committees: An Overview*, by Todd Garvey, Alissa M. Dolan, and Henry B. Hogue.

Ghio, R.S. The Iran-Contra Prosecutions and the Failure of Use Immunity. Stanford Law Review, v. 45, 1992: 229.

Grabow, John C. Congressional Investigations: Law and Practice. New Jersey: Prentice Hall Law and Business, 1988. KF4942.G73

Hamilton, James. The Power to Probe: A Study in Congressional Investigations. New York: Vintage Books, 1976. KF4942.H34

Hamilton, James and Grabow, John C. A Legislative Proposal for Resolving Executive Privilege Disputes Precipitated by Congressional Subpoenas. Harvard Journal Legislation, v. 21, Winter 1984: 145.

Iraola, Roberts. Congressional Oversight, Executive Privilege, and Requests for Information Relating to Federal Criminal Investigations and Prosecutions. Iowa Law Review, v. 87, 2002: 1559.

Moreland, Allen B. Congressional Investigations and Private Persons. Southern California Law Review, v. 40, Winter 1967: 189.

Peterson, Todd D. Prosecuting Executive Branch Officials For Contempt Of Congress. New York University Law Review, v. 66, 1991: 563.

_____.Congressional Oversight of Open Criminal Investigations. Notre Dame Law Review, v. 75, 2002: 1373.

Roberts, John C. Are Congressional Committees Constitutional? Radical Textualism, Separation of Powers, and the Enactment Process, and the Enactment Process. Case Western Rescue Law Review, v. 52, 2001: 489.

Rosenthal, Paul C. and Grossman, Robert S. Congressional Access to Confidential Information Collected by Federal Agencies. Harvard Journal of Legislation, v. 15, 1977: 74.

Rozell, Mark J. Executive Privilege: Presidential Power, Secrecy, and Accountability. Lawrence: University Press of Kansas, 2002 (2d edition, revised). JK468.S4 R67

Schlesinger, Arthur M., Jr., and Bruns, Rogers (eds.). Congress Investigates: 1792-1974. New York: Chelsea House Publishers. 1975 (5 Vols.). JK 1123.A2 S34

Shane, Peter M. Legal Disagreement and Negotiation in a Government of Laws: The Case of Executive Privilege Claims Against Congress. Minnesota Law Review, v. 71, February 1987: 461.

Shane, Peter M. Negotiation for Knowledge: Administrative Responses to Congressional Demands For Information. Administrative Law Review, v. 44, Spring 1992: 197.

Sklamberg, Harold. Investigation Versus Protection: The Constitutional Limits on Congress' Power to Immunize Witnesses. North Carolina Law Review, v. 78: November 1999: 153.

Stathis, Stephen W. Executive Cooperation: Presidential Recognition of the Investigative Authority of Congress and the Courts. Journal of Law and Politics, v. 3, Fall 1986: 187.

Taylor, Telford. Grand Inquest: The Story of Congressional Investigations. New York: Simon and Schuster, 1995. KF4942.T38

Tiefer, Charles. Congressional Oversight of the Clinton Administration and Congressional Procedure. Administrative Law Review, v. 50, 1998: 199.

_____.The Law: President Bush's First Executive Privilege Claim: The FBI/Boston Investigation. Presidential Studies Quarterly, v. 33, March 2003: 201.

Vermeule, Adrian. The Constitutional Law of Congressional Procedure. University of Chicago Law Review, v. 71, Spring 2004: 361.

Walsh, Lawrence E. The Independent Counsel and the Separation of Powers. Houston Law Review, v. 25, January 1988: 1.

Wald, Patricia and Siegel, Jay. The D.C. Circuit and the Struggle for Control of Presidential Information. Georgetown Law Journal, v. 90, March 2002: 737.

Wright, Ronald F. Congressional Use of Immunity Grants After Iran-Contra. Minnesota Law Review, v. 80, December 1995: 407.

Statutory Offices of Inspector General

CRS Report R40675, *Statutory Offices of Inspectors General (IGs): Methods of Appointment and Legislative Proposals*, by Vanessa K. Burrows.

CRS Report R40099, *The Special Inspector General for the Troubled Asset Relief Program (SIGTARP)*, by Vanessa K. Burrows.

Duffy, Diane T. and Frederick M. Kaiser. Into the Woods: Mapping New Directions for OIGs. Journal of Public Inquiry, Fall-Winter 1999.

Fong, Phyllis K., The IG Reform Act and the New IG Council: Dawn of a New Era, Journal of Public Inquiry, Fall-Winter 2008-2009, pp. 1-6.

Hendricks, Michael et al. Inspectors General: A New Force in Evaluation. San Francisco: Jossey-Bass, Inc., 1990.

Kaiser, Frederick M. The Watchers' Watchdog: The CIA Inspector General. International Journal of Intelligence and Counterintelligence, vol. 3, 1989. pp. 55-75.

Light, Paul C. Monitoring Government: Inspectors General and the Search for Accountability. Washington: Brookings, 1993. HJ9801.L54

Newcomer, Kathryn E. The Changing Nature of Accountability: The Role of the Inspectors General in Federal Agencies. Public Administration Review, vol. 58, March/April, 1998.

U.S. Congress. House. Committee on Government Operations. Establishment of Offices of Inspector General in Certain Executive Departments and Agencies. H. Rept. 95-584, 95th Cong., 1st sess. Washington: GPO, 1977.

_____. The Inspector General Act of 1978: A 10-Year Review. H. Rept. 100-1027, 100th Cong., 2nd sess. Washington: GPO, 1988.

U.S. Congress. House. Committee on Oversight and Government Reform. Improving Government Accountability. H.Rept. 110-354, 110th Cong., 1st sess. Washington: GPO, 2007.

U.S. Congress. House. Subcommittee on Government Efficiency. 25th Anniversary of the Inspector General Act. Hearings, 108th Cong., 1st sess. Washington: GPO, 2003.

U.S. Congress. House. Subcommittee on Government Management and Organization. Inspectors General: Independence and Accountability. Hearing, 110th Cong., 1st sess. Washington: GPO, 2007.

U.S. Congress. Senate. Committee on Governmental Affairs. Establishment of Inspector and Auditor General in Certain Executive Departments and Agencies. S. Rept. 95-1071, 95th Cong., 2nd sess. Washington: GPO, 1978.

_____. The Inspector General Act: 20 Years Later. Hearings, 105th Congress, 2nd session. Washington: GPO, 1998.

U.S. Congress. Senate. Committee on Homeland Security and Governmental Affairs. The Inspector General Reform Act of 2007. S.Rept. 110-262, 110th Cong., 1st sess. Washington: GPO, 2007.

U.S. Government Accountability Office (formerly, General Accounting Office). Designated Federal Entities: Survey of Governance Practices and the Inspector General Role. GAO Report GAO-09-270. Washington: GAO, 2009.

_____. Federal Inspectors General: An Historical Perspective. GAO Report T-AIMD-98-146. Washington: GAO, 1998.

_____.Highlights of the Comptroller General's Panel on Federal Oversight and the Inspectors General. GAO Report GAO-06-931SP. Washington: GAO, 2006.

_____. Inspectors General: Enhancing Federal Accountability. GAO Report GAO-04-117T. Washington: GAO, 2003.

_____. Inspectors General: Office Consolidation and Related Issues. GAO Report GAO-02-575. Washington: GAO, 2002.

_____. Inspectors General: Opportunities to Enhance Independence and Accountability. GAO Report GAO-07-1089T. Washington: GAO, 2007.

Reporting, Consultation, and Other Sources of Information

CRS Report RL31160, *Disapproval of Regulations by Congress: Procedure Under the Congressional Review Act*, by Richard S. Beth.

CRS Report RL30795, *General Management Laws: A Compendium*, by Clinton T. Brass et al.

CRS Report RL32339, *Federal Regulations: Efforts to Estimate Total Costs and Benefits of Rules*, by Curtis W. Copeland.

Collier, Ellen C. Reporting Requirements. In Joint Committee on the Organization of Congress. Congressional Reorganization: Proposals for Change. Senate Print 103-19, 103rd Congress, 1st session. Washington: GPO, 1993. p. 135.

_____. Foreign Policy by Reporting Requirement. The Washington Quarterly, vol. 11, Winter 1988.

Johannes, John. Statutory Reporting Requirements: Information and Influence for Congress. In Abdo Baaklini, ed., Comparative Legislative Reforms and Innovations. New York: SUNY Press, 1977. pp. 33-60.

Kerwin, Cornelius. Rulemaking: How Government Agencies Write Laws and Make Policy, 2nd ed. Washington: CQ Press, 1999.

U.S. General Accounting Office. Investigators' Guide to Sources of Information. GAO Report OSI-97-2. Washington: GAO, 1997.

U.S. General Accounting Office. A Systematic Management Approach Is Needed for Congressional Reporting Requirements. GAO Report PAD-82-12. Washington: GAO, 1981.

U.S. House of Representatives. Clerk. Reports To Be Made to Congress. House Document 108-14, 108th Congress, 1st session. Washington: GPO, 2003.

U.S. Vice President Al Gore. National Performance Review. Creating a Government That Works Better & Costs Less: Streamlining Management Control. Washington: Office of the Vice President, 1993 (Reduce the Burden of Congressionally Mandated Reports, pp. 33-36).

Resolutions of Inquiry

CRS Report RL31909, *House Resolutions of Inquiry*, by Christopher M. Davis.

History of the United States House of Representatives, 1789-1994, H. Doc. 103-324, 103rd Congress, 2nd session. Washington: GPO, 1994 (Resolutions of Inquiry, pp. 260-262).

Methods and Techniques

Art, Robert J. Congress and the Defense Budget: Enhancing Policy Oversight, Political Science Quarterly, v. 100, Summer 1985: 227-248.

Bowers, James R. Regulating the Regulators: An Introduction to the Legislative Oversight of Administrative Rulemaking. New York: Praeger, 1990. 140p. KF5411.B69

Hill, James P. The Third House of Congress Versus the Fourth Branch of Government: The Impact of Congressional Committee Staff on Agency Regulatory Decision-Making, John Marshall Law Review, v. 19, Winter 1986: 247-273.

Kaiser, Frederick M. Congressional Oversight of the Presidency, Annals of the American Academy of Political and Social Science, v. 499, September 1988: 75-89.

U.S. Congress. Senate. Committee on Government Operations [now titled Homeland Security and Governmental Affairs]. Subcommittee on Oversight Procedures. Committee Print. Congressional Oversight: Methods and Techniques. 94th Congress, 2nd session, July 1976. Washington: GPO, 1976. 254p.

Special Studies and Investigations by Staff and Others

Johannes, John R. To Serve the People: Congress and Constituency Service. Lincoln, University of Nebraska Press, 1984. JK1071.J63

Kaiser, Frederick M. *A Congressional Office of Constituent Assistance: Proposals, Rationales, and Possible Objections*. CRS Report 91-893 (out of print; available from the authors).

Pontius, John S. *Casework in a Congressional Office*. CRS Report 98-878 (out of print; available from the authors).

The Press and Media

Cook, Timothy E. Making Laws and Making News. Washington: The Brookings Institution, 1989. 210 p. JK1447.C66

Hess, Stephen. Live From Capitol Hill. Washington: The Brookings Institution, 1991. 178 p. PN4888.P6H48

Mann, Thomas and Norman Ornstein, eds. Congress, the Press, and the Public. Washington: The American Enterprise Institute and The Brookings Institution, 1994. 212 p. JK1140.C62

Ritchie, Donald A. Press Gallery: Congress and the Washington Correspondents. Cambridge, Mass.: Harvard University Press, 1991. PN4899.W3R58

Specialized Investigations

Congressional Quarterly. Guide to Congress. Washington: Congressional Quarterly, Inc., 2000, 5th ed. Vol. I, pp. 249-280.

Dimock, Marshall E. Congressional Investigating Committees. Baltimore: Johns Hopkins Press, 1929. KF4942.D5

Eberling, Ernest J. Congressional Investigations. New York: Columbia University Press, 1929. JK1123.A2E2

Fisher, Louis. Constitutional Conflicts between Congress and the President. Lawrence, Kansas: University Press of Kansas, 1997, 4th revised ed. pp. 160-195. KF4565.F57

Hamilton, James. The Power To Probe: A Study of Congressional Investigations. New York: Vintage Books, 1976. KF4942.H34

Kaiser, Frederick M. Impact and Implications of the Iran-Contra Affair on Congressional Oversight of the Executive. International Journal of Intelligence and Counterintelligence, vol. 7, Summer 1994, pp. 205-234.

Mayhew, David R. Divided We Govern: Party Control, Lawmaking, and Investigations, 1946-1990. New Haven: Yale University Press, 1991. JK2261.M36

Schlesinger, Arthur M. Jr. and Roger Bruns. Congress Investigates: A Documented History. New York: Chelsea House, 1975 (5 vols.). JK1123.A2S34

Taylor, Telford. The Grand Inquest: The Story of Congressional Investigations New York: Simon and Schuster, 1955. KF4942.T38

Appropriations Limitations and Riders

Banks, William C. and Peter Raven-Hansen. National Security Law and the Power of the Purse. New York, Oxford University Press, 1994. 260 p. KF4651.B36

Devins, Neal. Regulation of Government Agencies Through Limitation Riders, Duke Law Journal, v. 1987: 456.

Fisher, Louis. The Authorization-Appropriation Process in Congress: Formal Rules and Informal Practices, Catholic University Law Review, v. 29, 1979:5.

LeBoeuf, Jacques B. Limitations on the Use of Appropriations Riders by Congress to Effectuate Substantive Policy Changes, Hastings Constitutional Law Quarterly, v. 19, 1992: 457.

The Legislative Veto

Biden, Joseph R., Jr. Who Needs the Legislative Veto? Syracuse Law Review, v. 35, 1984: 685.

Breyer, Stephen. The Legislative Veto After *Chadha*. Georgetown Law Journal, v. 72, 1984: 785.

Craig, Barbara Hinson. Chadha: The Story of an Epic Constitutional Struggle. New York: Oxford University Press, 1988. KF228.C43C73

Fisher, Louis. The Legislative Veto: Invalidated, It Survives, Law & Contemporary Problems, v. 56, 1993: 273.

Gibson, Martha Liebler. Weapons of Influence: the Legislative Veto, American Foreign Policy, and the Irony of Reform. Boulder, Colo., Westview Press, 1992. 188p. JX1706.G53

Kaiser, Frederick M. Congressional Action to Overturn Agency Rules: Alternatives to the 'legislative veto.' Administrative Law Review, v. 32, 1980: 667.

Korn, Jessica. The Power of Separation: American Constitutionalism and the Myth of the Legislative Veto. Princeton, N.J.: Princeton University Press, 1996. 178p. JK305.K67

Independent Counsel

Eastland, Terry. Ethics, Politics and the Independent Counsel. Washington, National Legal Center for the Public Interest, 1989. 180 p. KF4568.E17 1989.

Harriger, Katy J. The Special Prosecutor in American Politics, 2d ed. revised. Lawrence: University Press of Kansas, 2000. 325 p. KF4568.H37

Jost, Kenneth. Independent Counsels: Should Congress make major changes in the law? CQ Researcher, v. 7, no. 7, February 21, 1997: 145-167.

Koukoutchos, Brian Stuart. Constitutional Kinetics: the Independent Counsel Case and the Separation of Powers. Wake Forest law review, v. 23, 1988: 635.

Maskell, Jack. The Independent Counsel Law. The Federal Lawyer, July 1998: 28-39.

Nolan, Beth. Removing Conflicts from the Administration of Justice: Conflicts of Interest and Independent Counsels Under the Ethics in Government Act. Georgetown Law Journal, v. 79, 1990: 1-80.

Walsh, Lawrence E. The Independent Counsel and the Separation of Powers. Houston Law Review, v. 25, 1988: 1.

General

Bimber, Bruce. Information as a Factor in Congressional Politics, Legislative Studies Quarterly, v. XVI, November 1991: 585-605.

Carnegie Commission on Science, Technology, and Government. Science, Technology, and Congress: Analysis and Advice from the Congressional Support Agencies. Washington: The Carnegie Commission, 1991. 70p.

Chubb, John E. Interest Groups and the Bureaucracy. Stanford, Calif.: Stanford University Press, 1983. 319 p.

Gilmour, Robert S. and Alexis A. Halley, eds. Who Makes Public Policy? Chatham, N.J.: Chatham House Publishers, Inc., 1994. 390 p. JK585.W48

Heinz, John P., et al. The Hollow Core: Private Interests in National Policy Making. Cambridge, Mass.: Harvard University Press, 1993. 450 p. JK1118.H55

U.S. Congress. Joint Committee on the Organization of Congress. Support Agencies. Hearing before the Joint Committee on the Organization of Congress. 103rd Congress, 1st session, June 10, 1993, Washington: GPO, 1993. 1577p. KF25.O7

Congressional Research Service http://www.crs.gov

Carney, Eliza Newlin. Billington's Book Wars, National Journal, v. 24, March 21, 1992: 695-698.

Cole, John Y. Jefferson's Legacy: A Brief History of the Library, Library of Congress Bulletin, v. 50, April 8, 1991: 124-130.

Dalrymple, Helen. Congressional Research Service: Think Tank, Policy Consultant and Information Factory, Library of Congress Information Bulletin, v. 49, September 24, 1990: 319-326.

Gude, Gilbert. Congressional Research Service: the Research and Information Arm of Congress, Government Information Quarterly, v. 2, January 1985: 5-11.

Robinson, William H. The Congressional Research Service: Policy Consultant, Think Tank, and Information Factory, In Organizations for Policy Analysis: Helping Government Think. edited by Carol H. Weiss. Newbury Park, Calif.: Sage Publications, 1992, pp. 181-200.

Government Accountability Office (formerly the General Accounting Office)
http://www.gao.gov

Abikoff, Kevin T. The Role of the Comptroller General in Light of Bowsher v. Synar, Columbia Law Review, v. 87, November 1987: 1539-1563.

_____.GAO Versus the CIA: Uphill Battles Against an Overpowering Force. International Journal of Intelligence and Counterintelligence, v. 15, 2002: 330-389.

Mosher, Frederick C. A Tale of Two Agencies: A Comparative Analysis of the General Accounting Office and the Office of Management and Budget. Baton Rouge, La.: Louisiana State University Press, 1984. 219 p. HJG802.M682

Rozell, Mark J. The Role of General Accounting Office Evaluation in the Post Reform Congress: The Case of General Revenue Sharing, International Journal of Public Administration, v. 7, September 1985: 267-290.

U.S. Congress. House. Committee on the Budget. Addressing Government Waste, Fraud, and Abuse. 108th Congress, 1st session. Washington: GPO, 2003. 421 p.

U.S. Congress. Senate. Committee on Governmental Affairs. The Roles, Mission and Operation of the U.S. General Accounting Office. Report prepared by the National Academy of Public Administration. Senate Print 103-87, 103rd Congress, 2nd session. Washington: GPO, 1994. 106 p.

U.S. Congress. House. Committee on Rules. Congressional Oversight: A "How-To" Series of Workshops. Committee Print. 106th Congress, 1st session. Washington: GPO, 2000. See pp. 90-143.

U.S. General Accounting Office. GAO History, 1921-1991, by Roger R. Trask. GAO Report OP-3-MP. Washington: GAO, 1991.

U.S. Government Accountability Office. Strategic Plan http://www.GAO.GOV.

Congressional Budget Office http://www.cbo.gov

Howard, James A. Government Economic Projections: A Comparison Between CBO and OMB, Public Budgeting & Finance, v. 7, Autumn 1987: 14-25.

CRS Report 98-720, *Manual on the Federal Budget Process*, by Robert Keith and Allen Schick, August 28, 1998.

CRS Report RL31880, *Congressional Budget Office: Appointment and Tenure of the Director and Deputy Director*, by Megan S. Lynch.

Schick, Allen. Congress and Money. Washington, D.C.: The Urban Institute, 1980. 604 p. H J2051.S34.

Twogood, R. Philip. Reconciling Politics and Budget Analysis: The Case of the Congressional Budget Office, Public Budgeting and Financial Management, v. 3, no. 1, 1991: 65-87.

Offices of Senate Legal Counsel and House General Counsel

Salokar, Rebecca Mae. Legal Counsel for Congress: Protecting Institutional Interests, Congress and the Presidency. vol. 20, No. 2, Autumn 1993: 131-155.

Tiefer, Charles. The Senate and House Counsel Offices: Dilemmas of Representing in Court the Institutional Congressional Client, Law and Contemporary Problems, v. 61, Spring 1998: 48-63.

Appendix D. Other Resources

Congressional Oversight Video Series[424]

Oversight: A Key Congressional Function. Former Representative Lee Hamilton delivered the keynote address to a 1999 series of CRS programs examining various aspects of congressional oversight. In this program, Mr. Hamilton emphasizes the importance of traditional oversight and reviews factors that contribute to successful oversight.

Program Length: 60 minutes. Product No.: MM70003.

The Constitutional Context of Oversight. Michael Stern, senior counsel with the House General Counsel's Office, and Michael Davidson, former Senate Legal Counsel, discuss the constitutional context of oversight. In addition, the two attorneys address a variety of oversight topics, including congressional investigations. Taped as part of a 1999 series of CRS programs examining various aspects of congressional oversight.

Program Length: 60 minutes. Product No.: MM70003, *1999 Congressional Oversight Seminars. Video Tape.*, by Walter J. Oleszek and Morton Rosenberg.

The "Rules & Tools" of Oversight. This program focuses on the formal institutional rules that committees must follow to insure the legitimacy and fairness of oversight proceedings. The nature of the formidable powers of inquiry available to congressional committees and the practicalities of their effective utilization are also explored. Taped as part of a 1999 series of CRS programs examining various aspects of congressional oversight.

Program Length: 60 minutes. Product No.: MM70003, *1999 Congressional Oversight Seminars. Video Tape.*, by Walter J. Oleszek and Morton Rosenberg.

Sources of Oversight Assistance. This session focuses on where congressional committees can obtain assistance in conducting oversight. Especially relevant are inspectors general, chief financial officers, and Congress's own support agencies, the Congressional Budget Office, Congressional Research Service, and Government Accountability Office. Taped as part of a 1999 series of CRS programs examining various aspect of congressional oversight.

Program Length: 46 minutes. Product No.: MM70003, *1999 Congressional Oversight Seminars. Video Tape.*, by Walter J. Oleszek and Morton Rosenberg.

Fiscal Oversight: "Follow the Money." This seminar examines congressional oversight of fiscal and budgetary activities, focusing on the role of the House and Senate Appropriations Committees in the annual budget cycle and key support activities of the Congressional Budget Office to Congress on budgetary matters generally. Taped as part of a 1999 series of CRS programs examining various aspects of congressional oversight.

Program Length: 45 minutes. Product No.: MM70007.

---

[424] These products are available from the authors of this report upon request.

Outside Actors in the Oversight Process. This program addresses how non-congressional individuals can assist in the investigative process and in monitoring executive branch performance. The panel includes a journalist, members of public and private interest groups, and a former counsel with the House Commerce Committee, Subcommittee on Oversight and Investigations. Taped as part of a 1999 series of CRS programs examining various aspects of congressional oversight.

Program Length: 50 minutes. Product No.: MM70003, *1999 Congressional Oversight Seminars. Video Tape.*, by Walter J. Oleszek and Morton Rosenberg.

Preparing for an Oversight Investigation. This program probes the "ins and outs" of how to prepare for Congressional Investigations from the perspective of both the investigator and those being investigated. Taped as part of a 1999 series of CRS programs examining various aspects of congressional oversight.

Program Length: 59:50. Product No.: MM70003, *1999 Congressional Oversight Seminars. Video Tape.*, by Walter J. Oleszek and Morton Rosenberg.

Congress, the President, the Courts, and the Separation of Powers. Product No.: MM70097.

Copies of CRS video programs are available on loan to congressional offices. For the schedule of CRS Programs on Channel 6 of the House and Channel 5 of the Senate, call 7-7009. For further information about any of these programs, please call 7-7547.

Author Contact Information

Alissa M. Dolan
Legislative Attorney
adolan@crs.loc.gov, 7-8433

Todd Garvey
Legislative Attorney
tgarvey@crs.loc.gov, 7-0174

Wendy Ginsberg
Analyst in American National Government
wginsberg@crs.loc.gov, 7-3933

L. Elaine Halchin
Specialist in American National Government
ehalchin@crs.loc.gov, 7-0646

Walter J. Oleszek
Senior Specialist in American National Government
woleszek@crs.loc.gov, 7-7854

Acknowledgments

Over time, authors of this report have included former CRS attorneys and analysts Louis Fisher, Rick Greenwood, T.J. Halstead, Frederick M. Kaiser, Mort Rosenberg, and Todd B. Tatelman.

CPSIA information can be obtained
at www.ICGtesting.com
Printed in the USA
LVHW060811200121
676895LV00009B/942